PRINCIPLES OF
COMPUTER SPEECH

PRINCIPLES OF
COMPUTER SPEECH

I. H. Witten

Man–Machine Systems Laboratory
Department of Computer Science
University of Calgary
Canada

1982

 ACADEMIC PRESS

A Subsidiary of Harcourt Brace Jovanovich, Publishers

LONDON · NEW YORK
PARIS · SAN DIEGO · SAN FRANCISCO
SÃO PAULO · SYDNEY · TOKYO · TORONTO

ACADEMIC PRESS INC. (LONDON) LTD.
24/28 Oval Road
London NW1

United States Edition published by
ACADEMIC PRESS INC.
111 Fifth Avenue
New York, New York 10003

British Library Cataloguing in Publication Data

Witten, I.H.
  Principles of computer speech.—(Computer and people)
  1. Speech processing systems
  2. Signal processing—Digital techniques
  I. Title   II. Series
  621.380′412   TK7882.S65

  ISBN 0-12-760760-9
  LCCCN 82-72336

Photoset in the United States of America by
Grafacon, Inc., Hudson, Massachusetts
Printed in Great Britain by
St Edmundsbury Press, Bury St Edmunds, Suffolk

PREFACE

Computer speech is changing rapidly from a specialist topic which embraces fields as far apart as phonetics and digital signal processing to a practical technology for man-computer interaction. Like its more exotic companion, speech recognition, its advantages in man–machine dialogue are manifold: hands-free and eyes-free operation, does not divert attention from the main task, distribution by the existing telephone network, no special terminal equipment needed, demands no unusual knowledge or skills of the user. Speech output, however, is technically much simpler than speech input because stereotyped utterances may be acceptable and the man can adapt to the machine's way of speaking much more easily than the machine could adapt to the man's.

Speech is still a rather esoteric communication medium for computers, despite its predominance in everyday human intercourse. It has, of course, long been of interest to linguists, who seek to wrest from nature the secrets of speech and sometimes even wish to demonstrate their understanding by generating it from a machine. A small body of engineers and computer scientists became interested in computer speech early in the 1960s, and research in the area grew slowly but surely over two decades. During the past four or five years, however, computer speech has exploded on to the commercial market. We now have talking toys, speaking language translators, reading machines for the blind. Cheap speech peripherals for computers large and small, professional and hobby, appear on the market almost monthly. Computer speech is moving out of research and into production.

The discipline of speech synthesis has been fortunate enough to mature at exactly the right time. The microprocessor revolution has bestowed the power to handle information in almost every walk of life, for information processing is now virtually free. It is communication between men and machines that constrains applications. The need for communication is there. Speech technology has matured. And the processing power to implement it cheaply has arrived.

This book presents a practical description of the technology of speech output from computers. It emphasizes the engineering, computing, and applications aspects of speech systems rather than the role of synthesis in exploring theories of spoken language. No prior phonetic or linguistic knowledge is assumed: what is needed is introduced in a fairly informal way. This

v

is not too difficult because we all share a great deal of common experience in producing speech sounds. The book has grown out of a decade of research by myself and collegues on speech output from computers. The subject is attractive from an academic point of view because it combines several disciplines—phonetics and linguistics, of course; a surprising amount of mathematics; electronics; computer hardware and software; and even psychology, physics, physiology—in a manner which provides a tangible, easy-to-appreciate, output. While my interest stemmed at first from electronics and low-level computer software, the fascination of speech led quickly into more distant territory. Now is the time to stand back and survey the whole scene. Fortuitously, the time is ripe for an entirely different reason. Growing numbers of engineers, computer scientists, and system designers need to know about the technology of computer speech.

There are two rather separate strands to the material in the book, both of which are necessary for a good understanding of computer speech. On the one hand are notions of signal processing: the nature of the speech waveform, mathematical techniques for analyzing it, extracting information, and re-synthesizing from a compressed representation; and the realization of these algorithms in electronic hardware or digital signal-processing software. On the other hand is higher-level knowledge of the linguistic structure of speech, and the software techniques needed to handle it, or even to derive it from plain text.

The book begins by explaining the motivation for speech output from computers, with several examples of actual systems which use speech in different ways. Then follows an introduction to the linguistic analysis of speech. Although this is necessarily rather cursory (after all, linguistics and phonetics are vast subjects in their own right), it provides a background which is quite adequate for understanding the later chapters on higher-level software/linguistic technology. Like the other chapters, it ends with a highly selected, and commented, book list for further reading.

Chapter 3 begins the first strand of signal processing for speech analysis and data compression by considering speech storage and coding in the time domain. We are primarily concerned with *digital* processing and synthesis of speech, for this is the dominant technology and is almost certain to remain so. Digitization of an analogue waveform involves both sampling in time, and quantization in amplitude. The properties of the speech signal make logarithmic rather than linear quantization, and differential rather than absolute coding, attractive. The next chapter moves from the time domain to the frequency domain, and presents an introduction to the theory of digital signal processing. It is intended to be a "plain man's guide" to the subject, but it must be admitted that a certain level of mathematical sophistication is necessary to follow the development in detail. The concept of frequency analysis of linear discrete-time systems using the z-transform is introduced, for it is essential for full understanding of the theory and practice of speech synthesizer design and linear prediction. The discrete Fourier transform and its use in cepstral analysis are covered, as are pitch extraction techniques using autocorrelation methods. Chapter 5 treats the design of resonance speech synthesizers. The theoretical development is expressed in terms of the Laplace transform, for this is familiar to most people with experience of filter design. However, both digital and analogue realizations are considered. Linear prediction forms the subject of Chapter 6. The autocorrelation and covariance methods are described, together with procedures for software implementation in Pascal. A new approach to lattice filters is developed which gives the flavour of the lattice methods, and the detailed structure of different lattice analysis and synthesis configurations is presented. A rigorous development of lattice filter theory is omitted, as the complexity that this would entail does not seem to yield sufficient rewards to make it worthwhile for most speech engineers.

The second strand of material, on linguistic as opposed to signal-processing structures, was begun in Chapter 2 and is continued in Chapter 7. Readers with insufficient time or background for the theoretical material on signal processing may wish to skip, or skim, chapters 3 through 6. Although some reference is made to these later on, the coupling is fairly loose. Chapter 7 studies various techniques for joining segments of speech, at the word level, the syllable level, and, most extensively, the phonetic level. An algorithm for speech synthesis by rule from phonetics is described in some detail. The next chapter proceeds to *prosodic* rather than *segmental* features. Here we begin to move from general principles to example problems and how they have been tackled, because of the paucity of hard results on prosodic synthesis. A system for transferring pitch from one utterance to another is described, together with the results of some experiments on how the utterances were perceived. Also considered is a specific algorithm for prosodic synthesis based upon fitting pre-defined intonation contours to tone groups. Chapter 9 describes the problems of generating speech from text. The regularities and irregularities of English pronunciation are discussed; some attention is also given to languages other than English. More important than pronunciation, though, is the task of deriving prosodic features from a textual representation of the utterance. In effect, the system must examine the text and understand it before it can generate a realistic reading. The chapter attempts to convey the sense in which "understanding" is necessary: actually accomplishing the task is presently an unsolved problem (and is likely to remain so for some time).

The final two chapters return to practical considerations when using speech output in actual computer systems. Chapter 10 discusses the design of the man–computer dialogue for speech systems. It turns out that special care has to be taken here, due to the transitory nature of the medium (as compared, say, with display on a VDU). The final chapter describes in detail four commercial speech output devices, chosen because they each represent rather different principles and architectures.

Calgary   *Ian H. Witten*
August, 1982

CONTENTS

ACKNOWLEDGEMENTS

I would like to thank the many friends and colleagues who have helped me in my frequent struggles with various aspects of the subject of computer speech. First and foremost, warm and grateful thanks go to David Hill, who introduced me to speech synthesis in the first place, overcoming by his enthusiasm my initial hesitations; and has nurtured my understanding and growth over the years with amazing generosity and patience. Brian Gaines has been especially influential in promoting a systems view of computer speech, encouraging me to consider the medium as another device to help people communicate with machines. He has also assisted my development in innumerable other ways over the years. These two have provided support in times of crisis and criticism in times of confidence.

Many students and colleagues have worked with me on aspects of speech communication: I would like to mention in particular Dorinda Bath, Angie Corbett, Paul Griffith, Rick Jenkins, Pete Madams, Paul Mermelstein, Linda Shockey and Alexandra Smith. Many of my ideas on the subject stem from fascinating conversations with Walter Lawrence. John Holmes and Wiktor Jassem have provided a great deal of stimulation for my work. Bruce Anderson, Rod Cuff, Kel Fidler, John Foster and Phil McCrea have all, perhaps unknowingly, contributed ideas to this book. I am heavily obliged to my reading squad: Gerard Chollet, Chris Corbett, Doug Girling and Danny Levinson for donating that most precious of all gifts—time—to help me to improve the presentation. Darrell Williamson helped a great deal by proof-reading much of the mathematics at very short notice.

I have been fortunate in obtaining support for my speech research from Bell-Northern Research, the Government Communications Headquarters, the National Sciences and Engineering Research Council of Canada, and the Science Research Council of Great Britain; as well as from the Department of Electrical Engineering Science, University of Essex, and the Department of Computer Science, University of Calgary. Figure 1.4 was kindly provided by Kurzweil Computer Products. Figures 2.3 and 2.4 were supplied by courtesy of the Joint Speech Research Unit, and are reproduced with the permission of the Controller of Her Majesty's Stationary Office (Crown Copyright, 1980). I am deeply grateful to several PDP-11 computers and a VAX for tirelessly printing and re-printing innumerable drafts.

Finally, and above all, I must thank Pam for putting up with it all. It was worse for her this second time for she knew what was in store.

1
WHY SPEECH OUTPUT?

Speech is our everyday, informal, communication medium. But although
we use it a lot, we probably don't assimilate as much information through
our ears as we do through our eyes, by reading or looking at pictures and
diagrams. You go to a technical lecture to get the feel of a subject—the
overall arrangement of ideas and the motivation behind them—and fill in
the details, if you still want to know them, from a book. You probably find
out more about the news from ten minutes with a newspaper than from a
ten-minute news broadcast. So it should be emphasized from the start that
speech output from computers is not a panacea. It doesn't solve the problems
of communicating with computers; it simply enriches the possibilities for
communication.

What, then, are the advantages of speech output? One good reason for
listening to a radio news broadcast instead of spending the time with a
newspaper is that you can listen while shaving, doing the housework, or
driving the car. Speech leaves hands and eyes free for other tasks. Moreover,
it is omnidirectional, and does not require a free line of sight. Related to
this is the use of speech as a secondary medium for status reports and
warning messages. Occasional interruptions by voice do not interfere with
other activities, unless they demand unusual concentration, and people can
assimilate spoken messages and queue them for later action quite easily and
naturally.

The second key feature of speech communication stems from the telephone. It is the universality of the telephone receiver itself that is important
here, rather than the existence of a world-wide distribution network; for
with special equipment (a modem and a VDU) one does not need speech
to take advantage of the telephone network for information transfer. But
speech needs no tools other than the telephone, and this gives it a substantial
advantage. You can go into a phone booth anywhere in the world, carrying
no special equipment, and have access to your computer within seconds.
The problem of data input is still there: perhaps your computer system has
a limited word recognizer, or you use the touchtone telephone keypad (or
a portable calculator-sized tone generator). Easy remote access without special equipment is a great, and unique, asset to speech communication.

The third big advantage of speech output is that it is potentially very' cheap. Being all-electronic, except for the loudspeaker, speech systems are well suited to high-volume, low-cost, LSI manufacture. Other computer output devices are at present tied either to mechanical moving parts or to the CRT. This was realized quickly by the computer hobbies market, where speech output peripherals have been selling like hot cakes since the mid-1970s.

A further point in favour of speech is that it is natural-seeming and somehow cuddly when compared with printers or VDU's. It would have been much more difficult to make this point before the advent of talking toys like Texas Instruments' "Speak 'n Spell" in 1978, but now it is an accepted fact that friendly computer-based gadgets can speak—there are talking pocket-watches that really do "tell" the time, talking microwave ovens, talking pinball machines, and of course, talking calculators. It is, however, difficult to assess whether the appeal stems from mechanical speech's novelty (it is still a gimmick) and also to what extent it is tied up with economic factors. After all, most of the population don't use high-quality VDUs, and their major experience of real-time interactive computing is through the very limited displays and keypads provided on video games and teletext systems.

Articles on speech communication with computers often list many more advantages of voice output (see Hill, 1971; Turn, 1974; Lea, 1980). For example, speech

—can be used in the dark
—can be varied from a (confidential) whisper to a (loud) shout
—requires very little energy
—is not appreciably affected by weightlessness or vibration.

However, these either derive from the three advantages we have discussed above, or relate mainly to exotic applications in space modules and divers' helmets.

Useful as it is at present, speech output would be even more attractive if it could be coupled with speech input. In many ways, speech input is its "big brother". Many of the benefits of speech output are even more striking for speech input. Although people can assimilate information faster through the eyes than the ears, the majority of us can generate information faster with the mouth than with the hands. Rapid typing is a relatively uncommon skill, and even high typing rates are much slower than speaking rates (although whether we can originate ideas quickly enough to keep up with fast speech is another matter!). To take full advantage of the telephone for interaction with machines, machine recognition of speech is obviously necessary. A microwave oven, calculator, pinball machine, or alarm clock that responds to spoken commands is certainly more attractive than one that just generates spoken status messages. A book that told you how to recognize speech by machine would undoubtedly be more useful than one like this that just discusses how to synthesize it! But the technology of speech recognition is nowhere near as advanced as that of synthesis: it's a much more difficult problem. However, because speech input is obviously complementary to speech output, and even very limited input capabilities will greatly enhance many speech output systems, it is worth summarizing the present state of the art of speech recognition.

Commercial speech recognizers do exist. Almost invariably, they accept words spoken in isolation, with gaps of silence between them, rather than connected utterances. It is not difficult to discriminate with high accuracy up to a hundred different words spoken by the same speaker, especially if the vocabulary is carefully selected to avoid words which sound similar. If several different speakers are to be comprehended, performance can be greatly improved if the machine is given an opportunity to calibrate their voices in a training session, and is informed at recognition time which one is to speak. With a large population of unknown speakers, accurate recognition is difficult for vocabularies of more than a few carefully chosen words.

A half-way house between isolated word discrimination and recognition of connected speech is the problem of spotting known words in continuous speech. This allows much more natural input, if the dialogue is structured as keywords which may be interspersed by unimportant "noise words". To speak in truly isolated words requires a great deal of self-discipline and concentration: it is surprising how much of ordinary speech is accounted for by vague sounds like um's and aah's, and false starts. Word spotting disregards these and so permits a more relaxed style of speech. Some progress has been made on it in research laboratories, but the vocabularies that can be accommodated are still very small.

The difficulty of recognizing connected speech depends crucially on what is known in advance about the dialogue: its pragmatic, semantic and syntactic constraints. Highly structured dialogues constrain very heavily the choice of the next word. Recognizers which can deal with vocabularies of over 1000 words have been built in research laboratories, but the structure of the input has been such that the average "branching factor"—the size of the set out of which the next word must be selected—is only around 10 (Lea, 1980). Whether such highly constrained languages would be acceptable in many practical applications is a moot point. One commercial recognizer, developed in 1978, can cope with up to five words spoken continuously from a basic 120-word vocabulary.

There has been much debate about whether it will ever be possible for a speech recognizer to step outside rigid constraints imposed on the utterances it can understand, and act, say, as an automatic dictation machine. Certainly the most advanced recognizers to date depend very strongly on a tight context being available. Informed opinion seems to accept that in ten years' time, voice data entry in the office will be an important and economically feasible prospect, but that it would be rash to predict the appearance of unconstrained automatic dictation by then.

Let's return now to speech output and take a look at some systems which use it, to illustrate the advantages and disadvantages of speech in practical applications.

1.1 Talking Calculator

Figure 1.1 shows a calculator that speaks. Whenever a key is pressed, the device confirms the action by saying the key's name. The result of any computation is also spoken aloud. For most people, the addition of speech output to a calculator is simply a gimmick. (Note incidentally that speech *input* is a different matter altogether. The ability to dictate lists of numbers

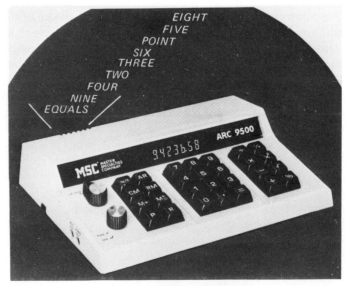

Fig. 1.1. Talking calculator.

and commands to a calculator, without lifting one's eyes from the page, would have very great advantages over keypad input.) Used-car salesmen find that speech output sometimes helps to clinch a deal: they key in the basic car price and their bargain-basement deductions, and the customer is so bemused by the resulting price being spoken aloud to him by a machine that he signs the cheque without thinking! More seriously, there may be some small advantage to be gained when keying a list of figures by touch from having their values read back for confirmation. For blind people, however, such devices are a boon, and there are many other applications, like talking elevators and talking clocks, which benefit from even very restricted voice output. Much more sophisticated is a typewriter with audio feedback, designed by IBM for the blind. Although blind typists can remember where the keys on a typewriter are without difficulty, they rely on sighted proof-readers to help check their work. This device could make them more useful as office typists and secretaries. As well as verbalizing the material (including punctuation) that has been typed, either by attempting to pronounce the words or by spelling them out as individual letters, it prompts the user through the more complex action sequences that are possible on the typewriter.

The vocabulary of the talking calculator comprises the 24 words of Table 1.1. This represents a total of about 13 seconds of speech. It is stored electronically in read-only memory (ROM), and Fig. 1.2 shows the circuitry of the speech module inside the calculator. There are three large integrated circuits. Two of them are ROMs, and the other is a special synthesis chip which decodes the highly compressed stored data into an audio waveform. Although the mechanisms used for storing speech by commercial devices are not widely advertised by the manufacturers, the talking calculator almost

Table 1.1. Vocabulary of a talking calculator.

zero	percent
one	low
two	over
three	root
four	em (m)
five	times
six	point
seven	overflow
eight	minus
nine	plus
times-minus	clear
equals	swap

Fig. 1.2. Circuitry of speech module within the talking calculator.

certainly uses linear predictive coding: a technique that we will examine in
Chapter 6. The speech quality is very poor because of the highly compressed
storage, and words are spoken in a grating monotone. However, because
of the very small vocabulary, the quality is certainly good enough for reliable
identification.

1.2 Computer-generated Wiring Instructions

I mentioned earlier that one big advantage of speech over visual output is
that it leaves the eyes free for other tasks. When wiring telephone equipment
during manufacture, the operator needs to use his hands as well as eyes to
keep his place in the task. For some time tape-recorded instructions have
been used for this in certain manufacturing plants. For example, the
instruction

Red 2.5   11A terminal strip   7A tube socket

directs the operator to cut 2.5″ of red wire, attach one end to a specified
point on the terminal strip, and attach the other to a pin of the tube socket.
The tape recorder is fitted with a pedal switch to allow a sequence of such
instructions to be executed by the operator at his own pace.

The usual way of recording the instruction tape is to have a human reader dictate them from a printed list. The tape is then checked against the list by another listener to ensure that the instructions are correct. Since wiring lists are usually stored and maintained in machine-readable form, it is natural to consider whether speech synthesis techniques could be used to generate the acoustic tape directly by a computer (Flanagan *et al.*, 1972).

Table 1.2 shows the vocabulary needed for this application. It is rather larger than that of the talking calculator (about 25 seconds of speech) but well within the limits of single-chip storage in ROM, compressed by the linear predictive technique. However, at the time that the scheme was investigated (1970–71), the method of linear predictive coding had not been fully developed, and the technology for low-cost microcircuit implementation was not available. But this is not important for this particular application, for there is no need to perform the synthesis on a miniature low-cost computer system, nor need it be accomplished in real time. In fact a technique of concatenating spectrally-encoded words was used (described in Chapter 7), and it was implemented on a minicomputer. Operating much slower than real-time, the system calculated the speech waveform and wrote it to disk storage. A subsequent phase read the pre-computed messages and recorded them on a computer-controlled analogue tape recorder.

Informal evaluation showed the scheme to be quite successful. Indeed, the synthetic speech, whose quality was not high, was actually preferred to natural speech in the noisy environment of the production line, for each instruction was spoken in the same format, with the same programmed

Table 1.2. Vocabulary needed for computer-generated wiring instructions.

A	green	seventeen
black	left	six
bottom	lower	sixteen
break	make	strip
C	nine	ten
capacitor	nineteen	terminal
eight	one	thirteen
eighteen	P	thirty
eleven	point	three
fifteen	R	top
fifty	red	tube socket
five	repeat coil	twelve
forty	resistor	twenty
four	right	two
fourteen	seven	upper

pause between the items. A list of 58 instructions of the form shown above was recorded and used to wire several pieces of apparatus without errors.

1.3 Telephone Enquiry Service

The computer-generated wiring scheme illustrates how speech can be used to give instructions without diverting visual attention from the task at hand. The next system we examine shows how speech output can make the telephone receiver into a remote computer terminal for a variety of purposes (Witten and Madams, 1977). The caller employs the touch-tone keypad shown in Figure 1.3 for input, and the computer generates a synthetic voice response. Table 1.3 shows the process of making contact with the system.

Advantage is taken of the disparate speeds of input (keyboard) and output (speech) to hasten the dialogue by imposing a question-answer structure on it, with the computer taking the initiative. The machine can afford to be slightly verbose if by so doing it makes the caller's response easier, and therefore more rapid. Moreover, operators who are experienced enough with the system to anticipate questions can easily forestall them just by typing ahead, for the computer is programmed to examine its input buffer before issuing prompts and to suppress them if input has already been provided.

Fig. 1.3. A touch-tone telephone terminal.

Table 1.3. Making contact with the telephone enquiry system.

CALLER:	Dials the service.
COMPUTER:	Answers telephone. "Hello, Telephone Enquiry Service. Please enter your user number".
CALLER:	Enters user number.
COMPUTER:	"Please enter your password".
CALLER:	Enters password.
COMPUTER:	Checks validity of password. If invalid, the user is asked to re-enter his user number. Otherwise, "Which service do you require?"
CALLER:	Enters service number.

An important aim of the system is to allow application programmers with no special knowledge of speech to write independent services for it. Table 1.4 shows an example of the use of one such application program, the Stores Information Service, which permits enquiries to be made of a database holding information on electronic components kept in stock. This subsystem is driven by *alphanumeric* data entered on the touch-tone keypad. Two or three letters are associated with each digit, in a manner which is fairly standard in touch-tone telephone applications. These are printed on a card overlay that fits the keypad (see Fig. 1.3). Although true alphanumeric data entry would require a multiple key press for each character, the ambiguity inherent in a single-key-per-character convention can usually be resolved by the computer, if it has a list of permissible entries. For example, the component names SN7406 and ZTX300 are read by the machine as "767406" and "189300", respectively. Confusion rarely occurs if the machine is expecting a valid component code. The same holds true of people's names, and file names—although with these one must take care not to identify a series of files by similar names, like TX38A, TX38B, TX38C. It is easy for the machine to detect the rare cases where ambiguity occurs, and respond by requesting further information: "The component name is SN7406. Is this correct?" (In fact, the Stores Information Service illustrated in Table 1.4 is defective in that it *always* requests confirmation of an entry, even when no ambiguity exists.) The use of a telephone keypad for data entry will be taken up again in Chapter 10.

A distinction is drawn throughout the system between data entries and commands, the latter being prefixed by a "*". In this example, the programmer chose to define a command for each possible question about a component, so that a new component name can be entered at any time without ambiguity. The price paid for the resulting brevity of dialogue is the burden of memorizing the meaning of the commands. This is an inherent disadvantage of a one-dimensional auditory display over the more con-

Table 1.4. The Stores Information Service.

COMPUTER:	"Stores Information Service. Please enter component name".
CALLER:	Enters "SN7406#".
COMPUTER:	"The component name is SN7406. Is this correct?"
CALLER:	Enters "*1#" (system convention for "yes").
COMPUTER:	"This component is in stores".
CALLER:	Enters "*7#" (command for "price").
COMPUTER:	"The component price is 35 pence".
CALLER:	Enters "*8#" (command for "minimum number").
COMPUTER:	"The minimum number of this component kept in stores is 10".
CALLER:	Enters "SN7417#".
COMPUTER:	"The component name is SN7417. Is this correct?"
CALLER:	Enters "*1#".
COMPUTER:	"This component is not in stores".
CALLER:	Enters "*9#" (command for "delivery time").
COMPUTER:	"The expected delivery time is 14 days".
CALLER:	Enters "*0#".
COMPUTER:	"Which service do you require?"

ventional graphical output: presenting menus by speech is tedious and long-winded. In practice, however, for a simple task such as the Stores Information Service it is quite convenient for the caller to search for the appropriate command by trying out all possibilities: there are only a few.

The problem of memorizing commands is alleviated by establishing some system-wide conventions. Each input is terminated by a "#", and the meaning of standard commands is given in Table 1.5.

A summary of services available on the system is given in Table 1.6. They range from simple games and demonstrations, through serious database services, to system maintenance facilities. A priority structure is imposed upon them, with higher service numbers being available only to higher priority users. Services in the lowest range (1–99) can be obtained by all, while those in the highest range (900–999) are maintenance services, available only to the system designers. Access to the lower-numbered "games"

Table 1.5. System-wide conventions for the service.

*#	—Erase this input line, regardless of what has been typed before the "*".
*0#	—Stop. Used to exit from any service.
*1#	—Yes.
*2#	—No.
*3#	—Repeat question or summarize state of current transaction.
# alone	—Short form of repeat. Repeats or summarizes in an abbreviated fashion.

Table 1.6. Summary of services on a telephone enquiry system.

1—tells the time
2—Biffo (a game of NIM)
3—MOO (a game similar to that marketed under the name "Mastermind")
4—error demonstration
5—speak a file in phonetic format
6—listening test
7—music (allows you to enter a tune and play it)
8—gives the date

100—squash ladder
101—stores information service
102—computes means and standard deviations
103—telephone directory

411—user information
412—change password
413—gripe (permits feedback on services from caller)

600—first year laboratory marks entering service

910—repeat utterance (allows testing of system)
911—speak utterance (allows testing of system)
912—enable/disable user 100 (a no-password guest user number)
913   mount a magnetic tape on the computer
914—set/reset demonstration mode (prohibits access by low-priority users)
915—inhibit games
916— inhibit the MOO game
917—disable password checking when users log in

---

services can be inhibited by a priority user: this was found necessary to prevent over-use of the system! Another advantage of telephone access to an information retrieval system is that some day-to-day maintenance can be done remotely, from the office telephone.

This telephone enquiry service, which was built in 1974, demonstrated that speech synthesis had moved from a specialist phonetic discipline into the province of engineering practicability. The speech was generated "by rule" from a phonetic input (the method is covered in Chapters 7 and 8), which has very low data storage requirements of around 75 bit/s of speech. Thus an enormous vocabulary and range of services could be accomodated on a small computer system. Despite the fairly low quality of the speech, the response from callers was most encouraging. Admittedly the user population was a self-selected body of University staff, which one might suppose to have high tolerance to new ideas, and a system designed for the general public would require more effort to be spent on developing speech of greater intelligibility. Although it was observed that some callers failed to understand parts of the responses, even after repetition, communication was largely unhindered in most cases, users being driven by a high motivation to help the system help them.

The use of speech output in conjunction with a simple input device requires careful thought for interaction to be successful and comfortable. It is necessary that the computer direct the conversation as much as possible, without seeming to be taking charge. Provision for eliminating prompts which are unwanted by sophisticated users is essential to avoid frustration. We will return to the topic of programming techniques for speech interaction in Chapter 10.

Making a computer system available over the telephone results in a sudden vast increase in the user population. Although people's reaction to a new computer terminal in every office was overwhelmingly favourable, careful resource allocation was essential to prevent the service being hogged by a persistent few. As with all multiaccess computer systems, it is particularly important that error recovery is effected automatically and gracefully.

1.4 Speech Output in the Telephone Exchange

The telephone enquiry service was an experimental vehicle for research on speech interaction, and was developed in 1974. Since then, speech has begun to be used in real commercial applications. One example is System X, the British Post Office's computer-controlled telephone exchange. This incorporates many features not found in conventional telephone exchanges. For example, if a number is found to be busy, the call can be attempted again by a "repeat last call" command, without having to re-dial the full number. Alternatively, the last number can be stored for future re-dialling, freeing the phone for other calls. "Short code dialling" allows a customer to associate short codes with commonly-dialled numbers. Alarm calls can be booked at specified times, and are made automatically without human intervention. Incoming calls can be barred, as can outgoing ones. A diversion service allows all incoming calls to be diverted to another telephone, either immediately, or if a call to the original number remains unanswered for a specified period of time, or if the original number is busy. Three-party calls can be set up automatically, without involving the operator.

Making use of these facilities presents the caller with something of a problem. With conventional telephone exchanges, feedback is provided on what is happening to a call by the use of four tones: the dial tone, the busy tone, the ringing tone and the number unavailable tone. For the more sophisticated interaction which is expected on the advanced exchange, a much greater variety of status signals is required. The obvious solution is to use computer-generated spoken messages to inform the caller when these services are invoked, and to guide him through the sequences of actions needed to set up facilities like call re-direction. For example, the messages used by the exchange when a user accesses the alarm call service are

Alarm call service. Dial the time of your alarm call followed by square*.
You have booked an alarm call for seven thirty hours.
Alarm call operator. At the third stroke it will be seven thirty.

Because of the rather small vocabulary, the number of messages that can be stored in their entirety rather then being formed by concatenation of smaller units, and the short time which was available for development, System X stores speech as a time waveform, slightly compressed by a time-domain encoding operation (such techniques are described in Chapter 3). Utterances which contain variable parts, like the time of alarm in the messages above, are formed by inserting separately-recorded digits in a fixed "carrier" message. No attempt is made to apply uniform intonation contours to the synthetic utterances. The resulting speech is of excellent quality (being a slightly compressed recording of a human voice), but sometimes exhibits somewhat anomalous pitch contours. For example, the digits comprising numbers often sound rather jerky and out-of-context; which indeed they are.

Even more advanced facilities can be expected on telephone exchanges in the future. A message storage capability is one example. Although automatic call recording machines have been available for years, a centralized facility could time and date a message, collect the caller's identity (using the telephone keypad), and allow the recipient to select messages left for him through an interactive dialogue so that he could control the order in which he listens to them. He could choose to leave certain messages to be dealt with later, or re-route them to a colleague. He may even wish to leave reminders for himself, to be dialled automatically at specified times (like alarm calls with user-defined information attached). The sender of a message could be informed automatically by the system when it is delivered. None of this requires speech recognition, but it does need economical speech *storage*, and also speech *synthesis* (for time and date tags).

1.5 Travel Consultant

Some current research in speech communication with computers is aimed at embedding the dialogue in a task environment which provides it with

---

* "Square" is the term used for the "#" key on the touch-tone telephone.

Table 1.7. A conversation with an airline flight information service (from Levinson and Shipley, 1980).

COMPUTER:	This is the Bell Laboratories flight information system. May I help you?
CALLER:	I would like to go to Chicago.
COMPUTER:	Please specify the day of your departure.
CALLER:	I want to leave at four p.m.
COMPUTER:	Please specify the day of your departure.
CALLER:	I want to depart on the two five May.
COMPUTER:	Flight number nine two leaves New York at four p.m. arrives in Chicago at five twenty five p.m.
CALLER:	What plane is on the flight?
COMPUTER:	The aircraft is a Boeing seven twenty seven
CALLER:	How much is the fare?
COMPUTER:	The round trip coach fare is one hundred forty two dollars.
CALLER:	I want a first class seat.
COMPUTER:	One seat thank you.
CALLER:	What is the fare?
COMPUTER:	The round trip first class fare is one hundred eighty four dollars.
CALLER:	Please repeat the arrival time.
COMPUTER:	The arrival time is five twenty five p.m.
CALLER:	I will take the flight.
COMPUTER:	Your reservation on flight number nine two to Chicago on Friday is confirmed. Thank you.

an overall contextual framework. This in fact was the motivation for the experimental telephone enquiry service described above, and it was observed that people are able to tolerate rather low-quality speech if they feel that the interaction is worthwhile. One step further is the use of speech *input* as well as output, and here the context of the conversation which is provided by the task environment can be used to improve recognition accuracy significantly. A system set up at Bell Telephone Laboratories indicates what we can expect to find operating commercially in the future (Levinson and Shipley, 1980). It provides timetable information about airline flights, and allows the user to make reservations.

An example dialogue is given in Table 1.7. The user dials the system from an ordinary telephone. The recognition side must be trained by each user, and accepts isolated words spoken with brief pauses between them. The voice response unit has a vocabulary of around 200 words, and synthesizes its answers by slotting words into "templates" evoked by the speech understanding part in response to a query. For example,

This flight makes—stops
Flight number—leaves—at—, arrives in—at—

are templates which when called with specific slot fillers could produce the utterances

> This flight makes three stops
> Flight number nine two leaves New York at four p.m., arrives in Chicago at five twenty-five p.m.

The chief research interest of the system is in its speech understanding capabilities, and the method used for speech output is relatively straight-forward. The templates and words are recorded, digitized, compressed slightly, and stored on disk files (totalling a few hundred thousand bytes of storage), using techniques similar to those of System X. Again, no in-dependent manipulation of pitch is possible, and so the utterances sound intelligible but the transition between templates and slot fillers is not com-pletely fluent. However, the overall context of the interaction means that the communication is not seriously disrupted even if the machine occasion-ally misunderstands the man or vice versa. The user's attention is drawn away from recognition accuracy and focussed on the exchange of information with the machine. The authors conclude that progress in speech recognition can best be made by studying it in the context of communication rather than in a vacuum or as part of a one-way channel, and the same is un-doubtedly true of speech synthesis as well.

1.6 Reading Machine for the Blind

Perhaps the most advanced attempt to provide speech output from a com-puter is the Kurzweil reading machine for the blind, first marketed in the late 1970s (Fig. 1.4). This device reads an ordinary book aloud. Users adjust

Fig. 1.4. The Kurzweil reading machine.

the reading speed according to the content of the material and their familiarity with it, and the maximum rate has recently been improved to around 225 words per minute—perhaps half as fast again as normal human speech rates.

As well as generating speech from text, the machine has to scan the document being read and identify the characters presented to it. A scanning camera is used, controlled by a program which searches for and tracks the lines of text. The output of the camera is digitized, and the image is enhanced using signal-processing techniques. Next each individual letter must be isolated, and its geometric features identified and compared with a pre-stored table of letter shapes. Isolation of letters is not at all trivial, for many type fonts have "ligatures" which are combinations of characters joined together (for example, the letters "fi" are often run together.) The machine must cope with many printed type fonts, as well as typewritten ones. The text-recognition side of the Kurzweil reading machine is in fact one of its most advanced features.

We will discuss the problem of speech generation from text in Chapter 9. It has many facets. First there is pronunciation, the translation of letters to sounds. It is important to take into account the morphological structure of words, dividing them into "root" and "endings". Many words have concatenated suffixes (like "like-li-ness"). These are important to detect, because a final "e" which appears on a root word is not pronounced itself but affects the pronunciation of the previous vowel. Then there is the difficulty that some words look the same but are pronounced differently, depending on their meaning or on the syntactic part that they play in the sentence. Appropriate intonation is extremely difficult to generate from a plain textual representation, for it depends on the meaning of the text and the way in which emphasis is given to it by the reader. Similarly the rhythmic structure is important, partly for correct pronunciation and partly for purposes of emphasis. Finally the sounds that have been deduced from the text need to be synthesized into acoustic form, taking due account of the many and varied contextual effects that occur in natural speech. This by itself is a challenging problem.

The performance of the Kurzweil reading machine is not good. While it seems to be true that some blind people can make use of it, it is far from comprehensible to an untrained listener. For example, it will miss out words and even whole phrases, hesitate in a stuttering manner, blatantly mispronounce many words, fail to detect "e"s which should be silent, and give completely wrong rhythms to words, making them impossible to understand. Its intonation is decidedly unnatural, monotonous, and often downright misleading. When it reads completely new text to people unfamiliar with its quirks, they invariably fail to understand more than an odd word here and there, and do not improve significantly when the text is repeated more than once. Naturally performance improves if the material is familiar or expected in some way. One useful feature is the machine's ability to spell out difficult words on command from the user.

While not wishing to denigrate the Kurzweil machine, which is a remarkable achievement in that it integrates together many different advanced technologies, there is no doubt that the state of the art in speech synthesis directly from unadorned text is extremely primitive, at present. It is vital not to overemphasize the potential usefulness of abysmal speech, which takes a great deal of training on the part of the user before it becomes at all intelligible. To make a rather extreme analogy, Morse code could be used as audio output, requiring a great deal of training, but capable of being understood at quite high rates by an expert. It could be generated very cheaply. But clearly the man in the street would find it quite unacceptable as an audio output medium, because of the excessive effort required to learn to use it. In many applications, very bad synthetic speech is just as useless. However, the issue is complicated by the fact that for people who use synthesizers regularly, synthetic speech becomes quite easily comprehensible. We will return to the problem of evaluating the quality of artificial speech later in the book (Chapter 8).

1.7 System Considerations for Speech Output

Fortunately, very many of the applications of speech output from computers do not need to read unadorned text. In all the example systems described above (except the reading machine), it is enough to be able to store utterances in some representation which can include pre-programmed cues for pronunciation, rhythm and intonation in a much more explicit way than ordinary text does.

Of course, techniques for storing audio information have been in use for decades. For example, a domestic cassette tape recorder stores speech at much better than telephone quality at very low cost. The method of direct recording of an analogue waveform is currently used for announcements in the telephone network to provide information such as the time, weather forecasts, and even bedtime stories. However, it is difficult to provide rapid access to messages stored in analogue form, and although some computer peripherals which use analogue recordings for voice-response applications have been marketed (they are discussed briefly at the beginning of Chapter 3) they have been superseded by digital storage techniques.

Although direct storage of a digitized audio waveform is used in some voice-response systems, the approach has certain limitations. The most obvious one is the large storage requirement: suitable coding can reduce the data-rate of speech to as little as one hundredth of that needed by direct digitization, and textual representations reduce it by another factor of ten or twenty. (Of course, the speech quality is inevitably compromised somewhat by data-compression techniques.) However, the cost of storage is dropping so fast that this is not necessarily an overriding factor. A more fundamental limitation is that utterances stored directly cannot sensibly be modified in any way to take account of differing contexts.

If the results of certain kinds of analyses of utterances are stored, instead of simply the digitized waveform, a great deal more flexibility can be gained. It is possible to separate out the features of intonation and amplitude from the articulation of the speech, and this raises the attractive possibility of regenerating utterances with pitch contours different from those with which they were recorded. The primary analysis technique used for this purpose is *linear prediction* of speech, and this is treated in some detail in Chapter 6. It also reduces drastically the data-rate of speech, by a factor of around 50. It is likely that many voice-response systems in the short- and medium-term future will use linear predictive representations for utterance storage.

For maximum flexibility, however, it is preferable to store a textual representation of the utterance. There is an important distinction between speech *storage*, where an actual human utterance is recorded, perhaps processed to lower the data-rate, and stored for subsequent regeneration when required, and speech *synthesis*, where the machine produces its own individual utterances which are not based on recordings of a person saying the same thing. The difference is summarized in Fig. 1.5. In both cases something is stored: for the first it is a direct representation of an actual human utterance, while for the second it is a typed *description* of the utterance in terms of the sounds, or phonemes, which constitute it. The accent and tone of voice of the human speaker will be apparent in the stored speech output, while for synthetic speech the accent is the machine's and the tone of voice is determined by the synthesis program.

Probably the most attractive representation of utterances in man-machine systems is ordinary English text, as used by the Kurzweil reading machine. But, as noted above, this poses extraordinarily difficult problems for the synthesis procedure, and these inevitably result in severely degraded speech. Although in the very long-term, these problems may indeed be solved, most speech output systems can adopt as their representation of an utterance a description of it which explicitly conveys the difficult features of intonation, rhythm, and even pronunciation. In the kind of applications described above (barring the reading machine), input will be prepared by a programmer as

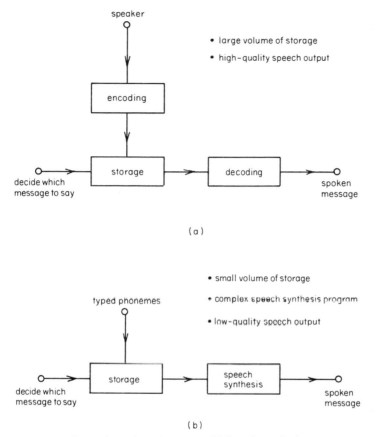

Fig. 1.5. (a) Speech storage, (b) Speech synthesis.

he builds the software system which supports the interactive dialogue. Although it is important that the method of specifying utterances be easily learned, it is not necessary that plain English is used. It should be simple for the programmer to enter new utterances and modify them on-line in cut-and-try attempts to render the man-machine dialogue as natural as possible. A phonetic input can be quite adequate for this, especially if the system allows the programmer to hear immediately the synthesized version of the message he types. Furthermore, markers which indicate rhythm and intonation can be added to the message so that the system does not have to deduce these features by attempting to "understand" the plain text.

This brings us to another disadvantage of speech storage as compared with speech synthesis. To provide utterances for a voice response system using stored human speech, one must assemble together special input hardware, a quiet room, and (probably) a dedicated computer. If the speech is to be heavily encoded, either expensive special hardware is required or the encoding process, if performed by software on a general-purpose computer, will take a considerable length of time (perhaps hundreds of times real-time). In either case, time-consuming editing of the speech will be necessary, with follow-up recordings to clarify sections of speech which turn out to be unsuitable or badly recorded. If at a later date the voice response system needs modification, it will be necessary to recall the same speaker, or re-record the entire utterance set. This discourages the application programmer from adjusting his dialogue in the light of experience. Synthesizing from a textual representation, on the other hand, allows him to change a speech prompt as simply as he could a VDU one, and evaluate its effect immediately.

We will return to methods of digitizing and compacting speech in Chapters 3 and 4, and carry on to consider speech synthesis in subsequent chapters. First, however, it is necessary to take a look at what speech is and how people produce it.

1.8 References

Flanagan, J.L., Rabiner, L.R., Schafer, R.W. and Denman, J.D. (1972). Wiring telephone apparatus from computer-generated speech. *Bell System Technical J.* **51** (2) 391–397.

Hill, D.R. (1971). Man-machine interaction using speech. *In* "Advances in computers 11", (F.L. Alt and M. Rubinoff, eds), pp 165–230. Academic Press, New York and London.

Lea, W.A. (editor) (1980). "Trends in speech recognition", Prentice Hall.

Levinson, S.E. and Shipley, K.L. (1980). A conversational-mode airline information and reservation system using speech input and output. *Bell System Technical J.* **59** (1) 119–137.

Turn, R. (1974). Speech as a man-computer communication channel. *Proc National Computer Conference*, 139–143.

Witten, I.H. and Madams, P.H.C. (1977). The Telephone Enquiry Service: a man-machine system using synthetic speech. *Int J Man-Machine Studies*, **9** (4) 449–464.

1.9 Further Reading

There are remarkably few general books on speech output, although a substantial specialist literature exists for the subject. In addition to the references listed above, I suggest that you look at the following.

Ainsworth, W.A. (1976). "Mechanisms of speech recognition", Pergamon.
    A nice, easy-going introduction to speech recognition, this book covers the acoustic structure of the speech signal in a way which makes it useful as

background reading for speech synthesis as well. It complements Lea, 1980, cited above; which presents more recent results in greater depth.

Flanagan, J.L. and Rabiner, L.R. (editors) (1973). "Speech synthesis", Dowden, Hutchinson and Ross, Stroundsburg, Pennsylvania.

This is a collection of previously-published research papers on speech synthesis, rather than a unified book. It contains many of the classic papers on the subject from 1940 to 1972, and is a very useful reference work.

LeBoss, B. (1980). Speech I/O is making itself heard. *Electronics*, 95–105, May 22.

The magazine *Electronics* is an excellent source of up-to-the-minute news, product announcements, titbits, and rumours in the commercial speech technology world. This particular article discusses the projected size of the voice output market and gives a brief synopsis of the activities of several interested companies.

Witten, I.H. (1980). "Communicating with microcomputers", Academic Press, London and New York.

A recent book on microcomputer technology, this is unusual in that it contains a major section on speech communication with computers (as well as ones on computer buses, interfaces and graphics).

2

WHAT IS SPEECH?

People speak by using their vocal cords as a sound source, and making rapid gestures of the articulatory organs (tongue, lips, jaw and so on). The resulting changes in shape of the vocal tract allow production of the different sounds that we know as the vowels and consonants of ordinary language.

What is it necessary to learn about this process for the purposes of speech output from computers? That depends crucially upon how speech is represented in the system. If utterances are stored as time waveforms (and this is what we will be discussing in the next chapter) the structure of speech is not important. If frequency-related parameters of particular natural utterances are stored, then it is advantageous to take into account some of the acoustic properties of the speech waveform.

This point can be brought into focus by contrasting the transmission (or storage) of speech with that of real-life television pictures, as has been proposed for a videophone service. Massive data reductions, of the order of 50:1, can be achieved for speech, using techniques that are described in later chapters. For pictures, data reduction is still an important issue, even more so for the videophone than for the telephone because of the vastly higher information rates involved. Unfortunately, the potential for data reduction is much smaller: nothing like the 50:1 figure quoted above. This is because speech sounds have definite characteristics, imparted by the fact that they are produced by a human vocal tract, which can be exploited for data reduction. Television pictures have no equivalent generative structure, for they show just those things that the camera points at.

Moving up from frequency-related parameters of *particular* utterances, it is possible to store such parameters in a *general* form which characterizes the sound segments that appear in spoken language. This immediately raises the issue of *classification* of sound segments, to form a basis for storing generalized acoustic information and for retrieval of the information needed to synthesize any particular utterance. Speech is by nature continuous, and any synthesis system based on discrete classification must come to terms with this by tackling the problems of transition from one segment to another, and local modification of sound segments as a function of their context.

This brings us to another level of representation. So far we have talked of the *acoustic* nature of speech, but when we have to cope with transitions between discrete sound segments, it may be fruitful to consider *articulatory* properties as well. Any model of the speech production process is in effect a model of the articulatory process that generates the speech. Some speech research is concerned with modelling the vocal tract directly, rather than modelling the acoustic output from it. One might specify, for example, position of tongue and posture of jaw and lips for a vowel, instead of giving frequency-related characteristics of it. This is a potent tool in linguistic research, for it brings one closer to human production of speech: in particular to the connection between brain and articulators.

Articulatory synthesis holds a promise of high-quality speech, for the transitional effects caused by tongue and jaw inertia can be modelled directly. However, this potential has not yet been realized. Speech from current articulatory models is of much poorer quality than that from acoustically-based synthesis methods. The major problem is in gaining data about articulatory behaviour during running speech: it is much easier to perform acoustic analysis on the resulting sound than it is to examine the vocal organs in action. Because of this, the subject is not treated in this book. We will only look at articulatory properties insofar as they help us to understand, in a qualitative way, the acoustic nature of speech.

Speech, however, is much more than mere articulation. Consider, admittedly a rather extreme and chauvinistic example, the number of ways a girl can say "yes". Breathy voice, slow tempo, low pitch: these are all characteristics which affect the utterance as a whole, rather than being classifiable into individual sound segments. Linguists call them "prosodic" or "suprasegmental" features, for they relate to overall aspects of the utterance, and distinguish them from "segmental" ones which concern the articulation of individual segments of syllables. The most important prosodic features are pitch, or fundamental frequency of the voice, and rhythm.

This chapter provides a brief introduction to the nature of the speech signal. Depending upon what speech output techniques we use, it may be necessary to understand something of the acoustic nature of the speech signal; the system that generates it (the vocal tract); commonly-used classifications of sound segments; and the prosodic aspects of speech. This material is little used in the early chapters of the book, but becomes increasingly important as the story unfolds. Hence you may skip the remainder of this chapter if you wish, but should return to it later to pick up more background whenever it becomes necessary.

2.1 The Anatomy of Speech

The so-called "voiced" sounds of speech, like the sound you make when you say "aaah", are produced by passing air up from the lungs through the larynx or voicebox, which is situated just behind the Adam's apple. The vocal tract from the larynx to the lips acts as a resonant cavity, amplifying certain frequencies and attenuating others.

The waveform generated by the larynx, however, is not simply sinusoidal. (If it were, the vocal tract resonances would merely give a sine wave of the same frequency but amplified or attenuated according to how close it was to the nearest resonance.) The larynx contains two folds of skin, the vocal cords, which blow apart and flap together again in each cycle of the pitch period. The pitch of a male voice in speech varies from as low as 50 Hz (cycles per second) to perhaps 250 Hz, with a typical median value of 100 Hz. For a female voice the range is higher, up to about 500 Hz in speech. Singing can go much higher: a top C sung by a soprano has a frequency of just over 1000 Hz, and some opera singers can reach substantially higher than this.

The flapping action of the vocal cords gives a waveform which can be approximated by a triangular pulse (this and other approximations will be discussed in Chapter 5). It has a rich spectrum of harmonics, decaying at around 12 dB/octave, and each harmonic is affected by the vocal tract resonances.

Vocal Tract Resonances

A simple model of the vocal tract is an organ-pipe-like cylindrical tube (Fig. 2.1), with a sound source at one end (the larynx) and open at the other (the lips). This has resonances at wavelengths $4L$, $4L/3$, $4L/5$, ..., where L is the length of the tube; and these correspond to frequencies $c/4L$, $3c/4L$, $5c/4L$, ... Hz; c being the speed of sound in air. Calculating these frequencies, using a typical figure for the distance between larynx and lips of 17 cm, and $c = 340$ m/s for the speed of sound, leads to resonances at approximately 500 Hz, 1500 Hz, 2500 Hz, ...

When excited by the harmonic-rich waveform of the larynx, the vocal tract resonances produce peaks known as *formants* in the energy spectrum of the speech wave (Fig. 2.2). The lowest formant, called formant one, varies from around 200 Hz to 1000 Hz during speech, the exact range depending on the size of the vocal tract. Formant two varies from around 500 to 2500 Hz, and formant three from around 1500 to 3500 Hz.

You can easily hear the lowest formant by whispering the vowels in the words "heed", "hid", "head", "had", "hod", "hawed", and "who'd". They appear to have a steadily descending pitch, yet since you are whispering there is no fundamental frequency. What you hear is the lowest resonance of the vocal tract: formant one. Some masochistic people can play simple tunes with this formant by putting their mouth in successive vowel shapes and knocking the top of their head with their knuckles—hard!

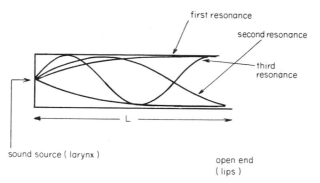

Fig. 2.1. Resonances in the organ-pipe model of the vocal tract.

A difficulty occurs when trying to identify the lower formants for speakers with high-pitched voices. When a formant frequency falls below the fundamental excitation frequency of the voice, its effect is diminished, although it is still present. The vibrato used by opera singers provides a very low-frequency excitation (at the vibrato rate) which helps to illuminate the lower formants even when the pitch of the voice is very high.

Of course, speech is not a static phenomenon. The organ-pipe model

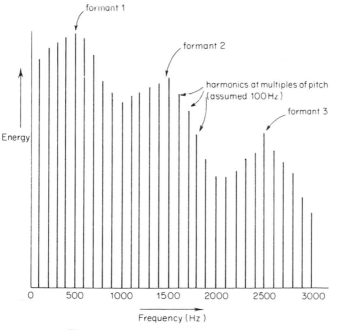
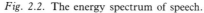

Fig. 2.2. The energy spectrum of speech.

describes the speech spectrum during a continuously held vowel with the mouth in a neutral position such as for "aaah". But in real speech the tongue and lips are in continuous motion, altering the shape of the vocal tract and hence the positions of the resonances. It is as if the organ-pipe were being squeezed and expanded in different places all the time. Say *ee* as in "heed" and feel how close your tongue is to the roof of your mouth, causing a constriction near the front of the vocal cavity.

Linguists and speech engineers use a special frequency analyser called a "sound spectrograph" to make a three-dimensional plot of the variation of the speech energy spectrum with time. Figure 2.3 shows a spectrogram of the utterance "go away". Frequency is given on the vertical axis, and a scale is shown at the beginning. Time is plotted horizontally, and energy is given by the darkness of any particular area. The lower few formants can be seen as dark bands extending horizontally, and they are in continuous motion. In the neutral first vowel of "away", the formant frequencies pass through approximately the 500 Hz, 1500 Hz, and 2500 Hz that we calculated earlier. (In fact, formants two and three are somewhat lower than these values.)

The fine vertical striations in the spectrogram correspond to single openings of the vocal cords. Pitch changes continuously throughout an utterance, and this can be seen on the spectrogram by the differences in spacing of the striations. Pitch change, or *intonation*, is singularly important in lending naturalness to speech.

On a spectrogram, a continuously held vowel shows up as a static energy spectrum. But beware: what we call a vowel in everyday language is not the same thing as a "vowel" in phonetic terms. Say "I" and feel how the tongue moves continuously while you're speaking. Technically, this is a *diphthong* or slide between two vowel positions, and not a single vowel. If you say *ar* as in "hard", and change slowly to *ee* as in "heed", you will obtain a diphthong not unlike that in "I". And there are many more phonetically different vowel sounds than the a, e, i, o, and u that we normally think of. The words "hood" and "mood" have different vowels, for example, as do "head" and "mead". The principal acoustic difference between the various vowel sounds is in the frequencies of the first two formants.

A further complication is introduced by the nasal tract. This is a large cavity which is coupled to the oral tract by a passage at the back of the mouth. The passage is guarded by a flap of skin called the "velum". You know about this because inadvertent opening of the velum while swallowing causes food or drink to go up your nose. The nasal cavity is switched in and out of the vocal tract by the velum during speech. It is used for consonants *m*, *n*, and the *ng* sound in the word "singing". Vowels are frequently nasalized too. A very effective demonstration of the amount of nasalization in ordinary speech can be obtained by cutting a nose-shaped

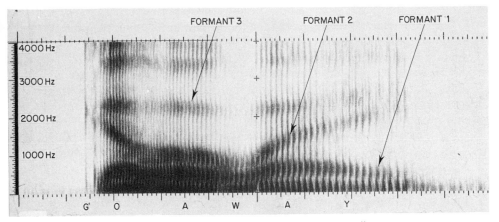

Fig. 2.3. Spectrogram of the utterance "go away".

hole in a large baffle which divides a room, speaking normally with one's nose in the hole, and having someone listen on the other side. The frequency of occurrence of nasal sounds, and the volume of sound that is emitted through the nose, are both surprisingly large. Interestingly enough, when we say in conversation that someone sounds "nasal", we usually mean "non-nasal". When the nasal passages are blocked by a cold, nasal sounds are missing: *n*'s turn into *d*'s, and *m*'s to *b*'s.

When the nasal cavity is switched in to the vocal tract, it introduces formant resonances, just as the oral cavity does. Although we cannot alter the shape of the nasal tract significantly, the nasal formant pattern is not fixed, because the oral tract does play a part in nasal resonances. If you say *m*, *n*, and *ng* continuously, you can hear the difference and feel how it is produced by altering the combined nasal/oral tract resonances with your tongue position. The nasal cavity operates in parallel with the oral one; this causes the two resonance patterns to be summed together, with resulting complications which will be discussed in Chapter 5.

Sound Sources

Speech involves sounds other than those caused by regular vibration of the larynx. When you whisper, the folds of the larynx are held slightly apart so that the air passing between them becomes turbulent, causing a noisy excitation of the resonant cavity. The formant peaks are still present, superimposed on the noise. Such "aspirated" sounds occur in the *h* of "hello", and for a very short time after the lips are opened at the beginning of "pit".

Constrictions made in the mouth produce hissy noises such as *ss*, *sh*, and *f*. For example in *ss*, the tip of the tongue is high up, very close to the roof of the mouth. Turbulent air passing through this constriction causes a random noise excitation known as "frication". Actually, the roof of the mouth is quite a complicated object. You can feel with your tongue a bony hump or ridge just behind the front teeth, and it is this that forms a constriction with the tongue for *s*. In *sh*, the tongue is flattened close to the roof of the mouth slightly farther back, in a position rather similar to that for *ee*, but with a narrower constriction; while *f* is produced with the upper teeth and lower lip. Because they are made near the front of the mouth, the resonances of the vocal tract have little effect on these fricative sounds.

To distinguish them from aspiration and frication, the ordinary speech sounds (like "aaah") which have their source in larynx vibration are known technically as "voiced". Aspirated and fricative sounds are called "unvoiced". Thus the three different sound types can be classified as

—voiced
—unvoiced (fricative)
—unvoiced (aspirated).

Can any of these types occur together? It would seem that voicing and aspiration can not, for the former requires the larynx to be vibrating regularly, but for the latter, it must be generating turbulent noise. However, there is a condition known technically as "breathy voice" which occurs when the vocal cords are slightly apart, still vibrating, but with a large volume of air passing between to create turbulence. Voicing can easily occur in conjunction with frication. Corresponding to *s*, *sh*, and *f* we get the *voiced* fricatives *z*, the sound in the middle of words like "vision" which I will call *zh*, and *v*. A simple illustration of voicing is to say "ffffvvvvffff ...". During the voiced part, you can feel the larynx vibrations with a finger on your Adam's apple, and it can be heard quite clearly if you stop up your ears. Technically, there is nothing to prevent frication and aspiration from occurring together (they do, for example, when a voiced fricative is whispered) but the combination is not an important one.

The complicated acoustic effects of noisy excitation in speech can be seen in the spectrogram in Fig. 2.4 of "high altitude jets whizz past screaming".

The Source-filter Model of Speech Production

We have been talking in terms of a sound source (be it voiced or unvoiced) exciting the resonances of the oral (and possibly the nasal) tract. This model, which is used extensively in speech analysis and synthesis, is known as the source-filter model of speech production. The reason for its success is that the effect of the resonances can be modelled as a frequency-selective filter, operating on an input which is the source excitation. Thus the frequency spectrum of the source is modified by multiplying it by the frequency characteristic of the filter (or adding it, if amplitudes are expressed logarithmically). This can be seen in Fig. 2.5, which shows a source spectrum and filter characteristic which combine to give the overall spectrum of Fig. 2.2.

Although, as mentioned above, the various fricatives are not subjected to the resonances of the vocal tract to the same extent that voiced and aspirated sounds are, they can still be modelled as a noise source followed by a filter to give them their different sound qualities.

The source-filter model is an oversimplification of the actual speech production system. There is inevitably some coupling between the vocal tract

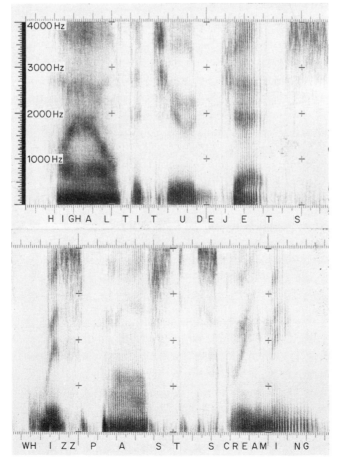

Fig. 2.4. Spectrogram of "high-altitude jets whizz past screaming".

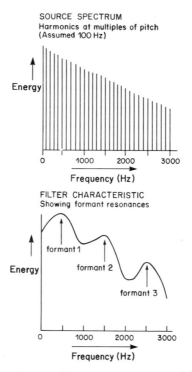

Fig. 2.5. The source-filter model: a source spectrum and filter characteristic.

and the lungs, through the glottis, during the period when it is open. This effectively makes the filter characteristics change during each individual cycle of the excitation. However, although the effect is of interest to speech researchers, it is probably not of great significance for practical speech output.

One very interesting implication of the source-filter model is that the prosodic features of pitch and amplitude are largely properties of the source, while segmental ones are introduced by the filter. This makes it possible to separate some aspects of overall prosody from the actual segmental content of an utterance, so that, for example, a human utterance can be stored initially and then spoken by a machine with a variety of different intonations.

2.2 Classification of Speech Sounds

The need to classify sound segments as a basis for storing generalized acoustic information and retrieving it was mentioned earlier. There is a real difficulty here because speech is by nature continuous and classifications are discrete. It is important to remember this difficulty because it is all too easy to criticize the complex and often confusing attempts of linguists to tackle the classification task.

Linguists call a written representation of the *sounds* of an utterance a "phonetic transcription" of it. The same utterance can be transcribed at different levels of detail: simple transcriptions are called "broad", and more specific ones are called "narrow". Perhaps the most logically satisfying kind of transcription employs units termed "phonemes". This is the broadest transcription, and is sometimes called a *phonemic* transcription to emphasize that it is in terms of phonemes. Unfortunately, the word "phoneme" is often used somewhat loosely. In its true sense, a phoneme is a *logical* unit, rather than a physical, acoustic, one, and is defined in relation to a particular language by reference to its use in discriminating different words. Classifications of sounds which are based on their semantic role as word-discriminators are called *phonological* classifications; we could ensure that there is no ambiguity in the sense with which we use the term "phoneme" by calling it a phonological unit, and the phonemic transcription could be called a phonological one.

Broad Phonetic Transcription

A phoneme is an abstract unit representing a set of different sounds. The issue is confused by the fact that the members of the set actually sound very similar, if not identical, to the untrained ear: precisely because the difference between them plays no part in distinguishing words from each other in the particular language concerned.

Take the words "key" and "caw", for example. Despite the difference in spelling, both of them begin with a *k* sound that belongs (in English) to the same phoneme set, called *k*. However, say them two or three times each, concentrating on the position of the tongue during the *k*. It is quite different in each case. For "key", it is raised, close to the roof of the mouth, in preparation for the *ee*, whereas in "caw" it is much lower down. The sound of the *k* is actually quite different in the two cases. Yet they belong to the same phoneme, for there is no pair of words which relies on this difference to distinguish them; "key" and "caw" are obviously distinguished by their vowels, not by the initial consonant. You probably cannot hear clearly the difference between the two *k*'s, precisely because they belong to the same phoneme and so the difference is not important (for English).

The point is sharpened by considering another language where we make a distinction (and hence can hear the difference) between two sounds that belong, in the language, to the same phoneme. Japanese does not distinguish *r* from *l*. Japanese people *do not hear* the difference between "lice" and "rice", in the same way that you do not hear the difference between the two *k*'s above. Cockneys do not hear, except with a special effort, the difference between "has" and "as", or "haitch" and "aitch", for the Cockney dialect does not recognize initial *h*'s.

So what is a phoneme? It is a set of sounds whose members do not discriminate between any words in the language under consideration. If you are mathematically minded, you could think of it as an equivalence class of sounds, determined by the relationship

*sound*₁ is related to *sound*₂ if *sound*₁ and *sound*₂ do not discriminate any pair of words in the language.

The *p* and *d* in "pig" and "dig" belong to different phonemes (in English), because they discriminate the two words. *b*, *f*, and *j* belong to different phonemes again. *i* and *a* in "hid" and "had" belong to different phonemes too. Proceeding like this, a list of phonemes can be drawn up.

Such a list is shown in Table 2.1, for British English. (The layout of the list does have some significance in terms of different categories of phonemes, which will be explained later.) In fact, linguists use an assortment of English letters, foreign letters, and special symbols to represent phonemes. In this book we use one- or two-letter codes, partly because they are more mnemonic, and partly because they are more suitable for communication to computers using standard peripheral devices. They are a direct transliteration of linguists' standard International Phonetic Association symbols.

We will discuss the sounds which make up each of these phoneme classes shortly. First, however, it is worthwhile pointing out some rather tricky points in the definition of these phonemes.

Table 2.1. The phonemes of British English.

uh	(the)	*p*	*t*	*k*	
a	(bud)	*b*	*d*	*g*	
e	(head)	*m*	*n*	*ng*	
i	(hid)				
o	(hod)	*r*	*w*	*l*	*y*
u	(hood)				
aa	(had)	*s*	*z*		
ee	(heed)	*sh*	*zh*		
er	(heard)	*f*	*v*		
uu	(food)	*th*	*dh*		
ar	(hard)	*ch*	*j*		
aw	(hoard)	*h*			

Phonological Difficulties

There are snags with phonological classification, as there are in any area where attempts are made to make completely logical statements about human activity. Consider *h* and the *ng* in "singing". (*ng* is certainly not an *n* sound followed by a *g* sound, although it is true that in some English accents "singing" is rendered with the *ng* followed by a *g* at each of its two occurrences.) No words end with *h,* and none begin with *ng.* (Notice that we are still talking about British English. In Chinese, the sound *ng* is a word in its own right, and is a common family name. But we must stick with one language for phonological classification.) Hence it follows that there is no pair of words which is distinguished by the difference between *h* and *ng.* Technically, they belong to the same phoneme. However, technical considerations in this case must take second place to common sense!

The *j* in "jig" is another interesting case. It can be considered to belong to a *j* phoneme, or to be a sequence of two phonemes, *d* followed by *zh* (the sound in "vision"). There is disagreement on this point in phonetics textbooks, and we do not have the time (nor, probably, the inclination!) to consider the pros and cons of this moot point. I have resolved the matter arbitrarily by writing it as a separate phoneme. The *ch* in "choose" is a similar case (*t* followed by the *sh* in "shoes").

Another difficulty, this time where Table 2.1 does not show how to distinguish between two sounds which *do* discriminate words in many people's English, is the *w* in "witch" and that in "which". The latter is conventionally transcribed as a sequence of two phonemes, *h w.*

The last few difficulties are all to do with deciding whether a sound belongs to a single phoneme class, or comprises a sequence of sounds each of which belongs to a phoneme. Are the *j* in "jug", the *ch* in "chug", and the *w* in "which", single phonemes or not? The definition above of a phoneme as a "set of sounds whose members do not discriminate any words in the language" does not help us to answer this question. As far as this definition is concerned, we could go so far as to call each and every word of the language an individual phoneme! It is clear that some acoustic evidence, and quite a lot of judgement, is being used when phonemes such as those of Table 2.1 are defined.

So much for the consonants. This same problem occurs in vowel sounds, particularly in diphthongs, which are sequences of two vowel-like sounds. Do the vowels of "main" and "man" belong to different phonemes? Clearly so, if they are both transcribed as single units, for they distinguish the two words. Notwithstanding the fact that they are sequences of separate sounds, a logically consistent system could be constructed which gave separate, unitary, symbols to each diphthong. However, it is usual to employ a compound symbol which indicates explicitly the character of the two vowel-like sounds involved. We will transcribe the diphthong of "main" as a sequence of two vowels, *e* (as in "head") and *i* (as in "hid", not "I"). This is done primarily for economy of symbols, choosing the constituent sounds on the basis of the closest match to existing vowel sounds. (Note that this again violates purely *logical* criteria for identifying phonemes.)

Categories of Speech Sounds

A phoneme is defined as a set of sounds whose members do not discriminate between any words in the language under consideration. The phonemes themselves can be classified into groups which reflect similarities between them. This can be done in many different ways, using various criteria for classification. In fact, one branch of linguistic research is concerned with defining a set of "distinctive features" such that a phoneme class is uniquely identified by the values of the features. Distinctive features are binary, and include such things as voiced–unvoiced, fricative–not fricative, aspirated–unaspirated. We will not be concerned here with such detailed classifications, but it is as well to know that they exist.

There is an everyday distinction between vowels and consonants. A vowel forms the nucleus of every syllable, and one or more consonants may optionally surround the vowel. But the distinction sometimes becomes a little ambiguous. Syllables like *sh* are commonly uttered and certainly do not contain a vowel. Furthermore, when we say "vowel" in everyday language, we usually refer to the *written* vowels a, e, i, o, and u; there are many more vowel sounds. A vowel in orthography is different to a vowel as a phoneme. Is a diphthong a phonetic vowel?—certainly, by the syllable-nucleus criterion; but it is a little different from ordinary vowels because it is a changing sound rather than a constant one.

Table 2.2 shows one classification of the phonemes of Table 2.1, which will be useful in our later studies of speech synthesis from phonetics. It shows twelve vowels, including the rather peculiar one, *uh* (which corresponds to the first vowel in the word "above"). This is the sound produced by the vocal tract when it is in a relaxed, neutral position; and it never occurs in prominent, stressed, syllables. The vowels later in the list are almost always longer than the earlier ones. In fact, the first six (*uh, a, e, i, o, u*) are often called "short" vowels, and the last five (*ee, er, uu, ar, aw*) "long" ones. The shortness or longness of the one in the middle (*aa*) is rather ambiguous. Diphthongs pose no problem here because we have not classified them as single phonemes.

The remaining categories are consonants. The glides are quite similar to vowels and diphthongs, though; for they are voiced, continuous sounds.

Table 2.2. Phoneme categories.

vowel	*uh a e i o u aa ee er uu ar aw*
diphthong	[not classified as individual phonemes]
glide (or liquid)	*r w l y*
stop	
unvoiced stop	*p t k*
voiced stop	*b d g*
nasal	*m n ng*
fricative	
unvoiced fricative	*s sh f th*
voiced fricative	*z zh v dh*
affricate	
unvoiced affricate	*ch*
voiced affricate	*j*
aspirate	*h*

You can say them and prolong them. (This is also true of the fricatives.) *r* is interesting because it can be realized acoustically in very different ways. Some people curl the tip of the tongue back: a so-called retroflex action of the tongue. Many people cannot do this, and their *r*'s sound like *w*'s. The stage Scotsman's *r* is a trill where the tip of the tongue vibrates against the roof of the mouth. *l* is also slightly unusual, for it is the only English phoneme which is "lateral": air passes either side of it, in two separate passages. Welsh has another lateral sound, a fricative, which is written "ll" as in "Llandudno".

The next category is the stops. These are formed by stopping up the mouth, so that air pressure builds up behind the lips, and releasing this pressure suddenly. The result is a little explosion (and the stops are often called "plosives"), which usually creates a very short burst of fricative noise (and in some cases, aspiration as well). They are further subdivided into voiced and unvoiced stops, depending upon whether voicing starts as soon as the plosion occurs (sometimes even before) or well after it. If you put your hand in front of your mouth when saying "pit", you can easily feel the puff of air that signals the plosion on the *p*, and probably on the *t* as well.

In a sense, nasals are really stops as well (and they are often called stops), for the oral tract is blocked although the nasal one is not. The peculiar fact that the nasal *ng* never occurs at the beginning of a word (in English) was mentioned earlier. Notice that for stops and nasals there is a similarity in the *vertical* direction of Table 2.2, between *p, b* and *m; t, d* and *n;* and *k, g* and *ng. p* is an unvoiced version of *b* (try saying them), and *m* is a nasalized version (for *b* is what you get when you have a cold and try to say *m*).

These three sounds are all made at the front of the mouth, while t, d and n, which bear the same resemblance to each other, are made in the middle; and k, g and ng are made at the back. This introduces another possible classification, according to *place of articulation*.

The unvoiced fricatives are quite straightforward, except perhaps for th, which is the sound at the beginning of "thigh". They are paired with the voiced fricatives on the basis of place of articulation. The voiced version of th is the dh at the beginning of "thy". zh is a fairly rare phoneme, which is heard in the middle of "vision". Affricates are similar to fricatives, but begin with a stopped posture, and as we mentioned earlier, there is some controversy as to whether they should be considered to be single phonemes, or sequences of stop phonemes and fricatives. Finally comes the lonely aspirate, h. Aspiration does occur elsewhere in speech, during the plosive burst of unvoiced stops.

Narrow Phonetic Transcription

The phonological classification outlined above is based upon a clear rationale for distinguishing between sounds according to how they affect meaning, although the rationale does become somewhat muddied in difficult cases. Narrower transcriptions are not so systematic. They use units called *allophones*, which are defined by reference to physical, acoustic, criteria rather than purely logical ones. ("Phone" is a more old-fashioned term for the same thing, and the misused word "phoneme" is often employed where allophone is meant, that is, as a physical rather than a logical unit.) Each phoneme has several allophones, more or less depending on how narrow or broad the transcription is, and the allophones are different acoustic realizations of the same logical unit. For example, the ks in "key" and "caw" may be considered as different allophones (in a slightly narrow transcription). Although we will not use symbols for allophones here, they are often indicated by diacritical marks in a text which modify the basic phoneme classes. For example, a tilde (˜) over a vowel means that it is nasalized, while a small circle underneath a consonant means that it is devoiced.

Allophonic variation in speech is governed by a mechanism called *coarticulation*, where a sound is affected by those that come either side of it. "Key"–"caw" is a clear example of this, where the tongue position in the k anticipates that of the following vowel: high in the first case, low in the second. Most allophonic variation in English is anticipatory, in that the sound is influenced by the following articulation rather than by preceding ones.

Nasalization is a feature which applies to vowels in English through anticipatory coarticulation. In many languages (for example, French) it is a *distinctive* feature for vowels, in that it serves to distinguish one vowel phoneme class from another. That this is not so in English sometimes tempts us to assume, incorrectly, that nasalization does not occur in vowels. It does, typically when the vowel is followed by a nasal consonant, and it is important for synthesis that nasalized vowel allophones are recognized and treated accordingly.

Coarticulation can be predicted by phonological rules, which show how a phonemic sequence will be realized by allophones. Such rules have been studied extensively by linguists.

The reason for coarticulation, and for the existence of allophones, lies in the physical constraints imposed by the motion of the articulatory organs, particularly their acceleration and deceleration. An immensely crude model is that the brain decides what phonemes to say (for it is concerned with semantic things, and the definition of a phoneme is a semantic one). It then takes this sequence and translates it into neural commands which actually move the articulators into target positions. However, other commands may be issued, and executed, before these targets are reached, and this accounts for coarticulation effects. Phonological rules for converting a phonemic sequence to an allophonic one are a sort of discrete model of the process. Particularly for work involving computers, it is possible that this rule-based approach will be overtaken by potentially more accurate methods which attempt to model the continuous articulatory phenomena directly.

2.3 Prosody

The phonetic classification introduced above divides speech into segments and classifies these into phonemes or allophones. Riding on top of this stream of segments are other, more global, attributes that dictate the overall prosody of the utterance. Prosody is defined by the Oxford English Dictionary as the "science of versification, laws of metre," which emphasizes the aspects of stress and rhythm that are central to classical verse. There are, however, many other features which are more or less global. These are collectively called prosodic or, equivalently, suprasegmental, features, for they lie above the level of phoneme or syllable segments.

Prosodic features can be split into two basic categories: features of voice quality and features of voice dynamics. Variations in voice quality, which are sometimes called "paralinguistic" phenomena, are accounted for by anatomical differences and long-term muscular idiosyncrasies (like a sore throat), and have little part to play in the kind of applications for speech output that have been sketched in Chapter 1. Variations in voice dynamics occur in three dimensions: pitch or fundamental frequency of the voice, time and amplitude. Within the first, the pattern of pitch variation, or *intonation*, can be distinguished from the overall range within which that variation occurs. The time dimension encompasses the rhythm of the speech, pauses, and the overall tempo: whether it is uttered quickly or slowly. The third dimension, amplitude, is of relatively minor importance. Intonation and rhythm work together to produce an effect commonly called "stress", and we will elaborate further on the nature of stress and discuss algorithms for synthesizing intonation and rhythm in Chapter 8.

These features have a very important role to play in communicating meaning. They are not fancy, optional components. It is their neglect which is largely responsible for the layman's stereotype of computer speech, a caricature of living speech (abrupt, arhythmic and in a grating monotone) which was well characterized by Isaac Asimov when he wrote of speaking "all in capital letters".

Timing has a syntactic function in that it sometimes helps to distinguish nouns from verbs (*ex*tract versus ex*tract*), and adjectives from verbs (*ap*proximate versus approxi*mate*), although segmental aspects play a part here too, for the vowel qualities differ in each pair of words. Nevertheless, if you make a mistake when assigning stress to words like these in conversation you are very likely to be queried as to what you actually said.

Intonation has a big effect on meaning too. Pitch often (but by no means always) rises on a question, the extent and abruptness of the rise depending on features like whether a genuine information-bearing reply or merely confirmation is expected. A distinctive pitch pattern accompanies the introduction of a new topic. In conjunction with rhythm, intonation can be used to bring out contrasts as in

"He didn't have a *red* car, he had a *black* one."

In general, the intonation patterns used by a reader depend not only on the text itself, but on his interpretation of it, and also on his expectation of the listener's interpretation of it. For example:

"He had a *red* car" (I think you thought it was black).
"He had a red *bi*cycle" (I think you thought it was a car).

In natural speech, prosodic features are significantly influenced by whether the utterance is generated spontaneously or read aloud. The variations in spontaneous speech are enormous. There are all sorts of emotions which are plainly audible in everyday speech: sarcasm, excitement, rudeness, disagreement, sadness, fright, love. Variations in voice quality certainly play a part here. Even with "ordinary" co-operative friendly conversation, the need to find words and somehow fit them into an overall utterance produces great diversity of prosodic structures. Applications for speech output from computers do not, however, call for spontaneous conversation, but for a controlled delivery which is like that when reading aloud. Here, the speaker is articulating utterances which have been set out for him, reducing his cognitive load to one of understanding and interpreting the text rather than generating it. Unfortunately for us, linguists are (quite rightly) primarily interested in living, spontaneous speech rather than pre-prepared readings.

Nevertheless, the richness of prosody in speech even when reading from a book should not be underestimated. Read aloud to an audience and listen to the contrasts in voice dynamics deliberately introduced for variety's sake. If stories are to be read, there is even a case for controlling voice *quality* to cope with quotations and affective imitations.

We saw earlier that the source-filter model is particularly helpful in distinguishing prosodic features, which are largely properties of the source, from segmental ones, which belong to the filter. Pitch and amplitude are primarily source properties. Rhythm and speed of speaking are not, but neither are they filter properties, for they belong to the source-filter system as a whole and not specifically to either part of it. The difficult notion of stress is, from an acoustic point of view, a combination of pitch, rhythm and amplitude. Even some features of voice quality can be attributed to the source (like laryngitis), although others (cleft palate, badly-fitting dentures) affect segmental features as well.

2.4 Further Reading

This chapter has been no more than a cursory introduction to some of the difficult problems of linguistics and phonetics. Here are some readable books which discuss these problems further.

Abercrombie, D. (1967). "Elements of general phonetics", Edinburgh University Press.
    This is an excellent book which covers all of the areas of this chapter, in much more detail than has been possible here.
Brown, G., Currie, K.L. and Kenworthy, J. (1980). "Questions of intonation", Croom Helm, London.
    An intensive study of the prosodics of colloquial, living speech is presented, with particular reference to intonation. Although not particularly relevant to speech output from computers, this book gives great insight into how conversational speech differs from reading aloud.
Fry, D.B. (1979). "The physics of speech", Cambridge University Press, Cambridge, England.
    This is a simple and readable account of speech science, with a good and completely non-mathematical introduction to frequency analysis.

Ladefoged, P. (1975). "A course in phonetics", Harcourt Brace Jovanovich, New York.

Usually books entitled "A course on ..." are dreadfully dull, but this is a wonderful exception. An exciting, readable, almost racy introduction to phonetics, full of little experiments you can try yourself.

Lehiste, I. (1970) "Suprasegmentals", MIT Press, Cambridge, Massachusetts.

This fairly comprehensive study of the prosodics of speech complements Ladefoged's book, which is mainly concerned with segmental phonetics.

O'Connor, J.D. (1973). "Phonetics", Penguin, London.

This is another introductory book on phonetics. It is packed with information on all aspects of the subject.

3

SPEECH STORAGE

The most familiar device that produces speech output is the ordinary tape recorder, which stores information in analogue form on magnetic tape. However, this is unsuitable for speech output from computers. One reason is that it is difficult to access different utterances quickly. Although random-access tape recorders do exist, they are expensive and subject to mechanical breakdown because of the stresses associated with frequent starting and stopping.

Storing speech on a rotating drum instead of tape offers the possibility of access to any track within one revolution time. For example, the IBM 7770 Audio Response Unit employs drums rotating twice a second which are able to store up to 32 500-msec words. These can be accessed randomly, within half a second at most. Although one can arrange to store longer words by allowing overflow on to an adjacent track at the end of the rotation period, the discrete time-slots provided by this system make it virtually impossible for it to generate connected utterances by assembling appropriate words from the store.

The Cognitronics Speechmaker has a similar structure, but with the analogue speech waveform recorded on photographic film. Storing audio waveforms optically is not an unusual technique, for this is how soundtracks are recorded on ordinary movie films. The original version of the "speaking clock" of the British Post Office used optical storage in concentric tracks on flat glass discs. It is described by Speight and Gill (1937), who include a fascinating account of how the utterances are synchronized. A 4 Hz signal from a pendulum clock was used to supply current to an electric motor, which drove a shaft equipped with cams and gears that rotated the glass discs containing utterances for seconds, minutes and hours at appropriate speeds!

A second reason for avoiding analogue storage is price. It is difficult to see how a random-access tape recorder could be incorporated into a talking pocket calculator or child's toy without considerably inflating the cost. Solid-state electronics is much cheaper than mechanics.

But the best reason is that, in many of the applications we have discussed, it is necessary to form utterances by concatenating separately-recorded parts. It is totally infeasible, for example, to store each and every possible telephone number as an individual recording! And utterances that are formed by concatenating individual words which were recorded in isolation, or in a different context, do not sound completely natural. For example in an early experiment, Stowe and Hampton (1961) recorded individual words on acoustic tape, spliced the tape with the words in a different order to make sentences, and played the result to subjects who were scored on the number of key words which they identified correctly. The overall conclusion was that while embedding a word in normally-spoken sentences *increases* the probability of recognition (because the extra context gives clues about the word), embedding a word in a constructed sentence, where intonation and rhythm are not properly rendered, *decreases* the probability of recognition. When the speech was uttered slowly, however, a considerable improvement was noticed, indicating that if the listener has more processing time he can overcome the lack of proper intonation and rhythm.

Nevertheless, many present-day voice response systems *do* store what amounts to a direct recording of the acoustic wave. However, the storage medium is digital rather than analogue. This means that standard computer storage devices can be used, providing rapid access to any segment of the speech at relatively low cost, for the economics of mass-production ensures a low price for random-access digital devices compared with random-access analogue ones. Furthermore, it reduces the amount of special equipment needed for speech output. One can buy very cheap speech input/output interfaces for home computers which connect to standard hobby buses. Another advantage of digital over analogue recording is that integrated circuit read-only memories (ROMs) can be used for hand-held devices which need small quantities of speech. Hence this chapter begins by showing how waveforms are stored digitally, and then describes some techniques for reducing the data needed for a given utterance.

3.1 Storing Waveforms Digitally

When an analogue signal is converted to digital form, it is made discrete both in time and in amplitude. Discretization in time is the operation of *sampling*, while in amplitude it is *quantizing*. It is worth pointing out that the transmission of analogue information by digital means is called "PCM" (standing for "pulse code modulation") in telecommunications jargon. Much of the theory of digital signal processing investigates signals which are sampled but not quantized (or quantized into sufficiently many levels to avoid inaccuracies). The operation of quantization, being non-linear, is not very amenable to theoretical analysis. Quantization introduces issues such as accumulation of round-off noise in arithmetic operations, which, although they are very important in practical implementations, can only be treated theoretically under certain somewhat unrealistic assumptions (in particular, independence of the quantization error from sample to sample).

Sampling

A fundamental theorem of telecommunications states that a signal can only be reconstructed accurately from a sampled version if it does not contain components whose frequency is greater than half the frequency at which the sampling takes place. Figure 3.1(a) shows how a component of slightly greater than half the sampling frequency can masquerade, as far as an observer with access only to the sampled data can tell, as a component at slightly less than half the sampling frequency. Call the sampling interval T seconds, so that the sampling frequency is $1/T$ Hz. Then components

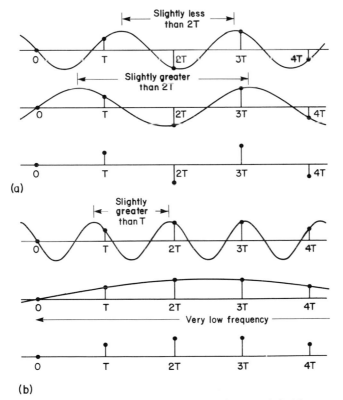

Fig. 3.1. Different sine waves which appear the same when sampled. (a) components near half the sampling frequency. (b) a component at just under the sampling frequency and its low-frequency equivalent.

at $1/2T + f$, $3/2T - f$, $3/2T + f$ and so on all masquerade as a component at $1/2T - f$. Similarly, components at frequencies just under the sampling frequency masquerade as very low-frequency components, as shown in Fig. 3.1(b). This phenomenon is often called "aliasing".

Thus the continuous, infinite, frequency axis for the unsampled signal, where two components at different frequencies can always be distinguished, maps into a repetitive frequency axis when the signal is sampled. As depicted in Fig. 3.2, the frequency interval $[1/T, 2/T)^*$ is mapped back into the band $[0, 1/T)$, as are the intervals $[2/T, 3/T)$, $[3/T, 4/T)$, and so on. Furthermore, the interval $[1/2T, 1/T)$ between half the sampling frequency and the sampling frequency, is mapped back into the interval below half the sampling frequency; but this time the mapping is backwards, with frequencies at just under $1/T$ being mapped to frequencies slightly greater than zero, and frequencies just over $1/2T$ being mapped to ones just under $1/2T$. The best way to represent a repeating frequency axis like this is as a circle. Figure 3.3 shows how the linear frequency axis for continuous systems maps on to a circular axis for sampled systems. For present purposes, it is easiest to imagine the bottom half of the circle as being reflected into the top half, so that traversing the upper semicircle in the anticlockwise direction corresponds to frequencies increasing from 0 to $1/2T$ (half the sample frequency), and returning along the lower semicircle is actually the same as coming back round the upper one, and corresponds to frequencies from $1/2T$ to $1/T$ being mapped into the range $1/2T$ to 0.

As far as speech is concerned, then, we must ensure that before sampling a signal no significant components at greater than half the sample frequency are present. Furthermore, the sampled signal will only contain information about frequency components less than this, so the sample frequency must be chosen as twice the highest frequency of interest. For example, consider telephone-quality speech. Telephones provide a familiar standard of speech quality which, although it can only be an approximate "standard", will be much used throughout this book. The telephone network aims to transmit only frequencies lower than 3.4 kHz. We saw in the previous chapter that this region will contain the information-bearing formants, and some (but not all) of the fricative and aspiration energy. Actually, transmitting speech through the telephone system degrades its quality very significantly, probably more than you realize since everyone is so accustomed to telephone speech. Try the dial-a-disc service and compare it with high-fidelity music for a striking example of the kind of degradation suffered.

---

* Intervals are specified in brackets, with a square bracket representing a closed end of the interval and a round one representing an open one. Thus the interval $[1/T, 2/T)$ specifies the range $1/T \leq frequency < 2/T$.

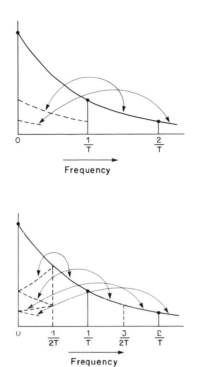

Fig. 3.2. How sampling "folds" the frequency spectrum.

For telephone speech, the sampling frequency must be chosen to be at least 6.8 kHz. Since speech contains significant amounts of energy above 3.4 kHz, it should be filtered before sampling to remove this; otherwise the higher components would be mapped back into the baseband and distort the low-frequency information. Because it is difficult to make filters that cut off very sharply, the sampling frequency is chosen rather greater than

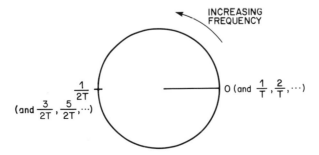

Fig. 3.3. The circular frequency axis of sampled systems.

twice the highest frequency of interest. For example, the digital telephone network samples at 8 kHz. The pre-sampling filter should have a cutoff frequency of 4 kHz; aim for negligible distortion below 3.4 kHz; and transmit negligible components above 4.6 kHz for these are reflected back into the band of interest, namely 0 to 3.4 kHz. Figure 3.4 shows a block diagram for the input hardware.

Quantization

Before considering specifications for the pre-sampling filter, let us turn from discretization in time to discretization in amplitude, that is, quantization. This is performed by an A/D converter (analogue-to-digital), which takes as input a constant analogue voltage (produced by the sampler) and generates a corresponding binary value as output. The simplest correspondence is *uniform* quantization, where the amplitude range is split into equal regions by points termed "quantization levels", and the output is a binary representation of the nearest quantization level to the input voltage. Typically, 11-bit conversion is used for speech, giving 2048 quantization levels, and the signal is adjusted to have zero mean so that half the levels correspond to negative input voltages and the other half to positive ones.

It is, at first sight, surprising that as many as 11 bits are needed for adequate representation of speech signals. Research on the digital telephone network, for example, has concluded that a signal-to-noise ratio of some 26–27 dB is enough to avoid undue harshness of quality, loss of intelligibility, and listener fatigue for speech at a comfortable level in an otherwise reasonably good channel. Rabiner and Schafer (1978) suggest that about 36 dB signal-to-noise ratio would "most likely provide adequate quality in a communications system". But 11-bit quantization seems to give a very much better signal-to-noise ratio than these figures. To estimate its magnitude, note that for N-bit quantization the error for each sample will lie between

$$-\frac{1}{2}.2^{-N} \quad \text{and} \quad +\frac{1}{2}.2^{-N}.$$

Assuming that it is uniformly distributed in this range (an assumption which is likely to be justified if the number of levels is sufficiently large) leads to

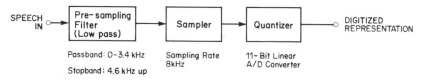

Fig. 3.4. Block diagram of input hardware for speech digitization.

a mean-squared error of

$$\int_{-2^{-N-1}}^{2^{-N-1}} e^2 p(e)de,$$

where $p(e)$, the probability density function of the error e, is a constant which satisfies the usual probability normalization constraint, namely

$$\int_{-2^{-N-1}}^{2^{-N-1}} p(e)de = 1.$$

Hence $p(e) = 2^N$, and so the mean-squared error is $2^{-2N}/12$. This is $10 \log_{10}(2^{-2N}/12)$ dB, or around -77 dB for 11-bit quantization.

This noise level is relative to the maximum amplitude range of the conversion. A maximum-amplitude sine wave has a power of -9 dB relative to the same reference, giving a signal-to-noise ratio of some 68 dB. This is far in excess of that needed for telephone-quality speech. However, look at the very peaky nature of the typical speech waveform given in Fig. 3.5. If clipping is to be avoided, the maximum amplitude level of the A/D converter must be set at a value which makes the power of the speech signal very much less than a maximum-amplitude sine wave. Furthermore, different people speak at very different volumes, and the overall level fluctuates constantly with just one speaker. Experience shows that while 8- or 9-bit quantization may provide sufficient signal-to-noise ratio to preserve telephone-quality speech if the overall speaker levels are carefully controlled, about 11 bits are generally required to provide high-quality representation of speech with a uniform quantization. With 11 bits, a sine wave whose amplitude is only 1/32 of the full-scale value would be digitized with a signal-to-noise ratio of around 36 dB, the most pessimistic figure quoted above for adequate quality. Even then it is useful if the speaker is provided with an indication of the amplitude of his speech; a traffic-light indicator with red signifying clipping overload, orange a suitable level, and green too low a value, is often convenient for this.

Logarithmic Quantization

For the purposes of speech *processing*, it is essential to have the signal quantized uniformly. This is because all of the theory applies to linear systems, and nonlinearities introduce complexities which are not amenable to analysis. Uniform quantization, although a nonlinear operation, is linear in the limiting case as the number of levels becomes large, and for most purposes its effect can be modelled by assuming that the quantized signal is obtained from the original analogue one by the addition of a small amount of uniformly-distributed quantizing noise, as in fact was done above. Usually the quantization noise is disregarded in subsequent analysis.

However, the peakiness of the speech signal illustrated in Fig. 3.5 leads one to suspect that a nonlinear representation, for example a logarithmic one, could provide a better signal-to-noise ratio over a wider range of input amplitudes, and hence be more useful than linear quantization, at least for speech storage (and transmission). And indeed this is the case. Linear quantization has the unfortunate effect that the absolute noise level is independent of the signal level, so that an excessive number of bits must be used if a reasonable ratio is to be achieved for peaky signals. It can be shown that a logarithmic representation like

$$y = 1 + k \log x,$$

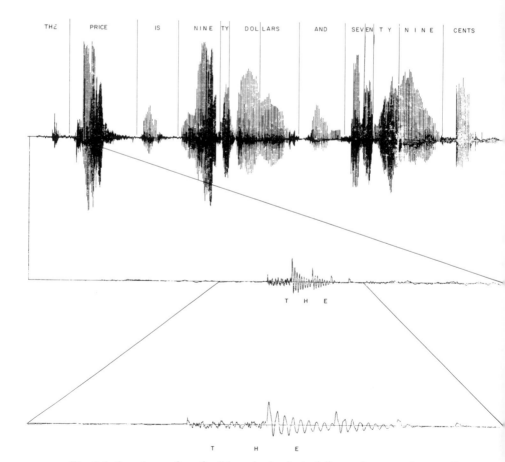

Fig. 3.5. Speech waveform for "the price is ninety dollars and seventy-nine cents".

where x is the original signal and y is the value which is to be quantized, gives a signal-to-noise *ratio* which is independent of the input signal level. This relationship cannot be realized physically, for it is undefined when the signal is negative and diverges when it is zero. However, realizable approximations to it can be made which retain the advantages of constant signal-to-noise ratio within a useful range of signal amplitudes. Figure 3.6 shows the logarithmic relation with one widely-used approximation to it, called the A-law. The idea of nonlinearly quantizing a signal to achieve adequate signal-to-noise ratios for a wide variety of amplitudes is called "companding", a contraction of "compressing-expanding". The original signal can be retrieved from its A-law compression by antilogarithmic expansion.

Figure 3.6 also shows one common coding scheme which is a piecewise linear approximation to the A law. This provides an 8-bit code, and gives the equivalent of 12-bit linear quantization for small signal levels. It approximates the A-law in 16 linear segments; 8 for positive and 8 for negative inputs. Consider the positive part of the curve. The first two segments, which are actually collinear, correspond exactly to 12-bit linear conversion. Thus the output codes 0 to 31 correspond to inputs from 0 to 31/2048, in equal steps. (Remember that both positive and negative signals must be converted, so a 12-bit linear converter will allocate 2048 levels for positive signals and 2048 for negative ones.) The next segment provides 11-bit linear quantization, output codes 32 to 47 corresponding to inputs from 16/1024 to 31/1024. Similarly, the next segment corresponds to 10-bit quantization, covering inputs from 16/512 to 31/512 and so on, the last section giving 6-bit quantization of inputs from 16/32 to 31/32, the full-scale positive value. Negative inputs are converted similarly. For signal levels of less than 32/2048, that is 2^{-6}, this implementation of the A-law provides full 12-bit precision. As the signal level increases, the precision decreases gradually to 6 bits at maximum amplitudes.

Logarithmic encoding provides what is in effect a floating-point representation of the input. The conventional floating-point format, however, is not used because many different codes can represent the same value. For example, with a 4-bit exponent preceding a 4-bit mantissa, the words 0000:1000, 0001:0100, 0010:0010 and 0011:0001 represent the numbers 0.1×2^0, 0.01×2^1, 0.001×2^2 and 0.0001×2^3 respectively, which are the same. (Some floating-point conventions assume that an unwritten "1" bit precedes the mantissa, except when the whole word is zero; but this gives decreased resolution around zero, which is exactly where we want the resolution to be greatest.) Table 3.1 shows the 8-bit A-law codes, according to the piecewise linear approximation of Figure 3.6, written in a notation which suggests floating point. Each linear segment has a different exponent except the first two segments, which as explained above are collinear.

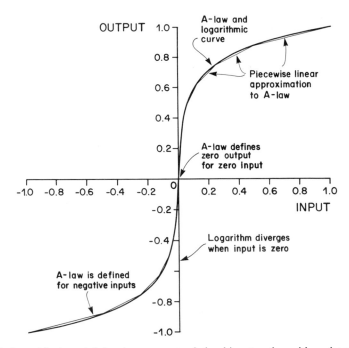

Fig. 3.6. Logarithmic and A-law input-output relationships, together with a piecewise linear approximation to the A-law.

Logarithmic encoders and decoders are available from many semiconductor manufacturers as single-chip devices called "codecs" (for "coder/decoder"). Intended for use on digital communication links, these generally provide a serial output bit-stream, which should be converted to parallel by a shift register if the data is intended for a computer. Because of the potentially vast market for codecs in telecommunications, they are made in great quantities and are consequently very cheap. Estimates of the speech quality necessary for telephone applications indicate that somewhat less than this accuracy is needed: 7-bit logarithmic encoding was used in early digital communications links, and it may be that even 6 bits are adequate. However, during the transition period when digital networks must coexist with the present analogue one, it is anticipated that a particular telephone call may have to pass through several links, some using analogue technology and some being digital. The possibility of several successive encodings and decodings has led telecommunications engineers to standardize on 8-bit representations, leaving some margin before additional degradation of signal quality becomes unduly distracting.

Unfortunately, world telecommunications authorities cannot agree on a single standard for logarithmic encoding. The A-law, which we have de-

Table 3.1. 8-bit A-law codes, with their floating-point equivalents.

8-bit codword:	bit 0	sign bit
	bits 1–3	3-bit exponent
	bits 4–7	4-bit mantissa

codeword	*interpretation*
0000 0000	$.0000 \times 2^{-7}$
...	...
0000 1111	$.1111 \times 2^{-7}$
0001 0000	$2^{-7} + .0000 \times 2^{-7}$
...	...
0001 1111	$2^{-7} + .1111 \times 2^{-7}$
0010 0000	$2^{-6} + .0000 \times 2^{-6}$
...	...
0010 1111	$2^{-6} + .1111 \times 2^{-6}$
0011 0000	$2^{-5} + .0000 \times 2^{-5}$
...	...
0011 1111	$2^{-5} + .1111 \times 2^{-5}$
0100 0000	$2^{-4} + .0000 \times 2^{-4}$
...	...
0100 1111	$2^{-4} + .1111 \times 2^{-4}$
0101 0000	$2^{-3} + .0000 \times 2^{-3}$
...	...
0101 1111	$2^{-3} + .1111 \times 2^{-3}$
0110 0000	$2^{-2} + .0000 \times 2^{-2}$
...	...
0110 1111	$2^{-2} + .1111 \times 2^{-2}$
0111 0000	$2^{-1} + .0000 \times 2^{-1}$
...	...
0111 1111	$2^{-1} + .1111 \times 2^{-1}$
1000 0000	$- .0000 \times 2^{-7}$ negative numbers treated
...	... as above, with a sign bit
1111 1111	$-2^{-1} - .1111 \times 2^{-1}$ of 1

scribed, is the European standard, but there is another system, called the μ-law, which is used universally in North America. It also is available in single-chip form with an 8-bit code. It has very similar quantization error characteristics to the A-law, and would be indistinguishable from it on the scale of Fig. 3.6.

The Pre-sampling Filter

Now that we have some idea of the accuracy requirements for quantization, let us discuss quantitative specifications for the pre-sampling filter. Figure 3.7 sketches the characteristics of this filter. Assume a sampling frequency of 8 kHz and a range of interest from 0 to 3.4 kHz. Although all components at frequencies above 4 kHz will fold back into the 0–4 kHz baseband, those below 4.6 kHz fold back above 3.4 kHz and are therefore outside the range of interest. This gives a "guard band" between 3.4 and 4.6 kHz which separates the passband from the stopband. The filter should transmit negligible components in the stopband above 4.6 kHz. To reduce the harmonic distortion caused by aliasing to the same level as the quantization noise in 11-bit linear conversion, the stopband attenuation should be around -68 dB (the signal-to-noise ratio for a full-scale sine wave). Passband ripple is not so critical, for two reasons. While the presence of aliased components means that information has been lost about the frequency components within the range of interest, passband ripple does not actually cause a loss of information but only a distortion, and could, if necessary, be compensated by a suitable filter acting on the digitized waveform. Secondly, distortion of the passband spectrum is not nearly so audible as the frequency images caused by aliasing. Hence one usually aims for a passband ripple of around 0.5 dB.

The pass and stopband targets we have mentioned above can be achieved with a 9'th order elliptic filter. While such a filter is often used in high-quality signal-processing systems, for telephone-quality speech much less stringent specifications seem to be sufficient. Figure 3.8, for example, shows a template which has been recommended by telecommunications authorities. A 5'th order elliptic filter can easily meet this specification. Such filters,

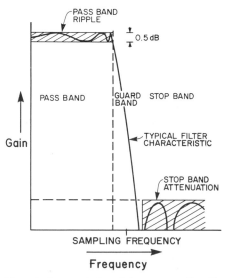

Fig. 3.7. General characteristics of the pre-sampling filter.

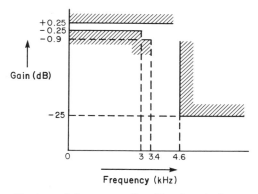

Fig. 3.8. Specifications of the pre-sampling filter for telephone-quality speech.

implemented by switched-capacitor means, are available in single-chip form. Integrated CCD (charge-coupled device) filters which meet the same specification are also marketed. Indeed, some codecs provide input filtering on the same chip as the A/D converter.

Instead of implementing a filter by analogue means to meet the aliasing specifications, digital filtering can be used. A high sample-rate A/D converter, operating at, say, 32 kHz, and preceded by a very simple low-pass pre-sampling filter, is followed by a digital filter which meets the desired specification, and its output is subsampled to provide an 8 kHz sample rate. While such implementations may be economic where a multichannel digitizing capability is required, as in local telephone exchanges where the subscriber connection is an analogue one, they are unlikely to prove cost-effective for a single channel.

Reconstructing the Analogue Waveform

Having digitized and stored a signal, it needs to be passed though a D/A converter (digital-to-analogue) and low-pass filter when replayed. D/A converters are cheaper than A/D converters, and the characteristics of the low-pass filter for output can be the same as those for input. However, the desampling operation introduces an additional distortion, which has an effect on the component at frequency f of

$$\frac{\sin(\pi f/f_s)}{\pi f/f_s},$$

where f_s is the sampling frequency. An "aperture correction" filter is needed to compensate for this, although many systems simply do without it. Such a filter is sometimes incorporated into the codec chip.

Summary

For telephone-quality speech, existing codec chips, coupled if necessary with integrated pre-sampling filters, can be used, at a remarkably low cost. For higher-quality speech storage the analogue interface can become quite complex. A comprehensive study of the problems as they relate to digitization of audio, which demands much greater fidelity than speech, has been made by Blesser (1978). He notes the following sources of error (among others):

—slew-rate distortion in the pre-sampling filter for signals at the upper end of the audio band;
—insufficient filtering of high-frequency input signals;
—noise generated by the sample-and-hold amplifier or pre-sampling filter;
—acquisition errors because of the finite settling time of the sample-and-hold circuit;
—insufficient settling time in the A/D conversion;
—errors in the quantization levels of the A/D and D/A converters;
—noise in the converters;
—jitter on the clock used for timing input or output samples;
—aperture distortion in the output sampler;
—noise in the output filter as a result of limited dynamic range of the integrated circuits;
—power-supply noise injection or ground coupling;
—changes in characteristics as a result of temperature or ageing.

Care must be taken with the analogue interface to ensure that the precision implied by the resolution of the A/D and D/A converters is not compromised by inadequate analogue circuitry. It is especially important to eliminate high-frequency noise caused by fast edges on nearby computer buses.

3.2 Coding in the Time Domain

There are several methods of coding the time waveform of a speech signal to reduce the data rate for a given signal-to-noise ratio, or alternatively to reduce the signal-to-noise ratio for a given data rate. They almost all require more processing, both at the encoding (for storage) and decoding (for regeneration) ends of the digitization process. They are sometimes used to economize on memory in systems using stored speech, for example the System X telephone exchange and the travel consultant described in Chapter 1, and so will be described here. However, it is to be expected that simple time-domain coding techniques will be superseded by the more complex linear predictive method, which is covered in Chapter 6, because this can give a much more substantial reduction in the data rate for only a small degradation in speech quality. Hence the aim of this section is to introduce the ideas in a qualitative way; theoretical development and summaries of results of listening tests can be found elsewhere (eg. Rabiner and Schafer, 1978). The methods we will examine are summarized in Table 3.2.

Syllabic Companding

We have already studied one time-domain encoding technique, namely logarithmic quantization, or log PCM (sometimes called "instantaneous companding"). A more sophisticated encoder could track slowly varying trends in the overall amplitude of the speech signal and use this information to adjust the quantization levels dynamically. Speech coding methods based on this principle are called adaptive pulse code modulation systems (APCM). Because the overall amplitude changes slowly, it is sufficient to adjust the quantization relatively infrequently (compared with the sampling rate), and this is often done at rates approximating the syllable rate of running speech, leading to the term "syllabic companding". A block floating-point format can be used, with a common exponent being stored every M samples (with M, say, 125 for a 100 msec block length at 8 kHz sampling), but the mantissa being stored at the regular sample rate. The overall energy in the block,

$$\sum_{n=h}^{h+M-1} x(n)^2 \quad (M = 125, \text{ say}),$$

is used to determine a suitable exponent, and every sample in the block— namely $x(h)$, $x(h + 1)$, ..., $x(h + M - 1)$—is scaled according to that exponent. Note that for speech transmission systems this method necessitates a delay of M samples at the encoder, and indeed some methods base the exponent

Table 3.2. Time-domain encoding techniques.

linear PCM	linearly-quantized pulse code modulation
log PCM	logarithmically-quantized pulse code modulation (instantaneous companding)
APCM	adaptively quantized pulse code modulation (usually syllabic companding)
DPCM	differential pulse code modulation
ADPCM	differential pulse code modulation with either adaptive quantization, or adaptive prediction, or both
DM	delta modulation (1-bit DPCM)
ADM	delta modulation with adaptive quantization

on the energy in the last block to avoid this. For speech storage, however, the delay is irrelevant. A rather different, nonsyllabic, method of adaptive PCM is continually to change the step size of a uniform quantizer, by multiplying it by a constant at each sample which is based on the magnitude of the previous code word.

Adaptive quantization exploits information about the amplitude of the signal, and, as a rough generalization, yields a reduction of one bit per sample in the data rate for telephone-quality speech over ordinary logarithmic quantization, for a given signal-to-noise ratio. Alternatively, for the same data rate an improvement of 6 dB in signal-to-noise ratio can be obtained. Some results for actual schemes are given by Rabiner and Schafer (1978). However, there is other information in the time waveform of speech, namely, the sample-to-sample correlation, which can be exploited to give further reductions.

Differential Coding

Differential pulse code modulation (DPCM), in its simplest form, uses the present speech sample as a prediction of the next one, and stores the prediction error: that is, the sample-to-sample difference. This is a simple case of predictive encoding. Referring back to the speech waveform displayed in Fig. 3.5, it seems plausible that the data rate can be reduced by transmitting the difference between successive samples instead of their absolute values; less bits are required for the difference signal for a given overall accuracy because it does not assume such extreme values as the absolute signal level. Actually, the improvement is not all that great; about 4 to 5 dB in signal-to-noise ratio, or just under one bit per sample for a given signal-to-noise ratio, for the difference signal can be nearly as large as the absolute signal level.

If DPCM is used in conjunction with adaptive quantization, giving one form of adaptive differential pulse code modulation (ADPCM), both the overall amplitude variation and the sample-to-sample correlation are exploited, leading to a combined gain of 10–11 dB in signal-to-noise ratio (or just under two bits reduction per sample for telephone-quality speech). Another form of adaptation is to alter the predictor by multiplying the previous sample value by a parameter which is adjusted for best performance. Then the transmitted signal at time n is

$$e(n) = x(n) - ax(n - 1),$$

where the parameter a is adapted (and stored) on a syllabic time-scale. This leads to a slight improvement in signal-to-noise ratio, which can be combined with that achieved by adaptive quantization. Much more substantial benefits can be realized by using a weighted sum of the past several (up to 15) speech samples, and adapting all the weights. This is the basic idea of linear prediction, which is developed in Chapter 6.

Delta Modulation

The coding methods presented so far all increase the complexity of the analogue-to-digital interface (or, if the sampled waveform is coded digitally, they increase the processing required before and after storage). One method which considerably *simplifies* the interface is the limiting case of DPCM with just 1-bit quantization. Only the sign of the difference between the current and last values is transmitted. Figure 3.9 shows the conversion hardware. The encoding part is essentially the same as a tracking D/A, where the value in a counter is forced to track the analogue input by incrementing or decrementing the counter accordingly as the input exceeds or falls short of the analogue equivalent of the counter's contents. However, for this encoding scheme, called "delta modulation", the increment–decrement signal itself forms the discrete representation of the waveform, instead of the counter's contents. The analogue waveform can be reconstituted from the bit stream with another counter and D/A converter. Alternatively, an all-analogue implementation can be used, both for the encoder and decoder, with a capacitor as integrator whose charging current is controlled digitally. This is a much cheaper realization.

It is fairly obvious that the sampling frequency for delta modulation will need to be considerably higher than for straightforward PCM. Figure 3.10

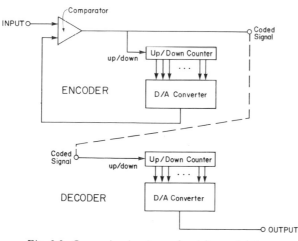

Fig. 3.9. Conversion hardware for delta modulation.

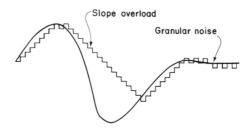

Fig. 3.10. Slope overload and granular noise in delta modulation.

shows an effect called "slope overload" which occurs when the sampling
rate is too low. Either a higher sample rate or a larger step size will reduce
the overload; however, larger steps increase the noise level of the alternate
1's and -1's that occur when no input is present (so-called "granular
noise"). A compromise is necessary between slope overload and granular
noise for a given bit rate. Delta modulation results in lower data rates than
logarithmic quantization for a given signal-to-noise ratio if that ratio is low
(poor-quality speech). As the desired speech quality is increased, its data
rate grows faster than that of logarithmic PCM. The crossover point occurs
at much lower than telephone quality speech, and so although delta modulation is used for some applications where the permissible data rate is
severely constrained, it is not really suitable for speech output from
computers.

It is profitable to adjust the step size, leading to *adaptive* delta modulation.
A common strategy is to increase or decrease the step size by a multiplicative
constant, which depends on whether the new transmitted bit will be equal
to or different from the last one. That is,

$$stepsize\ (n\ +\ 1)\ =\ stepsize\ (n)\ \times\ 2\ \text{if}\ x(n\ +\ 1) < x(n) < x(n\ -\ 1)\ \text{or}$$
$$x(n\ +\ 1) > x(n) > x(n\ -\ 1)\ \text{(slope overload condition)};$$
$$stepsize\ (n\ +\ 1)\ =\ stepsize\ (n)/2\ \text{if}\ x(n\ +\ 1),\ x(n\ -\ 1) < x(n)\ \text{or}$$
$$x(n\ +\ 1),\ x(n\ -\ 1) > x(n)\ \text{(granular noise condition)}.$$

Despite these adaptive equations, the step size should be constrained to lie
between a predetermined fixed maximum and minimum, to prevent it from
becoming so large or so small that rapid accommodation to changing input
signals is impossible. Then, in a period of potential slope overload the step
size will grow, preventing overload, possibly to its maximum value when
overload may resume. In a quiet period it will decrease to its minimum
value which determines the granular noise in the idle condition. Note that
the step size need not be stored, for it can be deduced from the bit changes
in the digitized data. Although adaptation improves the performance of delta
modulation, it is still inferior to PCM at telephone qualities.

Summary

It seems that ADPCM, with adaptive quantization and adaptive prediction, can provide a worthwhile advantage for speech storage, reducing the number of bits needed per sample of telephone-quality speech from 7 for logarithmic PCM to perhaps 5, and the data rate from 56 Kbit/s to 40 Kbit/s. Disadvantages are additional complexity in the encoding and decoding processes, and the fact that byte-oriented storage, with 8 bits/sample in logarithmic PCM, is more convenient for computer use. For low quality speech where hardware complexity is to be minimized, adaptive delta modulation could prove worthwhile, although the ready availability of PCM codec chips reduces the cost advantage.

3.3 References

Blesser, B.A. (1978). Digitization of audio: a comprehensive examination of theory, implementation and current practice. *J Audio Engineering Society*, **26**(10) 739 771.

Rabiner, L.R. and Schafer, R.W. (1978). "Digital processing of speech signals", Prentice Hall, Englewood Cliffs, New Jersey.

Speight, E.A. and Gill, O.W. (1937). The speaking clock Part II—the clock mechanism. *Post Office Electrical Engineering J* **XXIX**, 263–274.

Stowe, A.N. and Hampton, D.B. (1961). Speech synthesis with pre-recorded syllables and words. *J Acoustical Society of America*, **33**(6) 810–811.

3.4 Further Reading

Probably the best single reference on time-domain coding of speech is the book by Rabiner and Schafer (1978), cited above. However, this does not contain a great deal of information on practical aspects of the analogue-to-digital conversion process; this is covered by Blesser (1978) above, who is especially interested in high-quality conversion for digital audio applications, and Garrett (1978) below. There are many textbooks in the telecommunications area which are relevant to the subject of the chapter, although they concentrate primarily on fundamental theoretical aspects rather than the practical application of the technology.

Cattermole, K.W. (1969). "Principles of pulse code modulation", Iliffe, London.
    This is a standard, definitive, work on PCM, and provides a good grounding in the theory. It goes into the subject in much more depth than we have been able to here.

Garrett, P.H. (1978). "Analog systems for microprocessors and minicomputers", Reston Publishing Company, Reston, Virginia.
    Garrett discusses the technology of data conversion systems, including A/D and D/A converters and basic analogue filter design, in a clear and practical manner.

Inose, H. (1979). "An introduction to digital integrated communications systems",
    Peter Peregrinus, Stevenage, England.
        Inose's book is a recent one which covers the whole area of digital transmission
    and switching technology. It gives a good idea of what is happening to the
    telephone networks in the era of digital communications.
Steele, R. (1975). "Delta modulation systems", Pentech Press, London.
        Again a standard work, this time on delta modulation techniques. Steele gives
    an excellent and exhaustive treatment of the subject from a communications
    viewpoint.

4

SPEECH ANALYSIS

Digital recordings of speech provide a jumping-off point for further processing of the audio waveform, which is usually necessary for the purpose of speech output. It is difficult to synthesize natural sounds by concatenating individually-spoken words. Pitch is perhaps the most perceptually significant contextual effect which must be taken into account when forming connected speech out of isolated words. The intonation of an utterance, which manifests itself as a continually changing pitch, is a holistic property of the utterance and not the sum of components determined by the individual words alone. Happily, and quite coincidentally, communications engineers in their quest for reduced-bandwidth telephony have invented methods of coding speech that separate the pitch information from that carried by the articulation.

Although these analysis techniques, which were first introduced in the late 1930s (Dudley 1939), were originally implemented by analogue means (and in many systems still are (Blankenship, 1978, describes a recent switched-capacitor realization)), there is a continuing trend towards digital implementations, particularly for the more sophisticated coding schemes. It is hard to see how the technique of linear prediction of speech, which is described in detail in Chapter 6, could be accomplished in the absence of digital processing. Some groundwork is laid for the theory of digital signal analysis in this chapter. The ideas are not presented in a formal, axiomatic way; but are developed as and when they are needed to examine some of the structures that turn out to be useful in speech processing.

Most speech analysis views speech according to the source-filter model which was introduced in Chapter 2, and aims to separate the effects of the source from those of the filter. The frequency spectrum of the vocal tract filter is of great interest, and the technique of discrete Fourier transformation is discussed in this chapter. For many purposes it is better to extract the formant frequencies from the spectrum and use these alone (or in conjunction with their bandwidths) to characterize it. As far as the signal source in the source-filter model is concerned, its most interesting features are pitch and amplitude, the latter being easy to estimate. Hence we go on to look at pitch extraction. Related to this is the problem of deciding whether a segment of speech has voiced or unvoiced excitation, or both.

Estimating formant and pitch parameters is one of the messiest areas of speech processing. There is a delightful paper which points this out (Schroeder, 1970), entitled "Parameter estimation in speech: a lesson in unorthodoxy". It emphasizes that the most successful estimation procedures

> have often relied on intuition based on knowledge of speech signals and their production in the human vocal apparatus rather than routine applications of well-established theoretical methods.

Fortunately, the emphasis of the present book is on speech *output*, which involves parameter estimation only in so far as it is needed to produce coded speech for storage, and to illuminate the acoustic nature of speech for the development of synthesis by rule from phonetics or text. Hence the many methods of formant and pitch estimation are treated rather cursorily and qualitatively here; our main interest is in how to *use* such information for speech output.

If the incoming speech can be analysed into its formant frequencies, amplitude, excitation mode and pitch (if voiced), it is quite easy to resynthesize it directly from these parameters. Speech synthesizers are described in the next chapter. They can be realized in either analogue or digital hardware, the former being predominant in production systems and the latter in research systems, although, as in other areas of electronics, the balance is changing in favour of digital implementations.

4.1 The Channel Vocoder

A direct representation of the frequency spectrum of a signal can be obtained by a bank of bandpass filters. This is the basis of the *channel vocoder*, which was the first device that attempted to take advantage of the source-filter model for speech coding (Dudley, 1939). The word "vocoder" is a contraction of *voice coder*. The energy in each filter band is estimated by rectification and smoothing, and the resulting approximation to the frequency spectrum is transmitted or stored. The source properties are represented by the type of excitation (voiced or unvoiced), and if voiced, the pitch. It is not necessary to include the overall amplitude of the speech explicitly, because this is conveyed by the energy levels from the separate bandpass filters.

Figure 4.1 shows the encoding part of a channel vocoder which has been used successfully for many years (Holmes, 1980). We will discuss the block labelled "pre-emphasis" shortly. The shape of the spectrum is estimated by 19 bandpass filters, whose spacing and bandwidth decrease slightly with decreasing frequency to obtain the rather greater resolution that is needed

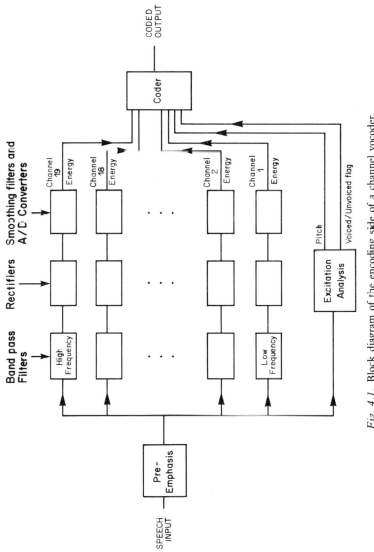

Fig. 4.1. Block diagram of the encoding side of a channel vocoder.

63

in the lower frequency region, as shown in Table 4.1. The 3 dB points of adjacent filters are halfway between their centre frequencies, so that there is some overlap between bands. The filter characteristics do not need to have very sharp edges, because the energy in neighbouring bands is fairly highly correlated. Indeed, there is a disadvantage in making them too sharp, because the phase delays associated with sharp cutoff filters induce "smearing" of the spectrum in the time domain. This particular channel vocoder uses second-order Butterworth bandpass filters.

For regenerating speech stored in this way, an excitation of unit impulses at the specified pitch period (for voiced sounds) or white noise (for unvoiced sounds) is produced and passed through a bank of bandpass filters similar to the analysis ones. The excitation has a flat spectrum, for regular impulses have harmonics at multiples of the repetition frequency which are all of the same size, and so the spectrum of the output signal is completely determined by the filter bank. The gain of each filter is controlled by the stored magnitude of the spectrum at that frequency.

The frequency spectrum and voicing pitch of speech change at much slower rates than the time waveform. The changes are due to movements of the articulatory organs (tongue, lips, etc.) in the speaker, and so are

Table 4.1. Filter specifications for a vocoder analyser (after Holmes, 1980)

Channel number	Centre frequency (Hz)	Analysis bandwidth (Hz)
1	240	120
2	360	120
3	480	120
4	600	120
5	720	120
6	840	120
7	1000	150
8	1150	150
9	1300	150
10	1450	150
11	1600	150
12	1800	200
13	2000	200
14	2200	200
15	2400	200
16	2700	200
17	3000	300
18	3300	300
19	3750	500

limited in their speed by physical constraints. A typical rate of production of phonemes is 15 per second, but in fact the spectrum can change quite a lot within a single phoneme (especially a stop sound). Between 10 and 25 msec (100 Hz and 40 Hz) is generally thought to be a satisfactory interval for transmitting or storing the spectrum, to preserve a reasonably faithful representation of the speech. Of course, the entire spectrum, as well as the source characteristics, must be stored at this rate. The channel vocoder described by Holmes (1980) uses 48 bits to encode the information. Repeated every 20 msec, this gives a data rate of 2400 bit/s: very considerably less than any of the time-domain encoding techniques.

It needs some care to encode the output of 19 filters, the excitation type, and the pitch into 48 bits of information. Holmes uses 6 bits for pitch, logarithmically encoded, and one bit for excitation type. This leaves 41 bits to encode the output of the 19 filters, and so a differential technique is used which transmits just the difference between adjacent channels, for the spectrum does not change abruptly in the frequency domain. Three bits are used for the absolute level in channel 1, and two bits for each channel-to-channel difference, giving a total of 39 bits for the whole spectrum. The remaining two bits per frame are reserved for signalling or monitoring purposes.

A 2400 bit/s channel vocoder degrades the speech in a telephone channel quite perceptibly. It is sufficient for interactive communication, where if you do not understand something, you can always ask for it to be repeated. It is probably not good enough for most voice response applications. However, the vocoder principle can be used with larger filter banks, and much higher bit rates, and still reduce the data rate substantially below that required by log PCM.

4.2 Pre-emphasis

There is an overall −6 dB/octave trend in speech radiated from the lips as frequency increases. We will discuss why this is so in the next chapter. Notice that this trend means that the signal power is reduced by a factor of 4, or the signal amplitude by a factor of 16, for each doubling in frequency. For vocoders, and indeed for other methods of spectral analysis of speech, it is usually desirable to equalize this by a +6 dB/octave lift prior to processing, so that the channel outputs occupy a similar range of levels. On regeneration, the output speech is passed through an inverse filter which provides 6 dB/octave of attenuation.

For a digital system, such pre-emphasis can either be implemented as an analogue circuit which precedes the presampling filter and digitizer, or as a digital operation on the sampled and quantized signal. In the former case, the characteristic is usually flat up to a certain breakpoint, which occurs somewhere between 100 Hz and 1 kHz (the exact position does not seem to be critical) at which point the +6 dB/octave lift begins. Although de-emphasis on output ought to have an exactly inverse characteristic, it is sometimes modified or even eliminated altogether in an attempt to counteract approximately the $\sin(\pi f/f_s)/(\pi f/f_s)$ distortion introduced by the desampling operation, which was discussed in the last chapter. Above half the sampling frequency, the characteristic of the pre-emphasis is irrelevant because any effect will be suppressed by the presampling filter.

The effect of a 6 dB/octave lift can also be achieved digitally, by differencing the input. The operation

$$y(n) = x(n) - ax(n - 1)$$

is suitable, where the constant parameter a is usually chosen between 0.9 and 1. The latter value gives straightforward differencing, and this amounts to creating a DPCM signal as input to the spectral analysis. Figure 4.2 plots the frequency response of this operation, with a sample frequency of 8 kHz, for two values of the parameter; together with that of a 6 dB/octave lift above 100 Hz. The vertical positions of the plots have been adjusted to give the same gain, 20 dB, at 1 kHz. The difference at 3.4 kHz, the upper end of the telephone spectrum, is just over 2 dB. At frequencies below the breakpoint, in this case 100 Hz, the difference between analogue and digital pre-emphasis can be very great. For $a = 0.9$, the attenuation at DC (zero frequency) is 18 dB below that at 1 kHz, which happens to be close to that of the analogue filter for frequencies below the breakpoint. However if the breakpoint had been at 1 kHz, there would have been 20 dB difference between the analogue and $a = 0.9$ plots at DC. And of course the $a = 1$

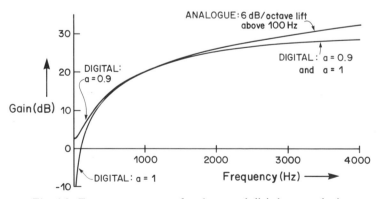

Fig. 4.2. Frequency response of analogue and digital pre-emphasis.

characteristic has infinite attenuation at DC. In practice, however, the exact form of the pre-emphasis does not seem to be at all critical.

The above remarks apply only to voiced speech. For unvoiced speech, there appears to be no real need for pre-emphasis; indeed, it may do harm by reinforcing the already large high-frequency components. There is a case for altering the parameter a according to the excitation mode of the speech: $a = 1$ for voiced excitation and $a = 0$ for unvoiced gives pre-emphasis just when it is needed. This can be achieved by expressing the parameter in terms of the autocorrelation of the incoming signal, as

$$a = \frac{R(1)}{R(0)},$$

where $R(1)$ is the correlation of the signal with itself delayed by one sample, and $R(0)$ is the correlation without delay (that is, the signal variance). This is reasonable intuitively because high sample-to-sample correlation is to be expected in voiced speech, so that $R(1)$ is very nearly as great as $R(0)$ and the ratio becomes 1; whereas little or no sample-to-sample correlation will be present in unvoiced speech, making the ratio close to 0. Such a scheme is reminiscent of ADPCM with adaptive prediction.

However, this sophisticated pre-emphasis method does not seem to be worthwhile in practice. Usually the breakpoint in an analogue pre-emphasis filter is chosen to be rather greater than 100 Hz to limit the amplification of fricative energy. In fact, the channel vocoder described by Holmes (1980) has the breakpoint at 1 kHz, limiting the gain to 12 dB at 4 kHz, two octaves above.

4.3 Digital Signal Analysis

You may be wondering how the frequency response for the digital pre-emphasis filters, displayed in Figure 4.2, can be calculated. Suppose a digitized sinusoid is applied as input to the filter

$$y(n) = x(n) - ax(n - 1).$$

A sine wave of frequency f has equation $x(t) = \sin 2\pi ft$, and when sampled at $t = 0, T, 2T, \ldots$ (where T is the sampling interval, 125 msec for an 8 kHz sample rate), this becomes $x(n) = \sin 2\pi fnT$. It is much more convenient to consider a complex exponential input, $e^{j2\pi fnT}$; the response to a sinusoid can then be derived by taking imaginary parts, if necessary. The output for this input is

$$y(n) = e^{j2\pi fnT} - ae^{j2\pi f(n-1)T} = (1 - ae^{-j2\pi fT})\, e^{j2\pi fnT},$$

a sinusoid at the same frequency as the input. The factor $1 - ae^{-j2\pi fT}$ is complex, with both amplitude and phase components. Thus the output will be a phase-shifted and amplified version of the input. The amplitude response at frequency f is therefore

$$|1 - ae^{-j2\pi fT}| = [1 + a^2 - 2a \cos 2\pi fT]^{1/2},$$

or

$$10 \log_{10}(1 + a^2 - 2a \cos 2\pi fT) \text{ dB}.$$

Normalizing to 20 dB at 1 kHz, and assuming 8 kHz sampling, yields

$$20 + 10 \log_{10}\left(1 + a^2 - 2a \cos \frac{\pi f}{4000}\right) - 10 \log_{10}\left(1 + a^2 - 2a \cos \frac{\pi}{4}\right) \text{ dB}.$$

With $a = 0.9$ and 1 this gives the graphs of Fig. 4.2.

Frequency responses for analogue filters are often plotted with a logarithmic frequency scale, as well as a logarithmic amplitude one, to bring out the asymptotes in dB/octave as straight lines. For digital filters the response is usually drawn on a *linear* frequency axis extending to half the sampling frequency. The response is symmetric about this point.

Analyses like the above are usually expressed in terms of the z-transform. Denote the unit delay operation by z^{-1}. The choice of the inverse rather than z itself is of course an arbitrary matter, but the convention has stuck. Then the filter can be characterized by Fig. 4.3, which signifies that the output is the input minus a delayed and scaled version of itself. The transfer function of the filter is

$$H(z) = 1 - az^{-1},$$

and we have seen that the effect of the system on a (complex) exponential of frequency f is to multiply it by

$$1 - ae^{-j2\pi fT}.$$

To get the frequency response from the transfer function, replace z^{-1} by

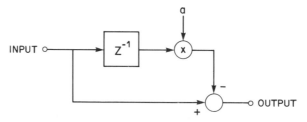

Fig. 4.3. Digital pre-emphasis filter.

$e^{-j2\pi fT}$. Amplitude and phase responses can then be found by taking the modulus and angle of the complex frequency response.

If z^{-1} is treated as an *operator*, it is quite in order to summarize the action of the filter by

$$y(n) = x(n) - az^{-1}x(n) = (1 - az^{-1})x(n).$$

However, it is usual to derive from the sequence $x(n)$ a *transform* $X(z)$ upon which z^{-1} acts as a *multiplier*. If the transform of $x(n)$ is defined as

$$X(z) = \sum_{n=-\infty}^{\infty} x(n)z^{-n},$$

then on multiplication by z^{-1} we get a new transform, say $V(z)$:

$$V(z) = z^{-1}X(z) = z^{-1}\sum_{n=-\infty}^{\infty} x(n)z^{-n} = \sum x(n)z^{-n-1} = \sum x(n-1)z^{-n}.$$

$V(z)$ can also be expressed as the transform of a new sequence, say $v(n)$, by

$$V(z) = \sum_{n=-\infty}^{\infty} v(n)z^{-n},$$

from which it becomes apparent that

$$v(n) = x(n-1).$$

Thus $v(n)$ is a delayed version of $x(n)$, and we have accomplished what we set out to do, namely to show that the delay *operator* z^{-1} can be treated as an ordinary *multiplier* in the z-transform domain, where z-transforms are defined as the infinite sums given above.

In terms of z-transforms, the filter can be written

$$Y(z) = (1 - az^{-1})X(z),$$

where z^{-1} is now treated as a multiplier. The transfer function of the filter is

$$H(z) = \frac{Y(z)}{X(z)} = 1 - az^{-1},$$

the ratio of the output to the input transform.

It may seem that little has been gained by inventing this rather abstract notion of transform, simply to change an operator to a multiplier. After all, the equation of the filter is no simpler in the transform domain than it was in the time domain using z^{-1} as an operator. However, we will need to go on to examine more complex filters. Consider, for example, the transfer function

$$H(z) = \frac{1 + az^{-1} + bz^{-2}}{1 + cz^{-1} + dz^{-2}}.$$

If z^{-1} is treated as an operator, it is not immediately obvious how this transfer function can be realized by a time-domain recurrence relation. However, with z^{-1} as an ordinary multiplier in the transform domain, we can make purely mechanical manipulations with infinite sums to see what the transfer function means as a recurrence relation.

It is worth noting the similarity between the z-transform in the discrete domain and the Fourier and Laplace transforms in the continuous domains. In fact, the z-transform plays an analogous role in digital signal processing to the Laplace transform in continuous theory, for the delay operator z^{-1} performs a similar service to the differentiation operator s. Recall first the continuous Fourier transform,

$$G(f) = \int_{-\infty}^{\infty} g(t)\, e^{-j2\pi ft}\, dt, \quad \text{where } f \text{ is real,}$$

and the Laplace transform,

$$F(s) = \int_{0}^{\infty} f(t)\, e^{-st}\, dt, \quad \text{where } s \text{ is complex.}$$

The main difference between these two transforms is that the range of integration begins at $-\infty$ for the Fourier transform and at 0 for the Laplace. Advocates of the Fourier transform, which typically include people involved with telecommunications, enjoy the freedom from initial conditions which is bestowed by an origin way back in the mists of time. Advocates of Laplace, including most analogue filter theorists, invariably consider systems where all is quiet before $t = 0$ (altering the origin of measurement of time to achieve this if necessary) and welcome the opportunity to include initial conditions explicitly *without* having to worry about what happens in the mists of time. Although there is a two-sided Laplace transform where the integration begins at $-\infty$, it is not generally used because it causes some convergence complications. Ignoring this difference between the transforms (by considering signals which are zero when $t < 0$), the Fourier spectrum can be found from the Laplace transform by writing $s = j2\pi f$; that is, by considering values of s which lie on the imaginary axis.

The z-transform is

$$H(z) = \sum_{n=0}^{\infty} h(n)z^{-n}, \quad \text{or} \quad H(z) = \sum_{n=-\infty}^{\infty} h(n)z^{-n},$$

depending on whether a one-sided or two-sided transform is used. The advantages and disadvantages of one- and two-sided transforms are the same as in the analogue case. z plays the role of e^{sT}, and so it is not surprising that the response to a (sampled) sinusoid input can be found by setting

$$z = e^{j2\pi fT}$$

in $H(z)$, as we proved explicitly above for the pre-emphasis filter.

The above relation between z and f means that real-valued frequencies correspond to points where $|z| = 1$, that is, the unit circle in the complex z-plane. As you travel anticlockwise around this unit circle, starting from the point $z = 1$, the corresponding frequency increases from 0, to $1/2T$ half-way round ($z = -1$), to $1/T$ when you get back to the beginning ($z = 1$) again. Frequencies greater than the sampling frequency are aliased back into the sampling band, corresponding to further circuits of $|z| = 1$ with frequency going from $1/T$ to $2/T$, $2/T$ to $3/T$, and so on. In fact, this is the circle of Fig. 3.3 which was used earlier to explain how sampling affects the frequency spectrum!

4.4 Discrete Fourier Transform

Let us return from this brief digression into techniques of digital signal analysis to the problem of determining the frequency spectrum of speech. Although a bank of bandpass filters such as is used in the channel vocoder is perhaps the most straightforward way to obtain a frequency spectrum, there are other techniques which are in fact more commonly used in digital speech processing.

It is possible to define the Fourier transform of a discrete sequence of points. To motivate the definition, consider first the ordinary Fourier transform (FT), which is

$$g(t) = \int_{-\infty}^{\infty} G(f)\, e^{+j2\pi ft}\, df \qquad G(f) = \int_{-\infty}^{\infty} g(t)\, e^{-j2\pi ft}\, dt.$$

This takes a continuous time domain into a continuous frequency domain. Sometimes you see a normalizing factor $1/2\pi$ multiplying the integral in either the forward or the reverse transform. This is only needed when the frequency variable is expressed in radians/s, and we will find it more convenient to express frequencies in Hz.

The Fourier series (FS), which should also be familiar to you, operates on a periodic time waveform (or, equivalently, one that only exists for a finite period of time, which is notionally extended periodically). If a period lies in the time range $[0, b)$, then the transform is

$$g(t) = \sum_{r=-\infty}^{\infty} G(r)\, e^{+j2\pi rt/b} \qquad G(r) = \frac{1}{b} \int_0^b g(t)\, e^{-j2\pi rt/b}\, dt.$$

The Fourier series takes a periodic time-domain function into a discrete frequency-domain one. Because of the basic duality between the time and frequency domains in the Fourier transforms, it is not surprising that another version of the transform can be defined which takes a periodic *frequency*-domain function into a discrete *time*-domain one.

Fourier transforms can only deal with a finite stretch of a time signal by assuming that the signal is periodic, for if $g(t)$ is evaluated from its transform $G(r)$ according to the formula above, and t is chosen outside the interval $[0, b)$, then a periodic extension of the function $g(t)$ is obtained automatically. Furthermore, periodicity in one domain implies discreteness in the other. Hence if we transform a *finite* stretch of a *discrete* time waveform, we get a frequency-domain representation which is also finite (or, equivalently, periodic), and discrete. This is the discrete Fourier transform (DFT), and takes a discrete periodic time-domain function into a discrete periodic frequency-domain one as illustrated in Fig. 4.4. It is defined by

$$g(n) = \frac{1}{N} \sum_{r=0}^{N-1} G(r)\, e^{+j2\pi rn/N} \qquad G(r) = \sum_{n=0}^{N-1} g(n)\, e^{-j2\pi rn/N},$$

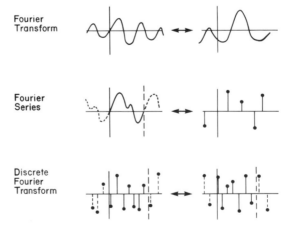

Fig. 4.4. Fourier transform, Fourier series, and discrete Fourier transform.

or, writing $W = e^{-j2\pi/N}$,

$$g(n) = \frac{1}{N} \sum_{r=0}^{N-1} G(r) W^{-rn} \qquad G(r) = \sum_{n=0}^{N-1} g(n) W^{rn}.$$

The $1/N$ in the first equation is the same normalizing factor as the $1/b$ in the Fourier series, for the finite time domain is $[0, N)$ in the discrete case and $[0, b)$ in the Fourier series case. It does not matter whether it is written into the forward or the reverse transform, but it is usually placed as shown above as a matter of convention.

As illustrated by Fig. 4.5, discrete Fourier transforms take an input of N real values, representing equally-spaced time samples in the interval $[0, b)$, and produce as output N complex values, representing equally-spaced frequency samples in the interval $[0, N/b)$. Note that the end-point of this frequency interval is the sampling frequency. It seems odd that the input is real and the output is the same number of *complex* quantities: we seem to be getting some numbers for nothing! However this isn't so, for it is easy to show that if the input sequence is real, the output frequency spectrum has a symmetry about its mid-point (half the sampling frequency). This can be expressed as

DFT symmetry: $G(\tfrac{1}{2}N + r) = G(\tfrac{1}{2}N - r)^*$ if g is real-valued,

where $*$ denotes the conjugate of a complex quantity (that is, $(a + jb)^* = a - jb$).

It was argued above that the frequency spectrum in the DFT is periodic, with the spectrum from 0 to the sampling frequency being repeated regularly up and down the frequency axis. It can easily be seen from the DFT equation that this is so. It can be written

DFT periodicity: $G(N + r) = G(r)$ always.

Figure 4.6 illustrates the properties of symmetry and periodicity.

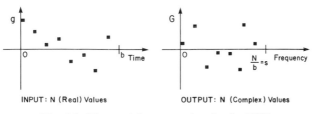

Fig. 4.5. Time and frequency domains for DFT.

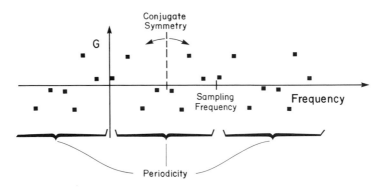

Fig. 4.6. Symmetry and periodicity in the DFT.

4.5 Estimating the Frequency Spectrum of Speech using the DFT

Speech signals are not exactly periodic. Although the waveform in a particular pitch period will usually resemble those in the preceding and following pitch periods, it will certainly not be identical to them. As the articulation of the speech changes, the formant positions will alter. As we saw in Chapter 2, the pitch itself is certainly not constant. Hence the fundamental assumption of the DFT, that the waveform is periodic, is not really justified. However, the signal is quasi-periodic, for changes from period to period will not usually be very great. One way of computing the short-term frequency spectrum of speech is to use *pitch-synchronous* Fourier transformation, where single pitch periods are isolated from the waveform and processed with the DFT. This gives a rather accurate estimate of the spectrum. Unfortunately, it is difficult to determine the beginning and end of each pitch cycle, as we shall see later in this chapter when discussing pitch extraction techniques.

If a finite stretch of a speech waveform is isolated and Fourier transformed, without regard to pitch of the speech, then the periodicity assumption will be grossly violated. Figure 4.7 illustrates that the effect is the same as multiplying the signal by a rectangular *window function*, which is 0 except during the period to be analysed, where it is 1. The windowed sequence will almost certainly have discontinuities at its edges, and these will affect the resulting spectrum. The effect can be analysed quite easily, but we will not do so here. It is enough to say that the high frequencies associated with the edges of the window cause considerable distortion of the spectrum. The effect can be alleviated by using a smoother window than a rectangular one, and several have been investigated extensively. The commonly-used windows of Bartlett, Blackman and Hamming are illustrated in Fig. 4.8.

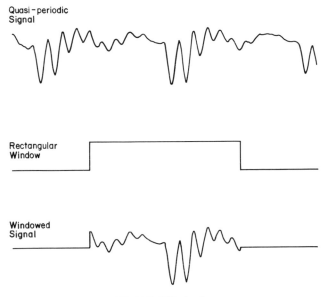

Quasi-periodic
Signal

Rectangular
Window

Windowed
Signal

Fig. 4.7. Windowing.

Because the DFT produces the same number of frequency samples, equally spaced, as there were points in the time waveform, there is a trade-off between frequency resolution and time resolution (for a given sampling rate). For example, a 256-point transform with a sample rate of 8 kHz gives the 256 equally-spaced frequency components between 0 and 8 kHz that are shown in Table 4.2. The top half of the frequency spectrum is of no interest, because it contains the complex conjugates of the bottom half (in reverse order), corresponding to frequencies greater than half the sampling frequency. Thus for a 30 Hz resolution in the frequency domain, 256 time samples, or a 32 msec stretch of speech, needs to be transformed. A common

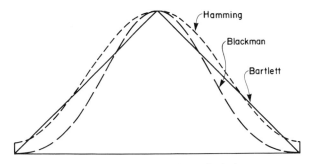

Hamming
Blackman
Bartlett

Fig. 4.8. Some commonly-used windows.

Table 4.2. Time domain and frequency domain samples for a 256-point DFT, with 8 kHz sampling.

Time domain		Frequency domain	
Sample number	Time	Sample number	Frequency
0	0 μsec	0	0 Hz
1	125	1	31
2	250	2	62
3	375	3	94
4	500	4	125
...	...	...	...
	...		...
	...		...
254	31 750	254	7938
255	31 875 μsec	255	7969 Hz

technique is to take overlapping periods in the time domain to give a new frequency spectrum every 16 msec. From the acoustic point of view this is a reasonable rate to re-compute the spectrum, for as noted above when discussing channel vocoders the rate of change in the spectrum is limited by the speed with which the speaker can move his vocal organs, and anything between 10 and 25 msec is a reasonable figure for transmitting or storing the spectrum.

The DFT is a complex transform, and speech is a real signal. It is possible to do two DFT's at once by putting one time waveform into the real parts of the input and another into the imaginary parts. This destroys the DFT symmetry property, for it only holds for real inputs. But given the DFT of a complex sequence formed in this way, it is easy to separate out the DFT's of the two real-time sequences. If the two time sequences are $x(n)$ and $y(n)$, then the transform of the complex sequence

$$g(n) = x(n) + jy(n)$$

(where $j^2 = -1$) is

$$G(r) = \sum_{n=0}^{N-1} [x(n)W^{rn} + jy(n)W^{rn}].$$

It follows that the complex conjugate of the aliased parts of the spectrum, in the upper frequency region, are

$$G(N - r)^* = \sum_{n-0}^{N-1} [x(n)W^{-(N-r)n} - jy(n)W^{-(N-r)n}],$$

and this is the same as

$$G(N - r)^* = \sum_{n=0}^{N-1} [x(n)W^{rn} - y(n)W^{rn}],$$

because W^N is 1 (recall the definition of W), and so W^{-Nn} is 1 for any integer n. Thus

$$X(r) = \frac{G(r) + G(N - r)^*}{2} \qquad Y(r) = \frac{G(r) - G(N - r)^*}{2j}$$

extracts the transforms $X(r)$ and $Y(r)$ of the original sequences $x(n)$ and $y(n)$.

With speech this trick is frequently used to calculate two spectra at once. Using 256-point transforms, a new estimate of the spectrum can be obtained every 16 msec by taking overlapping 32 msec stretches of speech, with a computational requirement of one 256-point transform every 32 msec.

4.6 The Fast Fourier Transform

Straightforward calculation of the DFT, expressed as

$$G(r) = \sum_{n=0}^{N-1} g(n)W^{nr},$$

for $r = 0, 1, 2, \ldots, N - 1$, takes N^2 operations, where each operation is a complex multiply and add (for W is, of course, a complex number). There is a better way, invented in the early sixties, which reduces this to $N \log_2 N$ operations: a very considerable improvement. Dubbed the "fast Fourier transform" (FFT) for historical reasons, it would actually be better called the "Fourier transform", with the straightforward method above known as the "slow Fourier transform"! There is no reason nowadays to use the slow method, except for tiny transforms. It is worth describing the basic principle of the FFT, for it is surprisingly simple. More details on actual implementations can be found in Brigham (1974).

It is important to realize that the FFT involves no approximation. It is an *exact* calculation of the values that would be obtained by the slow method (although it may be affected differently by round-off errors). Problems of aliasing and windowing occur in all discrete Fourier transforms, and they are neither alleviated nor exacerbated by the FFT.

To gain insight into the working of the FFT, imagine the sequence $g(n)$ split into two halves, containing the even and odd points respectively:

$$\text{even half } e(n) \text{ is } g(0)g(2) \cdots g(N - 2)$$
$$\text{odd half } o(n) \text{ is } g(1)g(3) \cdots g(N - 1).$$

Then it is easy to show that if G is the transform of g, E the transform of e, and O that of o, then

$$G(r) = E(r) + W^r O(r) \quad \text{for} \quad r = 0, 1, ..., \tfrac{1}{2}N - 1,$$

and

$$G(\tfrac{1}{2}N + r) = E(r) + W^{1/2N + r} O(r) \quad \text{for} \quad r = 0, 1, ..., \tfrac{1}{2}N - 1.$$

Calculation of the E and O transforms involves $(\tfrac{1}{2}N)^2$ operations each, while combining them together according to the above relationship occupies N operations. Thus the total is $N + \tfrac{1}{2}N^2$ operations, which is considerably less than N^2.

But don't stop there! The even half can itself be broken down into even and odd parts to expedite its calculation, and the same with the odd half. The only constraint is that the number of elements in the sequences splits exactly into two at each stage. Providing N is a power of 2, then, we are left at the end with some 1-point transforms to do. But transforming a single point leaves it unaffected! (Check the definition of the DFT.) A quick calculation shows that the number of operations needed is not $N + \tfrac{1}{2}N^2$, but $N \log_2 N$. Figure 4.9 compares this with N^2, the number of operations for straightforward DFT calculation, and it can be seen that the FFT is very much faster.

The only restriction on the use of the FFT is that N must be a power of two. If it is not, alternative, more complicated, algorithms can be used which give comparable computational advantages. However for speech processing, the number of samples that are transformed is usually arranged to be a power of two. If a pitch synchronous analysis is undertaken, the time stretch that is to be transformed is dictated by the length of the pitch period, and will vary from time to time. Then, it is usual to pad out the time waveform with zeros to bring the number of samples up to a power of two;

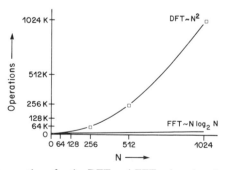

Fig. 4.9. Number of operations for the DFT and FFT, plotted against the size of transform.

otherwise, if different-length time stretches were transformed, the scale of the resulting frequency components would vary too.

The FFT provides very worthwhile cost savings over the use of a bank of bandpass filters for spectral analysis. Take the example of a 256-point transform with 8 kHz sampling, giving 128 frequency components spaced by 31.25 Hz from 0 up to almost 4 kHz. This can be computed on overlapping 32 msec stretches of the time waveform, giving a new spectrum every 16 msec, by a single FFT calculation every 32 msec (putting successive pairs of time stretches in the real and imaginary parts of the complex input sequence, as described earlier). The FFT algorithm requires $N \log_2 N$ operations, which is 2048 when $N = 256$. An additional 512 operations are required for the windowing calculation. Repeated every 32 msec, this gives a rate of 80 000 operations per second. To achieve a much lower frequency resolution with 20 bandpass filters, each of which are fourth order, will need a great deal more operations. Each filter will need between 4 and 8 multiplications per sample, depending on its exact digital implementation. But new samples appear every 125 *micro*seconds, and so somewhere around a million operations will be required every second. If we increased the frequency resolution to that obtained by the FFT, 128 filters would be needed, requiring between 4 and 8 million operations!

4.7 Formant Estimation

Once the frequency spectrum of a speech signal has been calculated, it may seem a simple matter to estimate the positions of the formants. But it is not! Spectra obtained in practice are not usually like the idealized ones of Fig. 2.2. One reason for this is that unless the analysis is pitch-synchronous, the frequency spectrum of the excitation source is mixed in with that of the vocal tract filter. There are other reasons, which will be discussed later in this section. But first, let us consider how to extract the vocal tract filter characteristics from the combined spectrum of source and filter. To do so we must begin to explore the theory of linear systems.

Discrete Linear Systems

Figure 4.10 shows an input signal exciting a filter to produce an output signal. For present purposes, imagine the input to be a glottal waveform, the filter a vocal tract one, and the output a speech signal (which is then subjected to high-frequency de-emphasis by radiation from the lips). We will consider here *discrete* systems, so that the input $x(n)$ and output $y(n)$

are sampled signals, defined only when n is integral. The theory is quite similar for continuous systems.

Assume that the system is *linear,* that is, if input $x_1(n)$ produces output $y_1(n)$ and input $x_2(n)$ produces output $y_2(n)$, then the sum of $x_1(n)$ and $x_2(n)$ will produce the sum of $y_1(n)$ and $y_2(n)$. It is easy to show from this that, for any constant multiplier a, the input $ax(n)$ will produce output $ay(n)$; it is pretty obvious when $a = 2$, or indeed any positive integer, for then $ax(n)$ can be written as $x(n) + x(n) + \dots$. Assume further that the system is *time-invariant,* that is, if input $x(n)$ produces output $y(n)$ then a time-shifted version of x, say $x(n + n_0)$ for some integer n_0, will produce the same output, only time-shifted; namely $y(n + n_0)$.

Now consider the discrete delta function $\delta(n)$, which is 0 except at $n = 0$ when it is 1. If this single impulse is presented as input to the system, the output is called the *impulse response,* and will be denoted by $h(n)$. The fact that the system is time-invariant guarantees that the response does not depend upon the particular time at which the impulse occurred, so that, for example, the impulsive input $\delta(n + n_0)$ will produce output $h(n + n_0)$. A delta-function input and corresponding impulse response are shown in Fig. 4.10.

The impulse response of a linear, time-invariant system is an extremely useful thing to know, for it can be used to calculate the output of the system for any input at all! Specifically, an input signal $x(n)$ can be written

$$x(n) = \sum_{k=-\infty}^{\infty} x(k)\delta(n - k),$$

because $\delta(n - k)$ is non-zero only when $k = n$, and so for any particular value of n, the summation contains only one non-zero term: that is, $x(n)$. The action of the system on each term of the sum is to produce an output $x(k)h(n - k)$, because $x(k)$ is just a constant, and the system is linear. Furthermore, the complete input $x(n)$ is just the sum of such terms, and since the system is linear, the output is the sum of $x(k)h(n - k)$. Hence

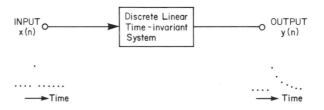

Fig. 4.10. Linear system with input and output, together with impulsive input and the corresponding impulse response.

the response of the system to an arbitrary input is

$$y(n) = \sum_{k=-\infty}^{\infty} x(k)h(n - k).$$

This is called a *convolution sum,* and is sometimes written

$$y(n) = x(n) \otimes h(n).$$

Let's write this in terms of z-transforms. The (two-sided) z-transform of $y(n)$ is

$$Y(z) = \sum_{n=-\infty}^{\infty} y(n)z^{-n} = \sum_{n} \sum_{k} x(k)h(n - k)z^{-n},$$

Writing z^{-n} as $z^{-(n-k)}z^{-k}$, and interchanging the order of summation, this becomes

$$Y(z) = \sum_{k} \left[\sum_{n} h(n - k)z^{-(n-k)} \right] x(k)z^{-k}$$

$$= \sum_{k} H(z)x(k)z^{-k} = H(z) \sum_{k} x(k)z^{-k} = H(z)X(z).$$

Thus convolution in the time domain is the same as multiplication in the z-transform domain, a very important result. Applied to the linear system of Fig. 4.10, this means that the output z-transform is the input z-transform multiplied by the z-transform of the system's impulse response.

What we really want to do is to relate the frequency spectrum of the output to the response of the system and the spectrum of the input. In fact, frequency spectra are very closely connected with z-transforms. A periodic signal $x(n)$ which repeats every N samples has DFT

$$\sum_{n=0}^{N-1} x(n)e^{-j2\pi rn/N},$$

and its z-transform is

$$\sum_{n=-\infty}^{\infty} x(n)z^{-n}.$$

Hence the DFT is the same as the z-transform of a single cycle of the signal, evaluated at the points $z = e^{j2\pi r/N}$ for $r = 0, 1, \ldots, N - 1$. In other words, the frequency components are samples of the z-transform at N equally-spaced points around the unit circle. Hence the frequency spectrum at the output of a linear system is the product of the input spectrum and the frequency response of the system itself (that is, the transform of its impulse response function). It should be admitted that this statement is somewhat questionable, because to get from z-transforms to DFT's we have assumed that a single cycle only is transformed, and the impulse response function of a system is not necessarily periodic. The real action of the system is to multiply z-transforms, not DFT's. However, it is useful in imagining the behaviour of the system to think in terms of products of DFT's, and in practice it is always these rather than z-transforms which are computed because of the existence of the FFT algorithm.

Figure 4.11 shows the frequency spectrum of a typical voiced speech signal. The overall shape shows humps at the formant positions, like those in the idealized Fig. 2.2. However, superimposed on this is an "oscillation" (in the frequency domain!) at the pitch frequency. This occurs because the transform of the vocal tract filter has been multiplied by that of the pitch pulse, the latter having components at harmonics of the pitch frequency. The oscillation must be suppressed before the formants can be estimated to any degree of accuracy.

One way of eliminating the oscillation is to perform pitch-synchronous analysis. This removes the influence of pitch from the frequency domain by dealing with it in the time domain! The snag is, of course, that it is not easy to estimate the pitch frequency: some techniques for doing so are discussed in the next main section. Another way is to use linear predictive analysis, which really does get rid of pitch information without having to estimate the pitch period first. A smooth frequency spectrum can be pro-

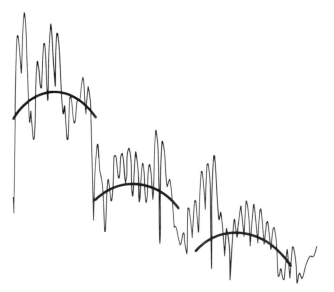

Fig. 4.11. Typical frequency spectrum of voiced speech.

duced using the analysis techniques described in Chapter 6, which provides a suitable starting-point for formant frequency estimation. The third method is to remove the pitch ripple from the frequency spectrum directly. This will be discussed in an intuitive rather than a theoretical way, because linear predictive methods are becoming dominant in speech processing.

Cepstral Processing of Speech

Suppose the frequency spectrum of Fig. 4.11 were actually a time waveform. To remove the high-frequency pitch ripple is easy: just filter it out! However, filtering removes *additive* ripples, whereas this is a *multiplicative* ripple. To turn multiplication into addition, take logarithms. Then the procedure would be

—compute the DFT of the speech waveform (windowed, overlapped);
—take the logarithm of the transform;
—filter out the high-frequency part, corresponding to pitch ripple.

Filtering is often best done using the DFT. If the rippled waveform of Fig. 4.11 is transformed, a strong component could be expected at the ripple frequency, with weaker ones at its harmonics. These components can be simply removed by setting them to zero, and inverse-transforming the result to give a smoothed version of the original frequency spectrum. A spectrum of the logarithm of a frequency spectrum is often called a *cepstrum*: a sort of backwards spectrum. The horizontal axis of the cepstrum, having the dimension of time, is called "quefrency"! Note that high-frequency signals have low quefrencies and vice versa. In practice, because the pitch ripple is usually well above the quefrency of interest for formants, the upper end of the cepstrum is often simply cut off from a fixed quefrency which corresponds to the maximum pitch expected. However, identifying the pitch peaks of the cepstrum has the useful by-product of giving the pitch period of the original speech.

To summarize, then, the procedure for spectral smoothing by the cepstral method is

—compute the DFT of the speech waveform (windowed, overlapped);
—take the logarithm of the transform;
—take the DFT of this log-transform, calling it the cepstrum;
—identify the lowest-quefrency peak in the spectrum as the pitch, confirming it by examining its harmonics, which should be equally spaced at the pitch quefrency;
—remove pitch effects from the cepstrum by cutting off its high-quefrency part above either the pitch quefrency or some constant representing

the maximum expected pitch (which is the minimum expected pitch quefrency);
—inverse DFT the resulting cepstrum to give a smoothed spectrum.

Estimating Formant Frequencies from Smoothed Spectra

The difficulties of formant extraction are not over even when a smooth frequency spectrum has been obtained. A simple peak-picking algorithm which identifies a peak at the k'th frequency component whenever

$$X(k - 1) < X(k) \quad \text{and} \quad X(k) > X(k + 1)$$

will quite often identify formants incorrectly. It helps to specify in advance minimum and maximum formant frequencies: say 100 Hz and 3 kHz for three-formant identification, and ignore peaks lying outside these limits. It helps to estimate the bandwidth of the peaks and reject those with bandwidths greater than 500 Hz, for real formants are never this wide. However, if two formants are very close, then they may appear as a single, wide, peak and be rejected by this criterion. It is usual to take account of formant positions identified in previous frames under these conditions.

Markel and Gray (1976) describe in detail several estimation algorithms. Their simplest uses the number of peaks identified in the raw spectrum (under 3 kHz, and with bandwidths greater than 500 Hz), to determine what to do. If exactly three peaks are found, they are used as the formant positions. It is claimed that this happens about 85% to 90% of the time. If only one peak is found, the present frame is ignored and the previously-identified formant positions are used (this happens less than 1% of the time). The remaining cases are two peaks (corresponding to omission of one formant) and four peaks (corresponding to an extra formant being included). More than four peaks never occurred in their data. Under these conditions, a nearest-neighbour measure is used for disambiguation. The measure is

$$v_{ij} = |F_i^{\Delta}(k) - F_j(k - 1)|,$$

where $F_j^{(k-1)}$ is the j'th formant frequency defined in the previous frame $k - 1$ and $F_i^{\Delta}(k)$ is the i'th raw data frequency estimate for frame k. If two peaks only are found, this measure is used to identify the closest peaks in the previous frame, and then the third peak of that frame is taken to be the missing formant position. If four peaks are found, the measure is used to determine which of them is furthest from the previous formant values, and this one is discarded.

This procedure works forwards, using the previous frame to disambiguate peaks given in the current one. More sophisticated algorithms work backwards as well, identifying *anchor points* in the data which have clearly-defined formant positions, and moving in both directions from these to disambiguate neighbouring frames of data. Finally, absolute limits can be imposed upon the magnitude of formant movements between frames to give an overall smoothing to the formant tracks.

Very often, people will refine the result of such automatic formant estimation procedures by hand, looking at the tracks, knowing what was said, and making adjustments in the light of their experience of how formants move in speech. Unfortunately, it is difficult to obtain high-quality formant tracks by completely automatic means.

One of the most difficult cases in formant estimation is where two formants are so close together that the individual peaks cannot be resolved. One simple solution to this problem is to employ "analysis-by-synthesis", whereby once a formant is identified, a standard formant shape at this position is synthesized and subtracted from the logarithmic spectrum (Coker, 1963). Then, even if two formants are right on top of each other, the second is not missed because it remains after the first one has been subtracted.

Unfortunately, however, the single peak which appears when two formants are close together usually does not correspond exactly with the position of either one. There is one rather advanced signal-processing technique that can help in this case. The frequency spectrum of speech is determined by *poles* which lie in the complex z-plane inside the unit circle. (They must be inside the unit circle if the system is stable. Those familiar with Laplace analysis of analogue systems may like to note that the left half of the s-plane corresponds with the inside of the unit circle in the z-plane.) As shown earlier, computing a DFT is tantamount to evaluating the z-transform at equally-spaced points around the unit circle. However, better resolution is obtained by evaluating around a circle which lies *inside* the unit circle, but *outside* the outermost pole position. Such a circle is sketched in Fig. 4.12.

Recall that the FFT is a fast way of calculating the DFT of a sequence. Is there a similarly fast way of evaluating the z-transform inside the unit circle? The answer is yes, and the technique is known as the "chirp z-

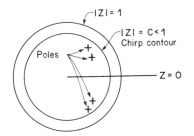

Fig. 4.12. Evaluating the z-transform on a circle inside the unit one.

transform", because it involves considering a signal whose frequency increases linearly, just like a radar chirp signal. The chirp method allows the
z-transform to be computed quickly at equally-spaced points along spirally-
shaped contours around the origin of the z-plane, corresponding to signals
of linearly increasing complex frequency. The spiral nature of these curves
is not of particular interest in speech processing. What *is* of interest, though,
is that the spiral can begin at any point on the $z = 0$ axis, and its pitch
can be set arbitrarily. If we begin spiralling at $z = 0.9$, say, and set the
pitch to zero, the contour becomes a circle inside the unit one, with radius
0.9. Such a circle is exactly what is needed to refine formant resolution.

4.8 Pitch Extraction

The last section discussed how to characterize the vocal tract filter in the
source-filter model of speech production; this one looks at how the most
important property of the source (that is, the pitch period) can be derived.
In many ways pitch extraction is more important from a practical point of
view than is formant estimation. In a voice-output system, formant estimation is only necessary if speech is to be stored in formant-coded form.
For linear predictive storage of speech, or for speech synthesis from phonetics or text, formant extraction is unnecessary; although of course general
information about formant frequencies and formant tracks in natural speech
is needed before a synthesis-from-phonetics system can be built. However,
knowledge of the pitch contour is needed for many different purposes. For
example, compact encoding of linearly predicted speech relies on the pitch
being estimated and stored as a parameter separate from the articulation.
Significant improvements in frequency analysis can be made by performing
pitch-synchronous Fourier transformations, because the need to window is
eliminated. Many synthesis-from-phonetics systems require the pitch contour for utterances to be stored rather than computed from markers in the
phonetic text.

Another issue which is closely bound up with pitch extraction is the
voiced–unvoiced distinction. A good pitch estimator ought to fail when
presented with aperiodic input such as an unvoiced sound, and so give a
reliable indication of whether the frame of speech is voiced or not.

One method of pitch estimation, which uses the cepstrum, has been
outlined above. It involves a substantial amount of computation, and has
a high degree of complexity. However, if implemented properly it gives
excellent results, because the source-filter structure of the speech is fully
utilized. Another method, using the linear prediction residual, will be described in Chapter 6. Again, this requires a great deal of computation of

a fairly sophisticated nature, and gives good results; although it relies on a somewhat more restricted version of the source-filter model than cepstral analysis.

Autocorrelation Methods

The most reliable way of estimating the pitch of a periodic signal which is corrupted by noise is to examine its short-time autocorrelation function. The autocorrelation of a signal $x(n)$ with lag k is defined as

$$\varphi(k) = \sum_{n=-\infty}^{\infty} x(n)x(n + k).$$

If the signal is quasi-periodic, with slowly varying period, a finite stretch of it can be isolated with a window $w(i)$, which is 0 when i is outside the range $[0, N)$. Beginning this window at sample m gives the windowed signal

$$x(n)w(n - m).$$

whose autocorrelation, the *short-time* autocorrelation of the signal x at point m, is

$$\varphi_m(k) = \sum_n x(n)w(n - m)x(n + k)w(n - m + k).$$

The autocorrelation function exhibits peaks at lags which correspond to the pitch periods and multiples of it. At such lags, the signal is in phase with a delayed version of itself, giving high correlation. The pitch of natural speech ranges about three octaves, from 50 Hz (low-pitched men) to around 400 Hz (children). To ensure that at least two pitch cycles are seen, even at the low end, the window needs to be at least 40 msec long, and the autocorrelation function calculated for lags up to 20 msec. The peaks which occur at lags corresponding to multiples of the pitch become smaller as the multiple increases, because the speech waveform will change slightly and the pitch period is not perfectly constant. If signals at the high end of the pitch range, 400 Hz, are viewed through a 40 msec autocorrelation window, considerable smearing of pitch resolution in the time domain is to be expected. Finally, for unvoiced speech, no substantial peaks of autocorrelation will occur.

If all deviations from perfect periodicity can be attributed to additive, white, Gaussian noise, then it can be shown from standard detection theory that autocorrelation methods are appropriate for pitch identification. Unfortunately, this is certainly not the case for speech signals. Although the short-time autocorrelation of voiced speech exhibits peaks at multiples of the pitch period, it is not clear that it is any easier to detect these peaks in the autocorrelation function than it is in the original time waveform! To take a simple example, if a signal contains a fundamental and in-phase first and second harmonics,

$$x(n) = a \sin 2\pi f nT + b \sin 4\pi f nT + c \sin 6\pi f nT,$$

then its short-time autocorrelation function is

$$\varphi_{m}(k) = \frac{a^2 \cos 2\pi f kT + b^2 \cos 4\pi f kT + c^2 \cos 6\pi f kT}{2}.$$

There is no reason to believe that detection of the fundamental period of this signal will be any easier in the autocorrelation domain than in the time domain.

The most common error of pitch detection by autocorrelation analysis is that the periodicities of the formants are confused with the pitch. This typically leads to the repetition time being identified as $T_{pitch} \pm T_{formant 1}$, where the T's are the periods of the pitch and first formant. Fortunately, there are simple ways of processing the signal non-linearly to reduce the effect of formants on pitch estimation using autocorrelation.

One way is to low-pass filter the signal with a cut-off above the maximum pitch period, say 600 Hz. However, formant 1 is often below this value. A different technique, which may be used in conjunction with filtering, is to "centre-clip" the signal as shown in Fig. 4.13. This removes many of the ripples which are associated with formants. However, it entails the use of an adjustable clipping threshold to cater for speech of varying amplitudes. Sondhi (1968), who introduced the technique, set the clipping level at 30% of the maximum amplitude. An alternative which achieves much the same effect without the need to fiddle with thresholds, is to cube the signal, or

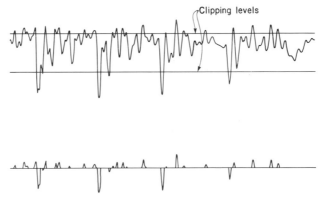

Fig. 4.13. Centre-clipping a speech signal.

raise it to some other high (odd!) power, before taking the autocorrelation. This highlights the peaks and suppresses the effect of low-amplitude parts.

For very accurate pitch detection, it is best to combine the evidence from several different methods of analysis of the time waveform. The autocorrelation function provides one source of evidence; and the cepstrum provides another. A third source comes from the time waveform itself. McGonegal *et al.* (1975) have described a semi-automatic method of pitch detection which uses human judgement to make a final decision based upon these three sources of evidence. This appears to provide highly accurate pitch contours at the expense of considerable human effort: it takes an experienced user 30 minutes to process each second of speech.

Speeding up Autocorrelation

Calculating the autocorrelation function is an arithmetic-intensive procedure. For large lags, it can best be done using FFT methods, although there are simpler arithmetic tricks which speed it up without going to such complexity. However, with the availability of analogue delay lines using charge-coupled devices, autocorrelation can now be done effectively and cheaply by analogue, sampled-data, hardware.

Nevertheless, some techniques to speed up digital calculation of short-time autocorrelations are in wide use. It is tempting to hard-limit the signal so that it becomes binary (Fig. 4.14a), thus eliminating multiplication. This can be disastrous, however, because hard-limited speech is known to retain considerable intelligibility and therefore the formant structure is still there. A better plan is to take centre-clipped speech and hard-limit that to a ternary signal (Figure 4.14b). This simplifies the computation considerably with essentially no degradation in performance (Dubnowski *et al.*, 1976).

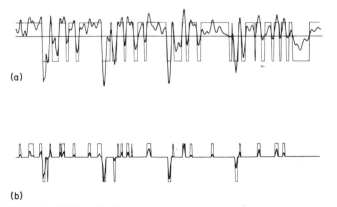

(a)

(b)

Fig. 4.14. (a) Hard-limited speech signal, (b) Ternary centre-clipping.

A different approach to reducing the amount of calculation is to perform a kind of autocorrelation which does not use multiplications. The "average magnitude difference function", which is defined by

$$d(k) = \sum_{n=-\infty}^{\infty} |x(n) - x(n + k)|,$$

has been used for this purpose with some success (Ross *et al.*, 1974). It exhibits dips at pitch periods (instead of the peaks of the autocorrelation function).

Feature-extraction Methods

Another possible way of extracting pitch in the time domain is to try to integrate information from different sources to give reliable pitch estimates. Several features of the time waveform can be defined, each of which provides an estimate of the pitch period, and an overall estimate can be obtained by majority vote.

For example, suppose that the only feature of the speech waveform which is retained is the height and position of the peaks, where a "peak" is defined by the simplistic criterion

$$x(n - 1) < x(n) \quad \text{and} \quad x(n) > x(n + 1).$$

Having found a peak which is thought to represent a pitch pulse, one could define a "blanking period", based upon the current pitch estimate, within which the next pitch pulse could not occur. When this period has expired, the next pitch pulse is sought. At first, a stringent criterion should be used for identifying the next peak as a pitch pulse, but it can gradually be relaxed if time goes on without a suitable pulse being located. Figure 4.15 shows a convenient way of doing this: a decaying exponential is begun at the end of the blanking period and when a peak shows above, it is identified as a pitch pulse. One big advantage of this type of algorithm is that the data

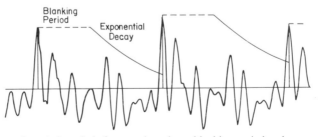

Fig. 4.15. Detecting pitch periods from peaks using a blanking period and exponential decay.

is greatly reduced by considering peaks only, which can be detected by simple hardware. Thus it can permit real-time operation on a small processor with minimal special-purpose hardware.

Such a pitch pulse detector is exceedingly simplistic, and will often identify the pitch incorrectly. However, it can be used in conjunction with other features to produce good pitch estimates. Gold and Rabiner (1969), who pioneered the approach, used six features:

—peak height
—valley depth
—valley-to-peak height
—peak-to-valley depth
—peak-to-peak height (if greater than 0)
—valley-to-valley depth (if greater than 0).

The features are symmetric with regard to peaks and valleys. The first feature is the one described above, and the second one works in exactly the same way. The third feature records the height between each valley and the succeeding peak, and fourth uses the depth between each peak and the succeeding valley. The purpose of the final two detectors is to eliminate secondary, but rather large, peaks from consideration. Figure 4.16 shows the kind of waveform on which the other features might incorrectly double the pitch, but the last two features identify correctly.

Gold and Rabiner also included the last two pitch estimates from each feature detector. Furthermore, for each feature, the present estimate was added to the previous one to make a fourth, and the previous one to the one before that to make a fifth, and all three were added together to make a sixth; so that for each feature there were 6 separate estimates of pitch. The reason for this is that if three consecutive estimates of the fundamental period are T_0, T_1 and T_2; then if some peaks are being falsely identified, the actual period could be any of

$$T_0 + T_1, \quad T_1 + T_2, \quad T_0 + T_1 + T_2.$$

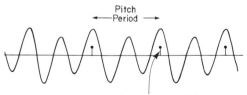

Pitch
←—Period —→

Peak- to- Peak Height
(Recorded only if Positive)

Fig. 4.16. A waveform which needs the peak-to-peak height feature for correct identification of pitch.

It is essential to do this, because a feature of a given type can occur more than once in a pitch period; secondary peaks usually exist.

Six features, each contributing six separate estimates, makes 36 estimates of pitch in all. An overall figure was obtained from this set by selecting the most popular estimate (within some pre-specified tolerance). The complete scheme has been evaluated extensively (Rabiner *et al.*, 1976) and compares favourably with other methods.

However, it must be admitted that this procedure seems to be rather *ad hoc* (as are many other successful speech parameter estimation algorithms!). Specifically, it is not easy to predict what kinds of waveforms it will fail on, and evaluation of it can only be pragmatic. When used to estimate the pitch of musical instruments and singers over a 6-octave range (40 Hz to 2.5 kHz), instances were found where it failed dramatically (Tucker and Bates, 1978). This is, of course, a much more difficult problem than pitch estimation for speech, where the range is typically 3 octaves. In fact, for speech the feature detectors are usually preceded by a low-pass filter to attenuate the myriad of peaks caused by higher formants, and this is inappropriate for musical applications.

There is evidence which shows that additional features can assist with pitch identification. The above features are all based upon the signal amplitude, and could be described as *secondary* features derived from a single *primary* feature. Other primary features can easily be defined. Tucker and Bates (1978) used a centre-clipped waveform, and considered only the peaks rising above the central region. They defined two further primary features, in addition to the peak amplitude: the *time width* of a peak (period for which it is outside the clipping level), and its *energy* (again, outside the clipping level). The primary features are shown in Fig. 4.17. Secondary features are defined, based on these three primary ones, and pitch estimates are made for each one. A further innovation was to combine the individual estimates in a way which is based upon autocorrelation analysis, reducing to some degree the "*ad-hoc*ery" of the pitch detection process.

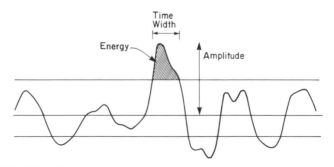

Fig. 4.17. Three features defined on the peaks and valleys of centre-clipped speech.

4.9 References

Blankenship, P.E. (1978). An NMOS LSI channel vocoder implementation. *Proc IEEE EASCON*, 684–692, Washington DC.

Brigham, E.O. (1974). "The fast Fourier transform", Prentice Hall, Englewood Cliffs, New Jersey.

Coker, C.H. (1963). Computer-simulated analyzer for a formant vocoder. *J. Acoustical Society of America*, **35**(11)1911(A), November.

Dubnowski, J.J., Schafer, R.W. and Rabiner, L.R. (1976). Real-time digital hardware pitch detector. *IEEE Trans Acoustics, Speech and Signal Processing*, **ASSP-24**(1)2–8, February.

Dudley, H. (1939). Remaking speech *J. Acoustical Society of America*, **11**(2)169–177, October.

Gold, B. and Rabiner, L.R. (1969). Parallel processing techniques for estimating pitch periods of speech in the time domain. *J. Acoustical Society of America*, **46**(2)442–448, August.

Holmes, J.N. (1980). The JSRU channel vocoder. *Proc Institute of Electrical Engineers*, **127**(F1)53–60, February.

Markel, J.D. and Gray, A.H. (1976). "Linear prediction of speech," Springer Verlag, Berlin.

McGonegal, C.A., Rabiner, L.R. and Rosenberg, A.E. (1975). A semi-automatic pitch detector (SAPD). *IEEE Trans Acoustics, Speech and Signal Processing*, **ASSP-23**, 570–574, December.

Rabiner, L.R., Cheng, M.J., Rosenberg, A.E. and McGonegal, C.A. (1976). A comparative performance study of several pitch detection algorithms. *IEEE Trans Acoustics, Speech and Signal Processing*, **ASSP-24**(5)399–418, October.

Ross, M.J., Schafer, H.L., Cohen, A., Freuberg, R. and Manley, H.J. (1974). Average magnitude difference function pitch extractor. *IEEE Trans Acoustics, Speech and Signal Processing*, **ASSP-22**(5)353–362, October.

Schroeder, M.R. (1970). Parameter estimation in speech: a lesson in unorthodoxy. *Proc. Institute of Electrical and Electronic Engineers*, **58**(5)707–712, May.

Sondhi, M.M. (1968). New methods of pitch extraction. *IEEE Trans Audio and Electroacoustics*, **AU-16**(2)262–266, June.

Tucker, W.H. and Bates, R.H.T. (1978). A pitch estimation algorithm for speech and music. *IEEE Trans Acoustics, Speech and Signal Processing*, **ASSP-26**(6)597–604, December.

4.10 Further Reading

There are a lot of books on digital signal analysis, although in general I find them rather turgid and difficult to read. The following are amongst the best.

Ackroyd, M.H. (1973). "Digital filters", Butterworths, London.
> Here is the exception to prove the rule. This book *is* easy to read. It provides a good introduction to digital signal processing, together with a wealth of practical design information on digital filters.

IEEE Digital Signal Processing Committee (1979). "Programs for digital signal processing", Wiley, New York.
> This is a remarkable collection of tried and tested Fortran programs for digital

signal analysis. They are all available from the IEEE in machine-readable form on magnetic tape. Included are programs for digital filter design, discrete Fourier transformation, and cepstral analysis, as well as others (like linear predictive analysis; see Chapter 6). Each program is accompanied by a concise, well-written description of how it works, with references to the relevant literature.

Oppenheim, A.V. and Schafer, R.W. (1975). "Digital signal processing", Prentice Hall, Englewood Cliffs, New Jersey.

This is one of the standard texts on most aspects of digital signal processing. It treats the z-transform, digital filters and discrete Fourier transformation in far more detail than we have been able to here.

Rabiner, L.R. and Gold, B. (1975). "Theory and application of digital signal processing", Prentice Hall, Englewood Cliffs, New Jersey.

This is the other standard text on digital signal processing. It covers the same ground as Oppenheim and Schafer (1975) above, but with a slightly faster (and consequently more difficult) presentation. It also contains major sections on special-purpose hardware for digital signal processing.

Rabiner, L.R. and Schafer, R.W. (1978). "Digital processing of speech signals", Prentice Hall, Englewood Cliffs, New Jersey.

Probably the best single reference for digital speech analysis, as it is for the time-domain encoding techniques of the last chapter. Unlike the books cited above, it is specifically oriented to speech processing.

5
RESONANCE SPEECH SYNTHESIZERS

This chapter considers the design of speech synthesizers which implement a direct electrical analogue of the resonance properties of the vocal tract by providing a filter for each formant whose resonant frequency is to be controlled. Another method is the channel vocoder, with a bank of fixed filters whose gains are varied to match the spectrum of the speech as described in Chapter 4. This is not generally used for synthesis from a written representation, however, because it is hard to get good quality speech. It *is* used sometimes for low-bandwidth transmission and storage, for it is fairly easy to analyse natural speech into fixed frequency bands. A second alternative to the resonance synthesizer is the linear predictive synthesizer, which at present is used quite extensively and is likely to become even more popular. This is covered in the next chapter. Another alternative is the articulatory synthesizer, which attempts to model the vocal tract directly, rather than modelling the acoustic output from it. Although, as noted in Chapter 2, articulatory synthesis holds a promise of high-quality speech— for the coarticulation effects caused by tongue and jaw inertia can be modelled directly—this has not yet been realized.

The source-filter model of speech production indicates that an electrical analogue of the vocal tract can be obtained by considering the source excitation and the filter that produces the formant frequencies separately. This approach was pioneered by Fant (1960), and we shall present much of his work in this chapter. There has been some discussion over whether the source-filter model really is a good one, and some synthesizers explicitly introduce an element of "sub-glottal coupling", which simulates the effect of the lung cavity on the vocal tract transfer function during the periods when the glottis is open (for an example see Rabiner, 1968). However, this is very much a low-order effect when considering speech synthesized by rule from a written representation, for the software which calculates parameter values to drive the synthesizer is a far greater source of degradation in speech quality.

5.1 Overall Spectral Considerations

Figure 5.1 shows the source-filter model of speech production. For voiced speech, the excitation source produces a waveform whose frequency components decay at about 12 dB/octave, as we shall see in a later section. The excitation passes into the vocal tract filter. Conceptually, this can best be viewed as an infinite series of formant filters, although for implementation purposes only the first few are modelled explicitly, and the effect of the rest is lumped together into a higher-formant compensation network. In either case the overall frequency profile of the filter is a flat one, upon which humps are superimposed at the various formant frequencies. Thus the output of the vocal tract filter falls off at 12 dB/octave just as the input does. However, measurements of actual speech show a 6 dB/octave decay with increasing frequency. This is explained by the effect of radiation of speech from the lips, which in fact has a "differentiating" action, producing a 6 dB/octave rise in the frequency spectrum. This 6 dB/octave lift is similar to that provided by a treble boost control on a radio or amplifier. Speech synthesized without it sounds unnaturally heavy and bassy.

These overall spectral shapes, which are derived from considering the human vocal tract, are summarized in the upper annotations in Fig. 5.1. But there is no real necessity for a synthesizer to model the frequency characteristics of the human vocal tract at intermediate points: only the output speech is of any concern. Because the system is a linear one, the filter blocks in the figure can be shuffled around to suit engineering requirements. One such requirement is the desire to minimize internally-generated noise in the electrical implementation, most of which will arise in the vocal tract filter (because it is much more complicated than the other components). For this reason an excitation source with a flat spectrum is often preferred, as shown in the lower annotations. This can be generated either by taking the desired glottal pulse shape, with its 12 dB/octave fall-off, and passing it through a filter giving 12 dB/octave lift at higher frequencies; or, if the pulse shape is to be stored digitally, by storing its second derivative instead. Then the radiation compensation, which is now more properly called "spectral equalization", will comprise a 6 dB/octave fall-off to give the required trend in the output spectrum.

For a given pitch period, this scheme yields exactly the same spectral

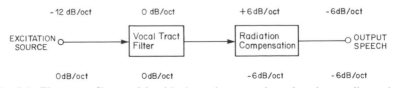

Fig. 5.1. The source-filter model, with alternative spectral trends at intermediate points.

characteristics as the original system which modelled the human vocal tract. However, when the pitch varies there will be a difference, for sounds with higher excitation frequencies will be attenuated by -6 dB/octave in the new system and $+6$ dB/octave in the old by the final spectral equalization. In practice, the pitch of the human voice lies quite low in the frequency region (usually below 400 Hz) and if all filter characteristics begin their roll-off at this frequency, the two systems will be the same. This simplifies the implementation with a slight compromise in its accuracy in modelling the spectral trend of human speech, for the overall -6 dB/octave decay actually begins at a frequency of around 100 Hz. If this is implemented, some adjustment will need to be made to the amplitudes to ensure that high-pitched sounds are not attenuated unduly.

The discussion so far pertains to voiced speech only. The source spectrum of the random excitation in unvoiced sounds is substantially flat, and combines with the radiation from the lips to give a $+6$ dB/octave rise in the output spectrum. Hence if spectral equalization is changed to -6 dB/octave to accomodate a voiced excitation with flat spectrum, the noise source should show a 12 dB/octave rise to give the correct overall effect.

5.2 The Excitation Sources

In human speech, the excitation source for voiced sounds is produced by two flaps of skin called the "vocal cords". These are blown apart by pressure from the lungs. When they come apart the pressure is relieved, and the muscles tensioning the skin cause the flaps to come together again. Subsequently, the lung pressure (called "sub-glottal pressure") builds up once more and the process is repeated. The factors which influence the rate and nature of vibration are muscular tension of the cords and the sub-glottal pressure. The detail of the excitation has considerable importance to speech synthesis because it greatly influences the apparent naturalness of the sound produced. For example, if you have inflamed vocal cords caused by laryngitis, the sound quality changes dramatically. Old people who do not have proper muscular control over their vocal cord tension produce a quavering sound. Shouted speech can easily be distinguished from quiet speech even when the volume cue is absent (you can verify this by fiddling with the volume control of a tape recorder) because when shouting, the vocal cords stay apart for a much smaller fraction of the pitch cycle than at normal volumes.

Voiced Excitation in Natural Speech

There are two basic ways to examine the shape of the excitation source in people. One is to use a dentist's mirror and high-speed photography to

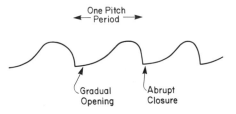

Fig. 5.2. Glottal excitation in natural speech.

observe the vocal cords directly. Although it seems a lot to ask someone to speak naturally with a mirror stuck down the back of his throat, the method has been used and photographs can be found, for example, in Flanagan (1972). The second technique is to process the acoustic waveform digitally, identifying the formant positions and deducting the formant contributions from the waveform by filtering. This leaves the basic excitation waveform, which can then be displayed. Such techniques lead to excitation shapes like those sketched in Fig. 5.2, in which the gradual opening and abrupt closure of the vocal cords can easily be seen.

It is a fact that if a periodic function has one or more discontinuities, its frequency spectrum will decay at sufficiently high frequencies at the rate of 6 dB/octave. For example, the components of the square wave

$$g(t) = 0 \quad \text{for} \quad 0 \leqslant t < h$$
$$1 \quad \text{for} \quad h \leqslant t < b$$

can be calculated from the Fourier series

$$G(r) = \frac{1}{b} \int_0^b g(t) \, e^{-j2\pi rt/b} \, dt = \frac{j}{2\pi r} (1 - e^{-j2\pi rh/b}),$$

so $|G(r)|$ is proportional to $1/r$, and the change in one octave is

$$20 \log_{10} \frac{|G(2r)|}{|G(r)|} = 20 \log_{10} \frac{1}{2} = -6 \text{ dB}.$$

However, if the discontinuities are ones of slope only, then the asymptotic decay at high frequencies is 12 dB/octave. Thus the glottal excitation of Fig. 5.2 will decay at this rate. Note that it is not the *number* but the *type* of discontinuities which are important in determining the asymptotic spectral trend.

Voiced Excitation in Synthetic Speech

There are several ways that glottal excitation can be simulated in a synthesizer, four of which are shown in Fig. 5.3. The square pulse and the

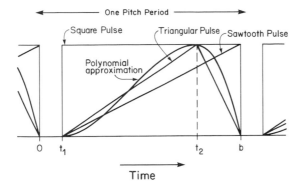

Fig. 5.3. Approximations to natural glottal excitation.

sawtooth pulse both exhibit discontinuities, and so will have the wrong asymptotic rate of decay (6 dB/octave instead of 12 dB/octave). A better bet is the triangular pulse. This has the correct decay, for there are only discontinuities of slope. However, although the asymptotic rate of decay is of first importance, the fine structure of the frequency spectrum at the lower end is also significant, and the fact that there are two discontinuities of slope instead of just one in the natural waveform means that the spectra cannot match closely.

Rosenberg (1971) has investigated several different shapes using listening tests, and he found that the polynomial approximation sketched in Fig. 5.3 was preferred by listeners. This has one slope discontinuity, and comprises three sections:

$$g(t) = 0 \quad \text{for} \quad 0 \leqslant t < t_1 \quad \text{(flat during the period of closure)}$$

$$g(t) = A \, u^2(3 - 2u),$$

where $\quad u = \dfrac{t - t_1}{t_2 - t_1}, \quad$ for $t_1 \leqslant t < t_2$ (opening phase)

$$g(t) = A(1 - v^2),$$

where $\quad v = \dfrac{t - t_2}{b - t_2}, \quad$ for $\quad t_2 \leqslant t < b$ (closing phase).

It is easy to see that the joins between the first and second section, and between the second and third section, are smooth; but that the slope of the third section at the end of the cycle when $t = b$ is

$$\frac{dg}{dt} = -2A.$$

A is the maximum amplitude of the pulse, and is reached when $t = t_2$.

A much simpler glottal pulse shape to implement is the filtered impulse. Passing an impulse through a continuous-time filter with characteristic

$$\frac{1}{(1 + sT)^2}$$

imparts a 12 dB/octave decay after frequency $1/T$. This gives a pulse shape of

$$g(t) = A\frac{t}{T}e^{1 - t/T},$$

which is sketched in Fig. 5.4. The pulse is the wrong way round in time when compared with the desired one, but this is not important under most listening conditions because phase differences are not noticeable (this point is discussed further below). The maximum is reached when $t = T$ and has height A. The value zero is never actually attained, for the decay to it is asymptotic, and if the slight discontinuity between pulses shown in the Figure is left, the asymptotic rate of decay of the frequency spectrum will be 6 dB/octave rather than 12 dB/octave. However, in a real implementation involving filtering an impulse there will be no such discontinuity, for the next pulse will start off where the last one ended.

This seems to be an attractive scheme because of its simplicity, and indeed is sometimes used in speech synthesis. However, it does not have the right properties when the pitch is varied, for in real glottal waveforms the maximum occurs at a fixed *fraction* of the period, whereas the filtered impulse's

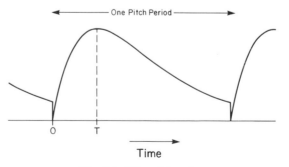

Fig. 5.4. Filtered impulse.

maximum is at a fixed time T. If T is chosen to make the system correct at high pitch frequencies (say 400 Hz), then the pulse will be much too narrow at low pitches and sound rather harsh. The only solution is to vary the filter parameters with the pitch, leading to complexity again.

Holmes (1973) has made an extensive study of the effect of the glottal waveshape on the naturalness of high-quality synthesized speech. He employed a rather special speech synthesizer, which provides far more comprehensive and sophisticated control than most. It was driven by parameters which were extracted from natural utterances by hand, but the process of generating and tuning them took many months of a skilled person's time. By using the pulse shape extracted from the natural utterance, he found that synthetic and natural versions could actually be made indistinguishable to most people, even under high-quality listening conditions using headphones. Performance dropped quite drastically when one of Rosenberg's pulse shapes, similar to the three-section one given above, was used. Holmes also investigated phase effects and found that while different pulse shapes with identical frequency spectra could easily be distinguished when listening over headphones, there was no perceptible difference if the listener was placed at a comfortable distance from a loudspeaker in a room. This is attributable to the fact that the room itself imposes a complex modification to the phase characteristics of the speech signal.

Although a great deal of care must be taken with the glottal pulse shape for very high-quality synthetic speech, for speech synthesized by rule from a written representation, the degradation which stems from incorrect control of the synthesizer parameters is much greater than that caused by using a slightly inferior glottal pulse. The triangular pulse illustrated in Fig. 5.3 has been found quite satisfactory for speech synthesis by rule.

Unvoiced Excitation

Speech quality is much less sensitive to the characteristics of the unvoiced excitation. Broadband white noise will serve admirably. It is quite acceptable to generate this digitally, using a pseudo-random feedback shift register. This gives a bit sequence whose autocorrelation is zero except at multiples of the repetition length. The repetition length can easily be made as long as the number of states in the shift register (less one); in this case, the configuration is called "maximal length" (Gaines, 1969). For example, an 18-bit maximal-length shift register will repeat every $2^{18} - 1$ cycles. If the bit-stream is used as a source of analogue noise, the autocorrelation function will have triangular parts whose width is twice the clock period, as shown in Fig. 5.5. According to a well-known result (the Weiner-Kinchine theorem; see for example Chirlian, 1973) the power density of the frequency spectrum

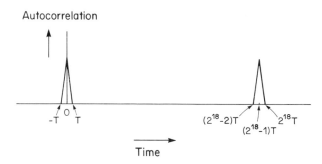

Fig. 5.5. Autocorrelation function of output from an 18-bit maximal-length feedback shift register, clocked every T seconds.

is the same as the Fourier transform of the autocorrelation function. Since the feedback shift register gives a periodic autocorrelation function, its transform is a Fourier series. The r'th frequency component is

$$G(r) = \frac{R^2}{4\pi^2 r^2 T}\left(1 - \cos\frac{2\pi r T}{R}\right).$$

Here, T is the clock period and $R = (2^N - 1)T$ is the repetition time of an N-bit shift register.

The spectrum is a bar spectrum, with components spaced at

$$\frac{1}{R} = \frac{1}{(2^N - 1)T}\text{ Hz.}$$

These are very close together, with $N = 18$ and sampling at 20 kHz (50 μsec) the spacing becomes under 0.1 Hz, and so it is reasonable to treat the spectrum as continuous, with

$$G(f) = \frac{1}{4\pi^2 f^2 T}(1 - \cos 2\pi f T).$$

This spectrum is sketched in Fig. 5.6(a), and the measured result of an actual implementation in Fig. 5.6(b). The 3 dB point occurs when

$$\frac{G(f)}{G(0)} = \frac{1}{2},$$

and $G(0)$ is $T/2$. Hence, at the 3 dB point,

$$\frac{1 - \cos 2\pi f T}{2\pi^2 f^2 T^2} = \frac{1}{2},$$

which has solution $f = 0.45/T$. Thus a pseudo-random shift register generates noise whose spectrum is substantially flat up to half the clock fre-

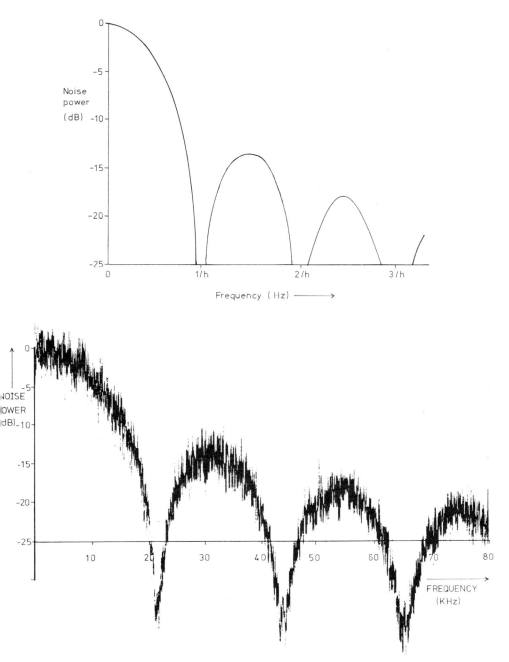

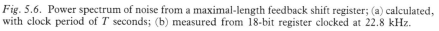

Fig. 5.6. Power spectrum of noise from a maximal-length feedback shift register; (a) calculated, with clock period of T seconds; (b) measured from 18-bit register clocked at 22.8 kHz.

quency. Anything over 10 kHz is therefore a suitable clocking rate for speech-quality noise. Choose 20 kHz to err on the conservative side. If the repetition occurs in less than 3 or 4 sec, it can be heard quite clearly; but above this figure it is not noticeable. An 18-bit shift register clocked at 20 kHz repeats every $(2^{18} - 1)/20000 = 13$ sec, which is more than adequate.

5.3 Simulating Vocal Tract Resonances

The vocal tract, from glottis to lips, can be modelled as an unconstricted tube of varying cross-section with no side branches and no sub-glottal coupling. This has an all-pole transfer function, which can be written in the form

$$H(s) = \frac{w_1^2}{s^2 + b_1 s + w_1^2} \cdot \frac{w_2^2}{s^2 + b_2 s + w_2^2} \cdots$$

There is an unspecified (conceptually infinite) number of terms in the product. Each of them produces a peak in the energy spectrum, and these are the formants we observed in Chapter 2.

Formants appear even in an over-simplified model of the tract as a tube of uniform cross-section, with a sound source at one end (the larynx) and open at the other (the lips). This extremely crude model was discussed in Chapter 2, and surprisingly perhaps, it gives a good approximation to the observed formant frequencies for a neutral, relaxed vowel such as that in "above".

Speech is made by varying the postures of the various organs of the vocal tract. Different vowels, for example, result largely from different tongue positions and lip postures. Naturally, such physical changes alter the frequencies of the resonances, and successful automatic speech synthesis depends upon successful movement of the formants. Fortunately, only the first three or four resonances need to be altered even for extremely realistic synthesis, and virtually all existing synthesizers provide control over these formants only.

Analysis of a Single Formant

Each formant is modelled as a second-order resonance, with transfer function

$$H(s) = \frac{w_c^2}{s^2 + bs + w_c^2}.$$

As will be shown below, w_c is the nominal resonant frequency in radians/s, and b is the approximate 3 dB bandwidth of the resonance. The term w_c^2 in the numerator adjusts the gain to be unity at DC ($s = 0$).

To calculate the frequency response of the formant, write $s = jw$. Then the energy spectrum is

$$|H(jw)|^2 = \frac{w_c^4}{(w^2 - w_c^2)^2 + b^2 w^2}$$

$$= \frac{w_c^4}{\left[w^2 - \left(w_c^2 - \frac{b^2}{2}\right)\right]^2 + b^2\left(w_c^2 - \frac{b^2}{4}\right)}.$$

This reaches a maximum when the squared term in the denominator of the second expression is zero, namely when $w = (w_c^2 - b^2/2)^{1/2}$. However formant bandwidths are low compared with their centre frequencies, and so to a good approximation, the peak occurs at $w = w_c$ and is of amplitude w_c/b; that is, $10 \log_{10} w_c/b$ dB above the DC gain. At frequencies higher than the peak, the energy falls off as $1/w^4$, a factor of $1/16$ for each doubling in frequency, and so the asymptotic decay is 12 dB/octave.

At the points which are 3 dB below the peak,

$$|H(jw_{3dB})|^2 = \frac{1}{2}|H(jw_{max})|^2 = \frac{1}{2} \times \frac{w_c^2}{b^2},$$

and it is easy to show that this is satisfied by $w_{3dB} = w_c \pm b/2$ to a good approximation (neglecting higher powers of b/w_c). Figure 5.7 summarizes the shape of an individual formant resonance.

The bandwidth of a formant is fairly constant, regardless of the formant frequency. This makes the formant filter a slightly unusual one: most engineering applications which use variable-frequency resonances require the bandwidth to be a constant proportion of the resonant frequency; the ratio w_c/b, often called the "Q" of the filter, is to be constant. For formants, we wish the Q to increase linearly with resonant frequency. Since the amplitude gain of the formant at resonance is w_c/b, this peak gain increases as the formant frequency is increased.

Although it is easy to measure formant frequencies on a spectrogram (cf. Chapter 2), it is not so easy to measure bandwidths accurately. One rather unusual method was reported by van den Berg (1955), who took a subject who had had a partial laryngectomy, an operation which left an opening into the vocal tract near the larynx position. Into this he inserted a sound source and made a swept-frequency calibration of the vocal tract! Almost as bizarre is a technique which involves setting off a spark inside the mouth of a subject as he holds his articulators in a given position.

The results of several different kinds of experiment are reported by Dunn

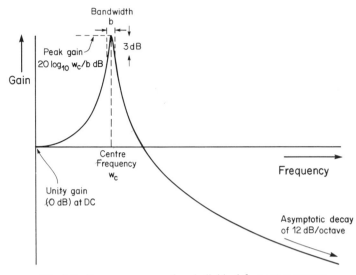

Fig. 5.7. Power spectrum of an individual formant resonance.

(1961), and are summarized in Table 5.1, along with the formant frequency ranges. Note that the bandwidths really are narrow compared with the resonant frequencies of the filters, except at the lower end of the formant 1 range. Choosing the lowest bandwidth estimate leads to an amplification factor at resonance of 50 for formant 2 when its frequency is at the top of its range; and formant 3 happens to give the same value.

Series Synthesizers

The simplest realization of the vocal tract filter is a chain of formant filters in series, as illustrated in Fig. 5.8. This leads to particular difficulties if the frequencies of two formants stray close together. The worst case occurs if

Table 5.1. Different estimates of formant bandwidths with range of formant frequencies for reference.

	Range of formant frequencies (Hz)	Range of bandwidths as measured in different experiments (Hz)
Formant 1	100–1100	45–130
Formant 2	500–2500	50–190
Formant 3	1500–3500	70–260

formants 2 and 3 have the same resonant frequencies, at the top of the range of formant 2, namely 2500 Hz. In this case, and if the bandwidths of the formants are set to the lowest estimates, a combined amplification factor of $(2500/50) \times (2500/70) = 1800$ is obtained at the point of resonance: that is, 65 dB above the DC value. This is enough to tax most analogue implementations, and can evoke clipping in the formant filters, with a very noticeable effect on speech quality. This extreme case will not occur during synthesis of realistic speech, for although the formant *ranges* overlap, the values for any particular (human) sound will not coincide exactly. However, it illustrates the difficulty of designing a series synthesizer which copes sensibly with arbitrary parameter settings, and explains why designers often choose formant bandwidths in the top half of the ranges given in Table 5.1.

The problem of excessive amplification within a series synthesizer can be alleviated to a small extent by choosing carefully the order in which the filters are placed in the chain. In a linear system, of course, the order in which the components occur does not matter. In physical implementations, however, it is advantageous to minimize extreme amplification at intermediate points. By placing the formant 1 filter between formants 2 and 3, the formant 2 resonance is attenuated somewhat before it reaches formant 3. Continuing with the extreme example above, where both formants 2 and 3 were set to 2500 Hz, assume that formant 1 is at its nominal value of 500 Hz. It provides attenuation at approximately 12 dB/octave above this, and so at the formant 2 peak, 2.3 octaves higher, the attenuation is 28 dB. Thus the gain at 2500 Hz, which is $20 \log_{10}2500/50 = 34$ dB after passing through the formant 2 filter, is reduced to 6 dB by formant 1, only to be increased by $20 \log_{10}2500/70 = 31$ dB to a value of 37 dB by formant 3. This avoids the extreme 65 dB gain of formants 2 and 3 combined.

Figure 5.8 shows only three formant filters modelled explicitly. The effect of the rest (and they do have an effect, although it is small at low frequencies) is incorporated by lumping them together into the "higher-formant correction" filter. To calculate the characteristics of this filter, assume that the lumped formants have the values given by the simple uniform-tube model of Chapter 2, namely 3500 Hz for formant 4, 4500 Hz for formant 5, and

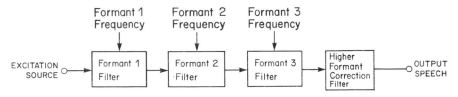

Fig. 5.8. Vocal-tract model in a series synthesizer.

in general, $500(2n - 1)$ Hz for formant n. The effect of each of these on the spectrum is

$$10 \log_{10} \frac{w_n^4}{(w^2 - w_n^2)^2 + b_n^2 w^2} = -10 \log_{10}\left[\left(1 - \frac{w^2}{w_n^2}\right)^2 + \frac{b_n^2 w^2}{w_n^4}\right] \text{dB},$$

following from what was calculated above. We will have to approximate this by assuming that b_n^2/w_n^2 is negligible (this is quite reasonable for these higher formants because Table 5.1 shows that the bandwidth does not increase in proportion to the formant frequency range) and approximate the logarithm by the first term of its series expansion:

$$-10 \log_{10}\left(1 - \frac{w^2}{w_n^2}\right)^2 = -20 \log_{10} e \, \log_e\left(1 - \frac{w^2}{w_n^2}\right) = 20 \log_{10} e \times \frac{w^2}{w_n^2}.$$

Now the total effect of formants 4, 5, ... at frequency f Hz (as distinct from w radians/s) is

$$20 \log_{10} e \times \sum_{n=4}^{\infty} \frac{f^2}{500^2 (2n - 1)^2}.$$

This expression is

$$20 \log_{10} e \times \frac{f^2}{500^2}\left(\sum_{n=1}^{\infty} \frac{1}{(2n - 1)^2} - \sum_{n=1}^{3} \frac{1}{(2n - 1)^2}\right).$$

The infinite sum can actually be calculated in closed form, and is equal to $\pi^2/8$. Hence the total correction is

$$20 \log_{10} e \times \frac{f^2}{500^2}\left(\frac{\pi^2}{8} - \sum_{n=1}^{3} \frac{1}{(2n - 1)^2}\right) = 2.87 \times 10^{-6} f^2 \text{ dB}.$$

Although this may at first seem to be a rather small correction, it is in fact 72 dB when $f = 5$ kHz! On further reflection this is not an unreasonable figure, for the 12 dB/octave decays contributed by formants 1, 2 and 3 must all be annihilated by the higher-formant correction to give an overall flat spectral trend. In fact, formant 1 will contribute 12 dB/octave from 500 Hz (3.3 octaves to 5 kHz, representing 40 dB); formant 2 will contribute 12 dB/octave from 1500 Hz (1.7 octaves to 5 kHz, representing 21 dB); and formant 3 will contribute 12 dB/octave from 2500 Hz (1 octave to 5 kHz, representing 12 dB). These sum to 73 dB.

If the first five formants are synthesized explicitly instead of just the first three, the correction is

$$20 \log_{10} e \times \frac{f^2}{500^2}\left(\frac{\pi^2}{8} - \sum_{n=1}^{5} \frac{1}{(2n - 1)^2}\right) = 1.73 \times 10^{-6} f^2 \text{ dB},$$

giving a rather more reasonable value of 43 dB when $f = 5$ kHz. In actual implementations, fixed filters are sometimes included explicitly for formants 4 and 5. Although this lowers the gain of the higher-formant correction filter, the total amplification at 5 kHz of the combined correction is still 72 dB. If one is less demanding and aims for a synthesizer that produces a correct spectrum only up to 3.5 kHz, it is 35 dB. This places quite stringent requirements on the preceding formant filters if the stray noise that they generate internally is not to be amplified to perceptible magnitudes by the correction filter at high frequencies.

Explicit inclusion of fixed filters for formants 4 and 5 undoubtedly improves the accuracy of the higher-formant correction. Recall that the above derivation of the correction filter characteristic used the first-order approximation

$$\log_e\left(1 - \frac{w^2}{w_n^2}\right) = -\frac{w^2}{w_n^2},$$

which is only valid if $w \ll w_n$. Thus it only holds at frequencies less than the highest explicitly synthesized formant, and so with formants 4 (3.5 kHz) and 5 (4.5 kHz) included a reasonable correction should be obtained for telephone-quality speech. However, detailed analysis with a second-order approximation shows that the coefficient of the neglected term is in fact small (Fant, 1960). A second, perhaps more compelling, reason for explicitly including a couple of fixed formants is that the otherwise enormous amplification provided by the correction can be distributed throughout the formant chain. We saw earlier why there is reason to prefer the order F3–F1–F2 over F1–F2–F3. With explicit formants 4 and 5, a suitable order which helps to keep the amplification at intermediate points in the chain within reasonable bounds is F3–F5–F2–F4–F1.

Parallel Synthesizers

A series synthesizer models the vocal tract resonances by a chain of formant filters in series. A parallel synthesizer utilizes a parallel connection of filters as illustrated in Fig. 5.9.

Consider a parallel combination of two formants with individually-controllable amplitudes. The combined transfer function is

$$H(s) = \frac{A_1 w_1^2}{s^2 + b_1 s + w_1^2} + \frac{A_2 w_2^2}{s^2 + b_2 s + w_2^2}$$

$$= \frac{(A_1 w_1^2 + A_2 w_2^2)s^2 + (A_1 b_2 w_1^2 + A_2 b_1 w_2^2)s + (A_1 + A_2)w_1^2 w_2^2}{(s^2 + b_1 s + w_1^2)(s^2 + b_2 s + w_2^2)}.$$

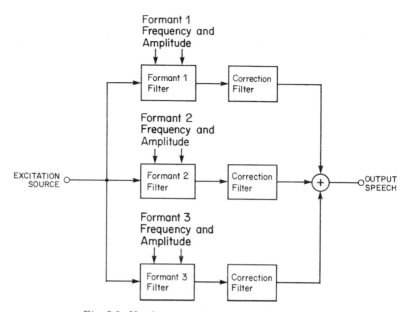

Fig. 5.9. Vocal-tract model in a parallel synthesizer.

If the formant bandwidths b_1 and b_2 are equal and the amplitudes are chosen as

$$A_1 = \frac{w_2^2}{w_2^2 - w_1^2} \qquad A_2 = -\frac{w_1^2}{w_2^2 - w_1^2},$$

then the transfer function becomes the same as that of a two-formant series synthesizer, namely

$$H(s) = \frac{w_1^2}{s^2 + b_1 s + w_1^2} \cdot \frac{w_2^2}{s^2 + b_2 s + w_2^2}.$$

The argument can be extended to any number of formants, under the assumption that the formant bandwidths are equal. Note that the signs of A_1 and A_2 differ: in general the formant amplitudes for a parallel synthesizer alternate in sign.

In theory, therefore, it would be possible to use five parallel formants to model a five-formant series synthesizer exactly. Then the same higher-formant correction filter would be needed for the parallel synthesizer as for the series one. If the formant amplitudes were set slightly incorrectly, however, the five filters would not combine to give a total of 60 dB/octave high-frequency decay above the resonances. It is easy to see this in the context of the simplified two-formant combination above: if the amplitudes were not chosen exactly right, then the s^2 term in the numerator would not be quite zero. Then, the decay in the two-formant combination would be -12 dB/octave instead of -24 dB/octave, and in the five-formant case the decay would in fact still be -12 dB/octave. Advantage can be taken of this to equalize the levels within the synthesizer so that large amplitude variations do not occur. This can best be done by associating relatively low-gain fixed correction filters with each formant instead of providing one comprehensive correction to the combined spectrum; these are shown in Fig. 5.9. Suitable correction filters have been determined empirically by Holmes (1972). They provide a 6 dB/octave lift above 640 Hz for formant 1, and 6 dB/octave lift above 300 Hz for formant 2. Formants 3 and 4 are uncorrected, while for formant 5, the correction begins as a 6 dB/octave decay above 600 Hz, and increases to an 18 dB/octave decay above 5.5 kHz.

The disadvantage of a parallel synthesizer is that the amplitudes of the formants must be specified as well as their frequencies. (Furthermore, the formant bandwidths should all be equal, but they are often chosen to be such in series synthesizers because of the uncertainty as to their exact values.) However, the extra amplitude parameters clearly give greater control over the frequency spectrum of the synthesized speech.

A good example of how this extra control can usefully be exploited is the synthesis of nasal sounds. Nasalization introduces a cavity parallel to the oral tract, as illustrated in Fig. 5.10, and this causes zeros in the transfer function. It is as if two different copies of the vocal tract transfer function, one for the oral and the other for the nasal passage, were added together. We have seen the effect of this above when considering parallel synthesis. The combination

$$H(s) = \frac{A_1 w_o^2}{s^2 + b_o s + w_o^2} + \frac{A_2 w_n^2}{s^2 + b_n s + w_n^2},$$

where the subscript "o" stands for oral and "n" for nasal, produces zeros in the numerator (unless the amplitudes are carefully adjusted to avoid them). These cannot be modelled by a series synthesizer, but they obviously can be by a parallel one.

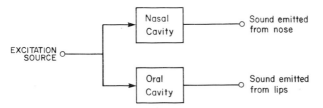

Fig. 5.10. Nasal and oral cavities in human speech production.

Although they are certainly needed for accurate imitation of human speech, transfer function zeros to simulate nasal sounds are not essential for synthesis of intelligible English. It is not difficult to get a sound like a nasal consonant (*n*, or *m*) with an all-pole synthesizer. Nevertheless, it is certainly true that a parallel synthesizer gives better *potential* control over the spectrum than a series one. Whether the added flexibility can be used properly by a synthesis-by-rule computer program is another matter.

Implementation of Formant Filters

Formant filters can be built in either analogue or digital form. A second-order resonance is needed, whose centre frequency can be controlled but whose bandwidth is fixed. If the control can be arranged as two tracking resistors, then the simple analogue configuration of Fig. 5.11, with two operational amplifiers, will suffice.

The transfer function of this arrangement is

$$-\frac{1/C_1R_1C_2R_2}{s^2 + \dfrac{1}{C_2R_2}s + \dfrac{1}{C_1R_1'C_2R_2}},$$

which characterizes it as a low-pass resonator with DC gain of $-R_1'/R_1$, bandwidth of $1/2\pi C_2R_2$ Hz, and centre frequency of $1/2\pi(C_1R_1'C_2R_2)^{1/2}$ Hz. Tracking R_1' with R_1 ensures that the DC gain remains constant, and that the centre frequency follows $R_1^{-1/2}$. Moreover, neither is especially sensitive to slight departures from exact tracking of R_1' with R_1. Such a filter has been used in a simple hand-controlled speech synthesizer, built for demonstration and amusement (Witten and Madams, 1978). However, the need for tracking resistors, and the inverse square root variation of the formant frequency with R_1, makes it rather unsuitable for serious applications.

A better analogue filter is the ring-of-three configuration shown in Fig.

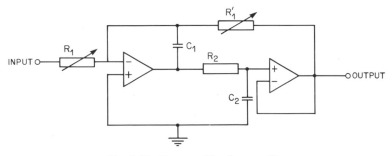

Fig. 5.11. Two-amplifier formant filter.

5.12 (ignore the secondary output for now). Control is achieved over the centre frequency by two multipliers, driven from the same control input k. These have a high-impedance output, producing a current kx if the input voltage is x. It is not too difficult to show that the transfer function of the circuit is

$$-\frac{\dfrac{k^2}{C^2}}{s^2 + \dfrac{2}{RC}s + \dfrac{1 + k^2R^2}{R^2C^2}}.$$

Suppose that R is chosen so that $k^2R^2 \gg 1$. Then this is a unity-gain resonator with constant bandwidth $1/\pi RC$ Hz and centre frequency $k/2\pi C$ Hz. Note that it is the combination of both multipliers that makes the centre frequency grow linearly with k: with one multiplier there would be a square-root relationship.

The ring-of-three filter of Fig. 5.12 is arranged in a slightly unusual way, with an inverting stage at the beginning and the two resonant stages following it. This ensures that the signal level at intermediate points in the filter does not exceed that at the output, and gives the filter the best chance of coping with a wide range of input amplitudes without clipping. This contrasts markedly with the resonator of Fig. 5.11, where the voltage at the output of the first integrator is w/b times the final output: a factor of 50 in the worst case.

For a digital implementation of a formant, consider the recurrence relation

$$y(n) = a_1 y(n-1) - a_2 y(n-2) + a_0 x(n),$$

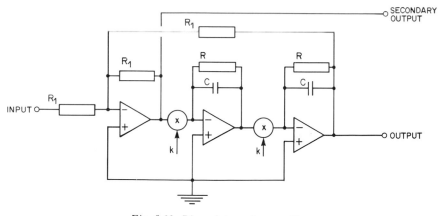

Fig. 5.12. Ring-of-three formant filter.

where $x(n)$ is the input and $y(n)$ the output at time n, $y(n - 1)$ and $y(n - 2)$ are the previous two values of the output, and a_0, a_1 and a_2 are (real) constants. The minus sign is in front of the second term because it makes a_2 turn out to be positive. To calculate the z-transform version of this relationship, multiply through by z^{-n} and sum from $n = -\infty$ to ∞:

$$\sum_{n=-\infty}^{\infty} y(n)z^{-n} = a_1 \sum_{n=-\infty}^{\infty} y(n-1)z^{-n} - a_2 \sum_{n=-\infty}^{\infty} y(n-2)z^{-n}$$

$$+ a_0 \sum_{n=-\infty}^{\infty} x(n)z^{-n}$$

$$= a_1 z^{-1} \sum y(n-1)z^{-(n-1)} - a_2 z^{-2} \sum y(n-2)z^{-(n-2)}$$

$$+ a_0 \sum x(n)x^{-n}.$$

Writing this in terms of z-transforms,

$$Y(z) = a_1 z^{-1}Y(z) - a_2 z^{-2}Y(z) + a_0 X(z).$$

Thus the input-output transfer function of the system is

$$H(z) = \frac{Y(z)}{X(z)} = \frac{a_0}{1 - a_1 z^{-1} + a_2 z^{-2}}.$$

We learned in the previous chapter that the frequency response is obtained from the z-transform of a system by replacing z^{-1} by $e^{-j2\pi fT}$, where f is the frequency variable in Hz. Hence the amplitude response of the digital formant filter is

$$|H(e^{j2\pi fT})|^2 = \left[\frac{a_0}{1 - a_1 e^{-j2\pi fT} + a_2 e^{-j4\pi fT}} \right]^2.$$

It is fairly obvious from this that a DC gain of 1 is obtained if

$$a_0 = 1 - a_1 + a_2,$$

for $e^{-j2\pi fT}$ is 1 at a frequency of 0 Hz. Some manipulation is required to show that, under the usual assumption that the bandwidth is small, the centre frequency is

$$\frac{1}{2\pi T} \cos^{-1} \frac{a_1}{2a_2^{1/2}} \text{ Hz.}$$

Furthermore, the 3 dB bandwidth of the resonance is given approximately by

$$-\frac{1}{2\pi T} \log_e a_2 \text{ Hz.}$$

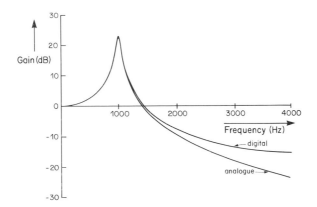

Fig. 5.13. Amplitude response of a digital and an analogue formant.

As an example, Fig. 5.13 shows an amplitude response for this digital filter. The parameters a_0, a_1 and a_2 were generated from the above relationships for a sampling frequency of 8 kHz, centre frequency of 1 kHz, and bandwidth of 75 Hz. It exhibits a peak of approximately the right bandwidth at the correct frequency, 1 kHz. Note that the response is flat at half the sampling frequency, for the frequency response from 4 kHz to 8 kHz is just a reflection of that up to 4 kHz. This contrasts sharply with that of an analogue formant filter also shown in Fig. 5.13, which slopes at − 12 dB/octave at frequencies above resonance.

The behaviour of a digital formant filter at frequencies above resonance actually makes it preferable to an analogue implementation. We saw earlier that considerable trouble must be taken with the latter to compensate for the cumulative effect of − 12 dB/octave at higher frequencies for each of the formants. This is not necessary with digital implementations, for the response of a digital formant filter is flat at half the sampling frequency. In fact, further study shows that digital synthesizers without any higher-pole correction give a closer approximation to the vocal tract than analogue ones with higher-pole correction (Gold and Rabiner, 1968).

Time-domain Methods

An interesting alternative to frequency-domain speech synthesis is to construct the formants in the time domain. When a second-order resonance is excited by an impulse, an exponentially decaying sinusoid is produced, as illustrated by Fig. 5.14. The oscillation occurs at the resonant frequency of the filter, while the decay is related to the bandwidth. In fact, if the formant filter has transfer function

$$\frac{w^2}{s^2 + bs + w^2},$$

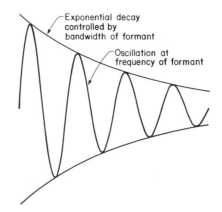

Fig. 5.14. Impulse response of a formant filter.

the time waveform for impulsive excitation is

$$x(t) = w \, e^{-bt/2} \sin wt \quad \text{(neglecting } b^2/w^2\text{)}.$$

It is the combination of several such time waveforms, coupled with the regular reappearance of excitation at the pitch period, that produces the characteristic wiggly waveform of voiced speech.

Now suppose we take a sine wave of frequency w and multiply it by a decaying exponential $e^{-bt/2}$. This gives a signal

$$x(t) = e^{-bt/2} \sin wt$$

which is identical with the filtered impulse except for a factor w. If there are several formants in parallel, all with the same bandwidth, the exponential factor is the same for each:

$$x(t) = e^{-bt/2}(A_1 \sin w_1 t + A_2 \sin w_2 t + A_3 \sin w_3 t).$$

A_1, A_2 and A_3 control the formant amplitudes, as in an ordinary parallel synthesizer, except that they need adjusting to account for the missing factors w_1, w_2 and w_3.

A neat way of implementing such a synthesizer digitally is to store one cycle of a sine wave in a read-only memory (ROM). Then, the formant frequencies can be controlled by reading the ROM at different rates. For example, if twice the basic frequency is desired, every second value should be read. Multiplication is needed for amplitude control of each formant: this can be accomplished by shifting the digital word (each place shifted accounts for 6 dB of attenuation). Finally, the exponential damping factor can be provided in analogue hardware by a single capacitor after the D/A converter. This implementation gives a system for hardware-software synthesis which involves an absolutely minimal amount of extra hardware apart from the computer, and does not need hardware multiplication for real-time operation. It could easily be made to work in real time with a microprocessor coupled to a D/A converter, damping capacitor, and fixed tone-control filter to give the required spectral equalization.

Because the overall spectral decay of an impulse exciting a second-order formant filter is 12 dB/octave, the appropriate equalization is +6 dB/octave lift at high frequencies, to give an overall −6 dB/octave spectral trend.

Note, however, that this synthesis model is an extremely basic one. Only impulsive excitation can be accommodated. For fricatives, which we will discuss in more detail below, a different implementation is needed. A hardware noise generator, with a few fixed filters (one for each fricative type) will suffice for a simple system. More damaging is the lack of aspiration, where random noise excites the vocal tract resonances. This cannot be simulated in the model. The *h* sound can be provided by treating it as a fricative, and although it will not sound completely realistic, because there will be no variation with the formant positions of adjacent phonemes, this can be tolerated because *h* is not too important for speech intelligibility. A bigger disadvantage is the lack of proper aspiration control for producing unvoiced stops, which as mentioned in Chapter 2 consist of a silent phase followed by a burst of aspiration. Experience has shown that although it is difficult to drive such a synthesizer from a software synthesis-by-rule system, quite intelligible output can be obtained if parameters are derived from real speech and tweaked by hand. Then, for each aspiration burst the most closely-matching fricative sound can be used.

5.4 Aspiration and Frication

The model of the vocal tract as a filter which affects the frequency spectrum of the basic voiced excitation breaks down if there are constrictions in it, for these introduce new sound sources caused by turbulent air. The generation of unvoiced excitation has been discussed earlier in this chapter: now we must consider how to simulate the filtering action of the vocal tract for unvoiced sounds.

Aspiration and frication need to be dealt with separately. The former is caused by excitation at the vocal cords: the cords are held so close together that turbulent noise is produced. This noise passes through the same vocal tract filter that modifies voiced sounds, and the same kind of formant structure can be observed. All that is needed to simulate it is to replace the voiced excitation source by white noise, as shown in the upper part of Fig. 5.15.

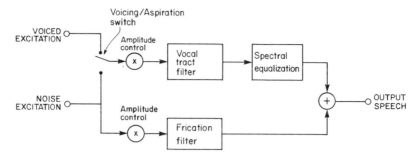

Fig. 5.15. Block diagram of a resonance synthesizer.

Speech can be whispered by substituting aspiration for voicing throughout. Of course, there is no fundamental frequency associated with aspiration. An interesting way of assessing informally the degradation caused by inadequate pitch control in a speech synthesis-by-rule system is to listen to whispered speech, in which pitch variations play no part.

Voiced and aspirative excitation are rarely produced at the same time in natural speech (but see the discussion in Chapter 2 about breathy voice). However, the excitation can change from one to the other quite quickly, and when this happens there is no discontinuity in the formant structure.

Fricative, or sibilant, excitation is quite different from aspiration, because it introduces a new sound source at a different place from the vocal cords. The constriction which produces the sound may be at the lips, the teeth, the hard ridge just behind the top front teeth, or further back along the palate. These positions each produce a different sound (*f*, *th*, *s* and *sh* respectively). However, smooth transitions from one of these sounds to another do not occur in natural speech, and dynamical movement of the frequency spectrum during a fricative is unnecessary for speech synthesis.

It is necessary, however, to be able to produce an approximation to the noise spectrum for each of these sound types. This is commonly achieved by a single high-pass resonance whose centre frequency can be controlled. This is the purpose of the secondary output of the formant filter of Fig. 5.12. Taking the output from this point gives a high-pass instead of a low-pass resonance, and this same filter configuration is quite acceptable for fricatives. Figure 5.15 shows the fricative sound path as a noise generator followed by such a filter.

Unlike aspiration, fricative excitation is frequently combined with voicing. This gives the voiced fricative sounds *v*, *dh*, *z* and *zh*. It is possible to produce frication and aspiration together, and although there are no examples of this in English, speech synthesis-by-rule programs often use a short burst of aspiration *and* frication when simulating the opening of unvoiced stops. Separate amplitude controls are therefore needed for voicing and frication, but the former can be used for aspiration as well, with a "glottal excitation type" switch to indicate aspiration rather than voicing.

5.5 Summary

A resonance speech synthesizer consists of a vocal tract filter, excited by either a periodic pitch pulse or aspiration noise. In addition, a set of sibilant sounds must be provided. The vocal tract filter is dynamic, with three controllable resonances. These, coupled with some fixed spectral compensation, give it a fairly high order: about 10 complex poles are needed. Although several different sibilant sound types must be simulated, dynamical movement is less important in fricative sound spectra than for voiced and aspirated sounds because smooth transitions between one fricative and another are not important in speech. However, fricative timing and amplitude must be controlled rather precisely.

The speech synthesizer is controlled by several parameters. These include fundamental frequency (if voiced), amplitude of voicing, frequency of the first few (typically three) formants, aspiration amplitude, sibilance amplitude, and frequency of one (or more) sibilance filters. Additionally, if the synthesizer is a parallel one, parameters for the amplitudes of individual formants will need to be included. It may be that some control over formant bandwidths is provided too. Thus synthesizers have from eight up to about 20 parameters (Klatt, 1980, describes one with 20 parameters).

The parameters are supplied to the synthesizer at regular intervals of time. For a 10-parameter synthesizer, the control can be thought of as a set of 10 graphs, each representing the time evolution of one parameter. They are usually called parameter *tracks*, the terminology dating from the days when a track was painted on a glass slide for each parameter to provide dynamic control of the synthesizer (Lawrence, 1953). The pitch track is often called a pitch *contour;* this is a common phonetician's usage. Do not confuse this with the everyday meaning of "contour" as a line joining points of equal height on a map: a pitch contour is just the time evolution of the pitch frequency.

For computer-controlled synthesizers, of course, the parameter tracks are sampled, typically every 5 to 20 msec. The rate is determined by the need to generate fast amplitude transitions for nasals and stop consonants. Contrast it with the 125 μsec sampling period needed to digitize telephone-quality speech. The raw data rate for a 10-parameter synthesizer updated every 10 msec is 1000 parameters/sec, or 6 Kbit/s if each parameter is represented by 6 bits. This is a substantial reduction over the 56 Kbit/s needed for PCM representation. For speech synthesis by rule (Chapter 7), these parameter tracks are generated by a computer program from a phonetic

Table 5.2. Implementation options for resonance speech synthesizers.

	Analogue	Digital
Series	Rice (1976)	Rabiner *et al.* (1971)
Parallel	Liljencrants (1968)	Holmes (1973)
Time-domain	unpublished	unpublished
High-order filter	—	Morris and Paillet (1972)

(or English) version of the utterance, lowering the data rate by a further one or two orders of magnitude.

Filters for speech synthesizers can be implemented in either analogue or digital form. High-order filters are usually broken down into second-order sections in parallel or in series. A third possibility, which has not been discussed above, is to implement a single high-order filter directly. Finally, the action of formant filters can be synthesized in the time domain. This gives eight possibilities which are summarized in Table 5.2. All but one have certainly been used as the basis for synthesis, and the table includes reference to published descriptions.

Each method has advantages and disadvantages. Series decomposition obviates the need for control over the amplitudes of individual formants, but does not allow synthesis of sounds which use the nasal tract as well as the oral one, for these are in parallel. Analogue implementation of series synthesizers is complicated by the need for higher-pole correction, and the fact that the gains at different frequencies can vary widely throughout the system. Higher-pole correction is not so important for digital synthesizers. Parallel decomposition eliminates some of these problems: higher-pole correction can be implemented individually for each formant. However, the formant amplitudes must be controlled rather precisely to simulate the vocal tract, which is essentially serial. Time-domain synthesis is associated with low hardware costs, but does not easily allow proper control over the excitation sources. In particular, it cannot simulate dynamical movement of the spectrum during aspiration. Implementation of the entire vocal tract model as a single high-order filter, without breaking it down into individual formants in series or parallel, is attractive from the computational point of view because less arithmetic operations are required. It is best analysed in terms of linear predictive coding, which is the subject of the next chapter.

5.6 References

van den Berg, J.W. (1955). Transmission of the vocal cavities. *J. Acoustical Society of America*, **27**(1)161–168, January.

Chirlian, P.M. (1973). "Signals, systems, and the computer", Intext Educational Publishers, New York.

Dunn, H.K. (1961). "Methods of measuring vowel formant bandwidths". *J. Acoustical Society of America*, **33**(12)1737–1746, December.

Fant, G. (1960). "Acoustic theory of speech production", Mouton, The Hague.

Flanagan, J.L. (1972). "Speech analysis, synthesis, and perception", (2nd, expanded, edition). Springer Verlag, Berlin.

Gaines, B.R. (1969). Stochastic computing systems. *In* "Advances in information systems science 2", (J. Tou, ed.), pp 37–172. Plenum.

Gold, B. and Rabiner, L.R. (1968). Analysis of digital and analogue formant synthesizers. *IEEE Trans Audio and Electroacoustics*, **AU-16**(1)81–94, March.

Holmes, J.N. (1972). "Speech synthesis", Mills and Boon, London.

Holmes, J.N. (1973). The influence of glottal waveform on the naturalness of speech from a parallel formant synthesizer. *IEEE Trans Audio and Electroacoustics*, **AU-21**(3)298–305, June.

Klatt, D.H. (1980). Software for a cascade/parallel formant synthesizer. *J. Acoustical Society of America*, **67**(3)971–995, March.

Lawrence, W. (1953). "The synthesis of speech from signals which have a low information rate" *In* "Communication theory", (W. Jackson, ed.). Pp 460–469. Butterworths, London.

Liljencrants, J.C.W.A. (1968). The OVE III speech synthesizer. *IEEE Trans Audio and Electroacoustics*, **AU-16**(1)137–140, March.

Morris, L.R. and Paillet, J.P. (1972). Real-time software speech synthesis. *IEEE Conference on Speech Communication and Processing*, 166–169.

Rabiner, L.R. (1968). Digital formant synthesizer for speech synthesis studies. *J. Acoustical Society of America*, **43**(4)822–828, April.

Rabiner, L.R., Jackson, L.B., Schafer, R.W. and Coker, C.H. (1971). A hardware realization of a digital formant synthesizer. *IEEE Trans Communication Technology*, **COM-19**(6)1016–1020, December.

Rice, D.L. (1976). Friends, humans and countryrobots: lend me your ears. *Byte*, **12**, 16–24.

Rosenberg, A.E. (1971). Effect of glottal pulse shape on the quality of natural vowels. *J. Acoustical Society of America*, **49**(2)583–590, February.

Witten, I.H. and Madams, P.H.C. (1978). The Chatterbox—a speech toy Parts 1 and II. *Wireless World*, **84**, 36–41, December, and **85**, 77–80, January 1979.

5.7 Further Reading

Historically-minded readers should look at the early speech synthesizer designed by Lawrence (1953). This and other classic papers on the subject are reprinted in Flanagan and Rabiner (1973). A good description of a quite sophisticated parallel synthesizer can be found in Holmes (1973), above, and another of a switchable series/parallel one in Klatt (1980), who even includes a listing of the Fortran program that implements it. Here are some useful books on speech synthesizers.

Fant, G. (1960). "Acoustic theory of speech production," Mouton, The Hague.
 Fant really started the study of the vocal tract as an acoustic system, and this book marks the beginning of modern speech synthesis.

Flanagan, J.L. (1972). "Speech analysis, synthesis, and perception", (2nd, expanded edition), Springer Verlag, Berlin.

This book is the speech researcher's bible, and like the bible, it's not all that easy to read. However, it is an essential reference source for speech acoustics and speech synthesis (as well as for human speech perception).

Flanagan, J.L. and Rabiner, L.R. (editors) (1973). "Speech synthesis", Dowden, Hutchinson and Ross, Stroudsburg, Pennsylvania.

I recommended this book at the end of Chapter 1 as a collection of classic papers on the subject of speech synthesis and synthesizers.

Holmes, J.N. (1972). "Speech synthesis", Mills and Boom, London.

This little book, by one of Britain's foremost workers in the field, introduces the subject of speech synthesis and speech synthesizers. It has a particularly good discussion of parallel synthesizers.

6

LINEAR PREDICTION OF SPEECH

The speech coding techniques which were discussed in Chapter 3 operate in the time domain, while the analysis and synthesis techniques of Chapters 4 and 5 are based in the frequency domain. Linear prediction is a relatively new method of speech analysis-synthesis, introduced in the early 1970s and used extensively since then, which is primarily a time-domain coding method but can be used to give frequency-domain parameters like formant frequency, bandwidth and amplitude.

It has several advantages over other speech analysis techniques, and is likely to become increasingly dominant in speech output systems. As well as bridging the gap between time- and frequency-domain techniques, it is of equal value for both speech storage and speech synthesis, and forms an extremely convenient basis for speech-output systems which use high-quality stored speech for routine messages and synthesis from phonetics or text for unusual or exceptional conditions. Linear prediction can be used to separate the excitation source properties of pitch and amplitude from the vocal tract filter which governs phoneme articulation, or in other words, to separate much of the prosodic from the segmental information. Hence it makes it easy to use stored segmentals with synthetic prosody, which is just what is needed to enhance the flexibility of stored speech by providing overall intonation contours for utterances formed by word concatenation (see Chapter 7).

The frequency-domain analysis technique of discrete Fourier transformation necessarily involves approximation because it applies only to periodic waveforms, and so the artificial operation of windowing is required to suppress the aperiodicity of real speech. In contrast, the linear predictive technique, being a time-domain method, can (in certain forms) deal more rationally with aperiodic signals.

The basic idea of linear predictive coding is exactly the same as one form of adaptive differential pulse code modulation which was introduced briefly in Chapter 3. There it was noted that a speech sample $x(n)$ can be predicted quite closely by the previous sample $x(n - 1)$. The prediction can be improved by multiplying the previous sample by a number, say a_1, which is adapted on a syllabic time-scale. This can be utilized for speech coding by transmitting only the prediction error

$$e(n) = x(n) - a_1x(n - 1),$$

and using it (and the value of a_1) to reconstitute the signal $x(n)$ at the receiver. It is worthwhile noting that exactly the same relationship was used for digital pre-emphasis in Chapter 4, with the value of a_1 being constant at about 0.9, although the possibility of adapting it to take into account the difference between voiced and unvoiced speech was discussed.

An obvious extension is to use several past values of the signal to form the prediction, instead of just one. Different multipliers for each would be needed, so that the prediction error could be written as

$$e(n) = x(n) - a_1x(n - 1) - a_2x(n - 2) - \cdots - a_px(n - p)$$

$$= x(n) - \sum_{k=1}^{p} a_kx(n - k).$$

The multipliers a_k should be adapted to minimize the error signal, and we will consider how to do this in the next section. It turns out that they must be re-calculated and transmitted on a time-scale that is rather faster than syllabic but much slower than the basic sampling rate: intervals of 10–25 msec are usually used (compare this with the 125 μsec sampling rate for telephone-quality speech). A configuration for high-order adaptive differential pulse code modulation is shown in Fig. 6.1.

Figure 6.2 shows typical time waveforms for each of the ten coefficients over a 1-second stretch of speech. Notice that they vary much more slowly than, say, the speech waveform of Fig. 3.5.

Turning the above relationship into z-transforms gives

$$E(z) = X(z) - \sum_{k=1}^{p} a_kz^{-k} X(z) = \left(1 - \sum_{k=1}^{p} a_kz^{-k}\right)X(z).$$

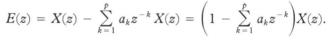

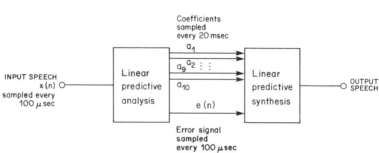

Fig. 6.1. Linear prediction used in high-order adaptive differential pulse code modulation.

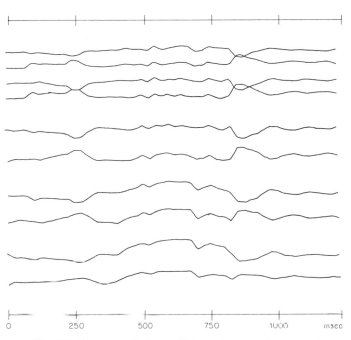

Fig. 6.2. Linear predictive coefficients for a sample of speech.

Rewriting the speech signal in terms of the error,

$$X(z) = \frac{1}{1 - \sum_{k=1}^{p} a_k z^{-k}} E(z).$$

Now let us bring together some facts from the previous chapter which will allow the time-domain technique of linear prediction to be interpreted in terms of the frequency-domain formant model of speech. Recall that speech can be viewed as an excitation source passing through a vocal tract filter, followed by another filter to model the effect of radiation from the lips. The overall spectral levels can be reassigned as in Fig. 5.1 so that the excitation source has a 0 dB/octave spectral profile, and hence is essentially impulsive. Considering the vocal tract filter as a series connection of digital formant filters, its transfer function is the product of terms like

$$\frac{1}{1 - b_1 z^{-1} + b_2 z^{-2}},$$

where b_1 and b_2 control the position and bandwidth of the formant resonances. The -6 dB/octave spectral compensation can be modelled by the first-order digital filter

$$\frac{1}{1 - bz^{-1}}.$$

The product of all these terms, when multiplied out, will have the form

$$\frac{1}{1 - c_1 z^{-1} - c_2 z^{-2} - \cdots - c_q z^{-q}},$$

where q is twice the number of formants plus one, and the c's are calculated from the positions and bandwidths of the formant resonances and the spectral compensation parameter. Hence the z-transform of the speech is

$$X(z) = \frac{1}{1 - \sum_{k=1}^{q} c_k z^{-k}} I(z),$$

where $I(z)$ is the transform of the impulsive excitation.

This is remarkably similar to the linear prediction relation given earlier! If p and q are the same, then the linear predictive coefficients a_k form a p'th order polynomial which is the same as that obtained by multiplying together the second-order polynomials representing the individual formants (together with the first-order one for spectral compensation). Furthermore, the predictive error $E(z)$ can be identified with the impulsive excitation $I(z)$. This raises the very interesting possibility of parametrizing the error signal by its frequency and amplitude (two relatively slowly-varying quantities) instead of transmitting it sample-by-sample (at an 8 kHz rate). This is how linear prediction separates out the excitation properties of the source from the vocal tract filter: the source parameters can be derived from the error signal and the vocal tract filter is represented by the linear predictive coefficients. Figure 6.3 shows how this can be used for speech transmission. Note that *no* signals need now be transmitted at the speech sampling rate, for the source parameters vary relatively slowly. This leads to an extremely low data rate.

Practical linear predictive coding schemes operate with a value of p between 10 and 15, corresponding approximately to 4-formant and 7-formant synthesis respectively. The a_k's are re-calculated every 10 to 25 msec, and transmitted to the receiver. Also, the pitch and amplitude of the speech are estimated and transmitted at the same rate. If the speech is unvoiced, there is no pitch value: an "unvoiced flag" is transmitted instead. Because the linear predictive coefficients are intimately related to formant frequencies and bandwidths, a "frame rate" in the region of 10 to 25 msec is appropriate because this approximates the maximum rate at which acoustic events happen in speech production.

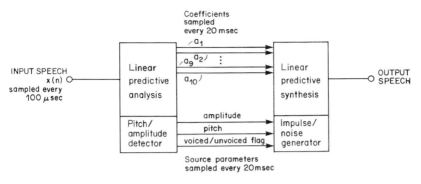

Fig. 6.3. Linear prediction used for very low bit-rate speech encoding by identifying the parameters of the excitation source.

At the receiver, the excitation waveform is reconstituted. For voiced speech, it is impulsive at the specified frequency and with the specified amplitude, while for unvoiced speech it is random, with the specified amplitude. This signal $e(n)$, together with the transmitted parameters $a_1, \ldots,$ a_p, is used to regenerate the speech waveform by

$$x(n) = e(n) + \sum_{k=1}^{p} a_k x(n - k),$$

which is the inverse of the transmitter's formula for calculating $e(n)$, namely

$$e(n) = x(n) - \sum_{k=1}^{p} a_k x(n - k).$$

This relies on knowing the past p values of the speech samples. Many systems set these past values to zero at the beginning of each pitch cycle.

Linear prediction can also be used for speech analysis, rather than for speech coding, as shown in Fig. 6.4. Instead of transmitting the coefficients

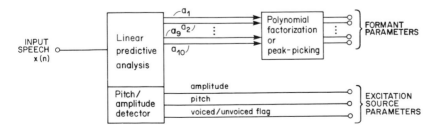

Fig. 6.4. Linear prediction used for formant analysis.

a_k, they are used to determine the formant positions and bandwidths. We saw above that the polynomial

$$1 - a_1 z^{-1} - a_2 z^{-2} - \cdots - a_p z^{-p},$$

when factored into a product of second-order terms, gives the formant characteristics (as well as the spectral compensation term). Factoring is equivalent to finding the complex roots of the polynomial, and this is fairly demanding computationally, especially if done at a high rate. Consequently, peak-picking algorithms are sometimes used instead. The absolute value of the polynomial gives the frequency spectrum of the vocal tract filter, and the formants appear as peaks: just as they do in cepstrally smoothed speech (see Chapter 4).

The chief deficiency in the linear predictive method, whether it is used for speech coding or for speech analysis, is that (like a series synthesizer) it implements an all-pole model of the vocal tract. We mentioned in Chapter 5 that this is rather simplistic, especially for nasalized sounds which involve a cavity in parallel with the oral one. Some research has been done on incorporating zeros into a linear predictive model, but it complicates the problem of calculating the parameters enormously. For most purposes, people seem to be able to live with the limitations of the all-pole model.

6.1 Linear Predictive Analysis

The key problem in linear predictive coding is to determine the values of the coefficients $a_1, \ldots, a_p$. If the error signal is to be transmitted on a sample-by-sample basis, as it is in adaptive differential pulse code modulation, then it can be most economically encoded if its mean power is as small as possible. Thus the coefficients are chosen to minimize

$$\sum_n e(n)^2$$

over some period of time. The period of time used is related to the frame rate at which the coefficients are transmitted or stored, although there is no need to make it exactly the same as one frame interval. As mentioned above, the frame size is usually chosen to be in the region of 10 to 25 msec. Some schemes minimize the error signal over as few as 30 samples (corresponding to 3 msec at a 10 kHz sampling rate). Others take longer: up to 250 samples (25 msec).

However, if the error signal is to be considered as impulsive and parametrized by its frequency and amplitude before transmission, or if the coefficients a_k are to be used for spectral calculations, then it is not immediately obvious how the coefficients should be calculated. In fact, it is still best to choose them to minimize the above sum. This is at least plausible, for an impulsive excitation will have a rather small mean power: most of the samples are zero. It can be justified theoretically in terms of *spectral whitening*, for it can be shown that minimizing the mean-square error produces an error signal whose spectrum is maximally flat. Now the only two waveforms whose spectra are absolutely flat are a single impulse and white noise. Hence if the speech is voiced, minimizing the mean-squared error will lead to an error signal which is as nearly impulsive as possible. Provided the time-frame for minimizing is short enough, the impulse will correspond to a single excitation pulse. If the speech is unvoiced, minimization will lead to an error signal which is as nearly white noise as possible.

How does one choose the linear predictive coefficients to minimize the mean-squared error? The total squared prediction error is

$$M = \sum_n e(n)^2 = \sum_n \left[x(n) - \sum_{k=1}^{p} a_k x_{n-k} \right]^2,$$

leaving the range of summation unspecified for the moment. To minimize M by choice of the coefficients a_j, differentiate with respect to each of them and set the resulting derivatives to zero.

$$\frac{dM}{da_j} = -2 \sum_n x(n-j) \left[x(n) - \sum_{k=1}^{p} a_k x(n-k) \right] = 0,$$

so

$$\sum_{k=1}^{p} a_k \sum_n x(n-j)x(n-k) = \sum_n x(n)x(n-j) \qquad j = 1, 2, ..., p.$$

This is a set of p linear equations for the p unknowns $a_1, ..., a_p$. Solving it is equivalent to inverting a $p \times p$ matrix. This job must be repeated at the frame rate, and so if real-time operation is desired quite a lot of calculation is needed.

The Autocorrelation Method

So far, the range of the n-summation has been left open. The coefficients of the matrix equation have the form

$$\sum_n x(n-j)x(n-k).$$

If a doubly-infinite summation were made, with $x(n)$ being defined as zero whenever $n < 0$, we could make use of the fact that

$$\sum_{n=-\infty}^{\infty} x(n-j)x(n-k) = \sum_{n=-\infty}^{\infty} x(n-j+1)x(n-k+1)$$

$$= \cdots = \sum_{n=-\infty}^{\infty} x(n)x(n+j-k)$$

to simplify the matrix equation. This just states that the autocorrelation of an infinite sequence depends only on the lag at which it is computed, and not on absolute time.

Defining $R(m)$ as the autocorrelation at lag m, that is,

$$R(m) = \sum_{n} x(n)x(n+m),$$

the matrix equation becomes

$$R(0)a_1 + R(1)a_2 + R(2)a_3 + \cdots = R(1)$$
$$R(1)a_1 + R(0)a_2 + R(1)a_3 + \cdots = R(2)$$
$$R(2)a_1 + R(1)a_2 + R(0)a_3 + \cdots = R(3)$$
etc.

An elegant method due to Durbin and Levinson exists for solving this special system of equations. It requires much less computational effort than is generally needed for symmetric matrix equations.

Of course, an infinite range of summation cannot be used in practice. For one thing, the power spectrum is changing, and only the data from a short time-frame should be used for a realistic estimate of the optimum linear predictive coefficients. Hence a windowing procedure,

$$x(n)^* = w_n x(n),$$

is used to reduce the signal to zero outside a finite range of interest. Windows were discussed in Chapter 4 from the point of view of Fourier analysis of speech signals, and the same sort of considerations apply to choosing a window for linear prediction.

This is known as the *autocorrelation method* of computing prediction parameters. Typically a window of 100 to 250 samples is used for analysis of one frame of speech.

Algorithm for the Autocorrelation Method

The algorithm for obtaining linear prediction coefficients by the autocorrelation method is quite simple. It is straightforward to compute the matrix

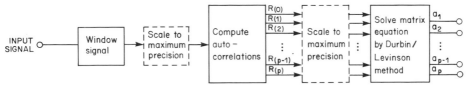

Fig. 6.5. Algorithm for the autocorrelation method.

coefficients $R(m)$ from the speech samples and window coefficients. The Durbin-Levinson method of solving matrix equations operates directly on this R-vector to produce the coefficient vector a_k. The complete procedure is given as Procedure 6.1, and is shown diagrammatically in Fig. 6.5.

This algorithm is not quite as efficient as it might be, for some multiplications are repeated during the calculation of the autocorrelation vector. Blankinship (1974) shows how the number of multiplications can be reduced by about half.

If the algorithm is performed in fixed-point arithmetic (as it often is in practice because of speed considerations), some scaling must be done. The maximum and minimum values of the windowed signal can be determined within the window calculation loop, and one extra pass over the vector will suffice to scale it to maximum significance. (Incidentally, if all sample values are the same, the procedure cannot produce a solution because E becomes zero, and this can easily be checked when scaling.)

The absolute value of the R-vector has no significance, and since $R(0)$ is always the greatest element, this can be set to the largest fixed-point number and the other R's scaled down appropriately after they have been calculated. These scaling operations are shown as dashed boxes in Fig. 6.5. E decreases monotonically as the computation proceeds, so it is safe to initialize it to $R(0)$ without extra scaling. The remainder of the scaling is straightforward, with the linear prediction coefficients a_k appearing as fractions.

The Covariance Method

One of the advantages of linear predictive methods that was promised earlier was that it allows us to escape from the problem of windowing. To do this, we must abandon the requirement that the coefficients of the matrix equation have the symmetry property of autocorrelations. Instead, suppose that the range of n-summation uses a fixed number of elements, say N, starting at $n = h$, to estimate the prediction coefficients between sample number h and sample number $h + N$.

```
const N = 256; p = 15; type svec = array [0..N − 1] of real; cvec = array [1..p]
of real;

procedure autocorrelation (signal: vec; window: svec; var coeff: cvec);

{computes linear prediction coefficients by autocorrelation method in
coeff [1..p]}

var R, temp: array [0..p] of real; n: [0..N − 1]; i, j: [0..p]; E: real;

begin {window the signal}
    for n:=0 to N−1 do signal[n] := signal[n]*window[n];

    {compute autocorrelation vector}
    for i:=0 to p do begin
      R[i] := 0;
      for n:=0 to N−1−i do R[i] := R[i] + signal[n]*signal[n+i]
    end;

    {solve the matrix equation by the Durbin-Levinson method}
    E := R[0];
    coeff[1] := R[1]/E;
    for i:=2 to p do begin
      E := (1 − coeff[i − 1]*coeff[i − 1])*E;
      coeff[i] := R[i];
      for j:=1 to i−1 do coeff[i] := coeff[i] − R[i−j]*coeff[j];
      coeff[i] := coeff[i]/E;
      for j:=1 to i−1 do temp[j] := coeff[j] − coeff[i]*coeff[i−j];
      for j:=1 to i−1 do coeff[j] := temp[j]
    end
end.
```

Procedure 6.1. Pascal algorithm for the autocorrelation method.

This leads to the matrix equation

$$\sum_{k=1}^{p} a_k \sum_{n=h}^{h+N-1} x(n-j)x(n-k) = \sum_{n=h}^{h+N-1} x(n)x(n-j) \qquad j = 1, 2, ..., p.$$

Alternatively, we could write

$$\sum_{k=1}^{p} a_k Q_{jk}^h = Q_{0j}^h \qquad j = 1, 2, ..., p;$$

where

$$Q_{jk}^h = \sum_{n=h}^{h+N-1} x(n-j)x(n-k).$$

Note that some values of $x(n)$ outside the range $h \leq n < h + N$ are required:
these are shown diagrammatically in Fig. 6.6.

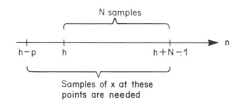

Fig. 6.6. Points at which input samples are needed for the covariance method.

Now $Q_{jk}^h = Q_{kj}^h$, so the equation has a diagonally symmetric matrix; and in fact the matrix Q^h can be shown to be positive semidefinite, and is almost always positive definite in practice. Advantage can be taken of these facts to provide a computationally efficient method for solving the equation. According to a result called Cholesky's theorem, a positive definite symmetric matrix Q can be factored into the form $Q = LL^T$, where L is a lower triangular matrix. This leads to an efficient solution algorithm.

This method of computing prediction coefficients has become known as the *covariance method*. It does not use windowing of the speech signal, and can give accurate estimates of the prediction coefficients with a smaller analysis frame than the autocorrelation method. Typically, 50 to 100 speech samples might be used to estimate the coefficients, and they are re-calculated every 100 to 250 samples.

Algorithm for the Covariance Method

An algorithm for the covariance method is given in Procedure 6.2, and is shown diagrammatically in Fig. 6.7. The algorithm shown is not terribly efficient from a computation and storage point of view, although it is workable. For one thing, it uses the obvious method for computing the covariance matrix by calculating Q_{01}^h, Q_{02}^h, ..., Q_{0p}^h, Q_{11}^h, ..., in turn, which repeats most of the multiplications p times: not an efficient procedure. A simple alternative is to precompute the necessary multiplications and store them in a $(N + h) \times (p + 1)$ diagonally symmetric table, but even apart from the extra storage required for this, the number of additions which must be

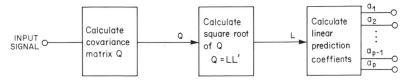

Fig. 6.7. Algorithm for the covariance method.

performed subsequently to give the Q's is far larger than necessary. It is possible, however, to write a procedure which is both time- and space-efficient (Witten, 1980).

```
const N = 100; p = 15; type svec = array [-p..N-1] of real; cvec = array
[1..p] of real;

procedure covariance (signal: svec; var coeff: cvec);

{computes linear prediction coefficients by covariance method in coeff[1..p]}

var Q: array [0..p,0..p] of real; n: [0..N-1]; i,j,r: [0..p]; X: real;

begin {calculate upper-triangular covariance matrix in Q}
    for i:=0 to p do
      for j:=i to p do begin
        Q[i,j]:=0;
        for n:=0 to N-1 do
          Q[i,j] := Q[i,j] + signal[n-i]*signal[n-j]
      end;

    {calculate the square root of Q}
    for r:=2 to p do
      begin
        for i:=2 to r-1 do
          for j:=1 to i-1 do
            Q[i,r] := Q[i,r] - Q[j,i]*Q[j,r];
          for j:=1 to r-1 do
            begin
              X := Q[j,r];
              Q[j,r] := Q[j,r]/Q[j,i];
              Q[r,r] := Q[r,r] - Q[j,r]*X
            end
      end;

    {calculate coeff[1..p]}
    for r:=2 to p do
      for i:=1 to r-1 do Q[0,r] := Q[0,r] - Q[i,r]*Q[0,i];
    for r:=1 to p do Q[0,r] := Q[0,r]/Q[r,r];
    for r:=p-1 downto 1 do
      for i:=r+1 to p do Q[0,r] := Q[0,r] - Q[r,i]*Q[0,i];
    for r:=1 to p do coeff[r] := Q[0,r]
end.
```

Procedure 6.2. Pascal algorithm for the covariance method.

The scaling problem is rather more tricky for the covariance method than for the autocorrelation method. The x-vector should be scaled initially in the same way as before, but now there are $p + 1$ diagonal elements of the covariance matrix, any of which could be the greatest element. Of course,

$$Q_{jk} \leq Max \, (Q_{11}, \, Q_{22}, \, ..., \, Q_{pp}),$$

but despite the considerable communality in the summands of the diagonal elements, there are no *a priori* bounds on the ratios between them.

The only way to scale the Q matrix properly is to calculate each of its p diagonal elements and use the greatest as a scaling factor. Alternatively, the fact that

$$Q_{jk} \leq N \times Max(x_n^2)$$

can be used to give a bound for scaling purposes; however, this is usually a rather conservative bound, and as N is often around 100, several bits of significance will be lost.

Scaling difficulties do not cease when Q has been determined. It is possible to show that the elements of the lower-triangular matrix L which represents the square root of Q are actually *unbounded*. In fact there is a slightly different variant of the Cholesky decomposition algorithm which guarantees bounded coefficients but suffers from the disadvantage that it requires square roots to be taken (Martin *et al.*, 1965). However, experience with the method indicates that it is rare for the elements of L to exceed 16 times the maximum element of Q, and the possibility of occasional failure to adjust the coefficients may be tolerable in a practical linear prediction system.

Comparison of Autocorrelation and Covariance Analysis

There are various factors which should be taken into account when deciding whether to use the autocorrelation or covariance method for linear predictive analysis. Furthermore, there is a rather different technique, called the "lattice method", which will be discussed shortly. The autocorrelation method involves windowing, which means that in practice, a rather longer stretch of speech should be used for analysis. We have illustrated this by setting $N = 256$ in the autocorrelation algorithm and 100 in the covariance one. Offsetting the extra calculation that this entails is the fact that the Durbin-Levinson method of inverting a matrix is much more efficient than Cholesky decomposition. In practice, this means that similar amounts of computation are needed for each method: a detailed comparison is made in Witten (1980).

A factor which weighs against the covariance method is the difficulty of scaling intermediate quantities within the algorithm. The autocorrelation method can be implemented quite satisfactorily in fixed-point arithmetic, and this makes it more suitable for hardware implementation. Furthermore, serious instabilities sometimes arise with the covariance method, whereas it can be shown that the autocorrelation one is always stable. Nevertheless, the approximations inherent in the windowing operation, and the smearing effect of taking a larger number of sample points, mean that covariance-method coefficients tend to represent the speech more accurately, if they can be obtained.

One way of using the covariance method which has proved to be rather satisfactory in practice is to synchronize the analysis frame with the beginning of a pitch period, when the excitation is strongest. Pitch synchronous techniques were discussed in Chapter 4 in the context of discrete Fourier transformation of speech. The snag, of course, is that pitch peaks do not occur uniformly in time, and furthermore it is difficult to estimate their locations precisely.

6.2 Linear Predictive Synthesis

If the linear predictive coefficients and the error signal are available, it is easy to regenerate the original speech by

$$x(n) = e(n) + \sum_{k=1}^{p} a_k x(n - k).$$

If the error signal is parametrized into the sound source type (voiced or unvoiced), amplitude, and pitch (if voiced), it can be regenerated by an impulse repeated at the appropriate pitch frequency (if voiced), or white noise (if unvoiced).

However, it may be that the filter represented by the coefficients a_k is unstable, causing the output speech signal to oscillate wildly. In fact, it is only possible for the covariance method to produce an unstable filter, and not the autocorrelation method; although even with the latter, truncation of the a_k's for transmission may turn a stable filter into an unstable one. Furthermore, the coefficients a_k are not suitable candidates for quantization, because small changes in them can have a dramatic effect on the characteristics of the synthesis filter.

Both of these problems can be solved by using a different set of numbers, called *reflection coefficients*, for quantization and transmission. Thus, for example, in Figs 6.1 and 6.3 these reflection coefficients could be derived at the transmitter, quantized, and used by the receiver to reproduce the speech waveform. They can be related to reflection and transmission parameters at the junctions of an acoustic tube model of the vocal tract; hence the name. Procedure 6.3 shows an algorithm for calculating the reflection coefficients from the filter coefficients a_k.

Although we will not go into the theoretical details here, reflection coefficients are bounded by ± 1 for stable filters, and hence form a useful test for stability. Having a limited range makes them easy to quantize for transmission, and in fact they behave better under quantization than do the filter coefficients. One could resynthesize speech from reflection coefficients by first converting them to filter coefficients and using the synthesis method

const p = 15; **type** cvec = **array** [1..p] **of** real;

procedure reflection(coeff: cvec; **var** refl: cvec);

{computes reflection coefficients in refl[1..p] corresponding to linear prediction coefficients in coeff[1..p]}

var temp: cvec; i, m: 1..p;

begin
```
        for m:=p downto 1 do begin
          refl[m] :=  coeff[m];
          for i:= 1 to m − 1 do temp[i] :=  coeff[i];
          for i:= 1 to m − 1 do
            coeff[i] :=
              (coeff[i] +  refl[m]*temp[m − i]) / (1 −  refl[m]*refl[m]);
        end
end.
```

Procedure 6.3. Pascal algorithm for producing reflection coefficients from filter coefficients.

described above. However, it is natural to seek a single-stage procedure which can regenerate speech directly from reflection coefficients.

Such a procedure does exist, and is called a *lattice filter*. Figure 6.8 shows one form of lattice for speech synthesis. The error signal (whether transmitted or synthesized) enters at the upper left-hand corner, passes along the top forward signal path, being modified on the way, to give the output signal at the right-hand side. Then it passes back through a chain of delays along the bottom, backward, path, and is used to modify subsequent forward signals. Finally it is discarded at the lower left-hand corner.

There are p stages in the lattice structure of Fig. 6.8, where p is the order of the linear predictive filter. Each stage involves two multiplications by the appropriate reflection coefficients, one by the backward signal (the result of which is added into the forward path) and the other by the forward signal (the result of which is subtracted from the backward path). Thus the number of multiplications is twice the order of the filter, and hence twice as many as for the realization using coefficients a_k. If the labour necessary to turn the reflection coefficients into a_k's is included, the computational load be-

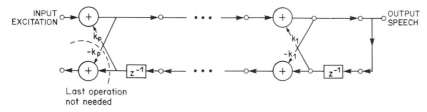

Fig. 6.8. A lattice filter for synthesis from reflection coefficients.

comes the same. Moreover, since the reflection coefficients need fewer quantization bits than the a_k's (for a given speech quality), the word lengths are smaller in the lattice realization.

The advantages of the lattice method of synthesis over direct evaluation of the prediction using filter coefficients a_k, then, are:

—the reflection coefficients are used directly
—the stability of the filter is obvious from the reflection coefficient values
—the system is more tolerant to quantization errors in fixed-point implementations.

Although it may seem unlikely that an unstable filter would be produced by linear predictive analysis, instability is in fact a real problem in non-lattice implementations. For example, coefficients are often interpolated at the receiver, to allow longer frame times and smooth over sudden transitions, and it is quite likely that an unstable configuration is obtained when interpolating filter coefficients between two stable configurations. This cannot happen with reflection coefficients, however, because a necessary and sufficient condition for stability is that all coefficients lie in the interval $(-1, +1)$.

6.3 Lattice Filtering

Lattice filters are an important new method of linear predictive *analysis* as well as synthesis, and so it is worth considering the theory behind them a little further.

Theory of the Lattice Synthesis Filter

Figure 6.9 shows a single stage of the synthesis lattice given earlier. There are two signals at each side of the lattice, and the z-transforms of these have been labelled X^+ and X^- at the left-hand side, and Y^+ and Y^- at the right-hand side. The direction of signal flow is forwards along the upper ("positive") path and backwards along the lower ("negative") one.

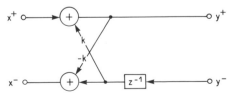

Fig. 6.9. Single stage of a synthesis lattice filter.

The signal flows show that the following two relationships hold:

$$Y^+ = X^+ + kz^{-1}Y^- \qquad \text{for the forward (upper) path}$$
$$X^- = -kY^+ + z^{-1}Y^- \qquad \text{for the backward (lower) path.}$$

Re-arranging the first equation yields

$$X^+ = Y^+ - kz^{-1}Y^-,$$

and so we can describe the function of the lattice by a single matrix equation:

$$\begin{bmatrix} X^+ \\ X^- \end{bmatrix} = \begin{bmatrix} 1 & -kz^{-1} \\ -k & z^{-1} \end{bmatrix} \begin{bmatrix} Y^+ \\ Y^- \end{bmatrix}.$$

It would be nice to be able to call this an input-output equation, but it is not; for the input signals to the lattice stage are X^+ and Y^-, and the outputs are X^- and Y^+. We have written it in this form because it allows a multi stage lattice to be described by cascading these matrix equations.

A single-stage lattice filter has Y^+ and Y^- connected together, forming its output (call this X_{output}), while the input is X^+ (X_{input}). Hence the input is related to the output by

$$\begin{bmatrix} X_{\text{input}} \\ \blacksquare \end{bmatrix} = \begin{bmatrix} 1 & -kz^{-1} \\ -k & z^{-1} \end{bmatrix} \begin{bmatrix} X_{\text{output}} \\ X_{\text{output}} \end{bmatrix},$$

so

$$X_{\text{input}} = (1 - kz^{-1}) \, X_{\text{output}},$$

or

$$\frac{X_{\text{output}}}{X_{\text{input}}} = \frac{1}{1 - kz^{-1}}.$$

(The symbol $\blacksquare$ is used here and elsewhere to indicate an unimportant element of a vector or matrix.) This certainly has the form of a linear predictive synthesis filter, which is

$$\frac{X(z)}{E(z)} = \frac{1}{1 - \Sigma_{k=1}^{p} a_k z^{-k}} = \frac{1}{1 - a_1 z^{-1}} \qquad \text{when } p = 1.$$

The behaviour of a second-order lattice filter, shown in Fig. 6.10, can be described by

$$\begin{bmatrix} X_3^+ \\ X_3^- \end{bmatrix} = \begin{bmatrix} 1 & -k_2 z^{-1} \\ -k_2 & z^{-1} \end{bmatrix} \begin{bmatrix} X_2^+ \\ X_2^- \end{bmatrix}$$

$$\begin{bmatrix} X_2^+ \\ X_2^- \end{bmatrix} = \begin{bmatrix} 1 & -k_1 z^{-1} \\ -k_1 & z^{-1} \end{bmatrix} \begin{bmatrix} X_1^+ \\ X_1^- \end{bmatrix}$$

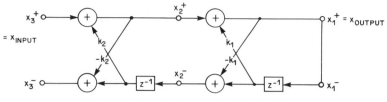

Fig. 6.10. Second-order synthesis lattice filter.

with

$$X_3^+ = X_{\text{input}}$$
$$X_1^+ = X_1^- = X_{\text{output}}.$$

X_2^+ and X_2^- can be eliminated by substituting the second equation into the first, which yields

$$\begin{bmatrix} X_{\text{input}} \\ \blacksquare \end{bmatrix} = \begin{bmatrix} 1 & -k_2z^{-1} \\ -k_2 & z^{-1} \end{bmatrix} \begin{bmatrix} 1 & -k_1z^{-1} \\ -k_1 & z^{-1} \end{bmatrix} \begin{bmatrix} X_{\text{output}} \\ X_{\text{output}} \end{bmatrix}$$

$$= \begin{bmatrix} 1 + k_1k_2z^{-1} & -k_1z^{-1} - k_2z^{-2} \\ \blacksquare & \blacksquare \end{bmatrix} \begin{bmatrix} X_{\text{output}} \\ X_{\text{output}} \end{bmatrix}.$$

This leads to an input-output relationship

$$\frac{X_{\text{output}}}{X_{\text{input}}} = \frac{1}{1 + k_1(k_2 - 1)z^{-1} - k_2z^{-2}},$$

which has the required form, namely

$$\frac{1}{1 - \Sigma_{k=1}^{p} a_k z^{-k}} \qquad (p = 2)$$

when

$$a_1 = -k_1(k_2 - 1)$$
$$a_2 = k_2.$$

A third-order filter is described by

$$\begin{bmatrix} X_{\text{input}} \\ \blacksquare \end{bmatrix} = \begin{bmatrix} 1 & -k_3z^{-1} \\ -k_3 & z^{-1} \end{bmatrix} \begin{bmatrix} 1 & -k_2z^{-1} \\ -k_2 & z^{-1} \end{bmatrix} \begin{bmatrix} 1 & -k_1z^{-1} \\ -k_1 & z^{-1} \end{bmatrix} \begin{bmatrix} X_{\text{output}} \\ X_{\text{output}} \end{bmatrix},$$

and brave souls can verify that this gives an input-output relationship

$$\frac{X_{\text{output}}}{X_{\text{input}}} = \frac{1}{1 + [k_2k_3 + k_1(k_2 - 1)]z^{-1} + [k_1k_3(1 - k_2) - k_2]z^{-2} - k_3z^{-3}}.$$

It is fairly obvious that a p'th order lattice filter will give the required all-pole p'th order synthesis form,

$$\frac{1}{1 - \sum_{k=1}^{p} a_k z^{-k}}.$$

We have not shown that the algorithm given in Procedure 6.3 for producing reflection coefficients from filter coefficients gives those values for k_i which are necessary to make the lattice filter equivalent to the ordinary synthesis filter. However, this is the case, and it is easy to verify by hand for the first, second and third-order cases.

Different Lattice Configurations

The lattice filters of Figures 6.8, 6.9 and 6.10 have two multipliers per section. This is called a "two-multiplier" configuration. However, there are other configurations which achieve the same effect, but require different numbers of multiplies. Figure 6.11 shows one-multiplier and four-multiplier configurations, along with the familiar two-multiplier one. It is easy to verify

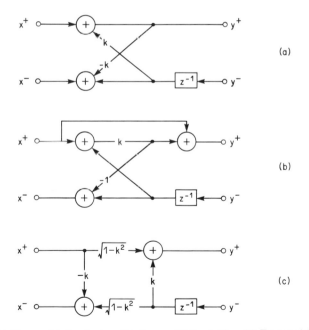

Fig. 6.11. (a) Two-multiplier lattice, (b) One-multiplier lattice, (c) Four-multiplier lattice.

that the three configurations can be modelled in matrix terms by

$$\begin{bmatrix} X^+ \\ X^- \end{bmatrix} = \begin{bmatrix} 1 & -kz^{-1} \\ -k & z^{-1} \end{bmatrix} \begin{bmatrix} Y^+ \\ Y^- \end{bmatrix} \qquad \text{two-multiplier configuration}$$

$$\begin{bmatrix} X^+ \\ X^- \end{bmatrix} = \begin{bmatrix} \dfrac{1-k}{1+k} \end{bmatrix}^{1/2} \begin{bmatrix} 1 & -kz^{-1} \\ -k & z^{-1} \end{bmatrix} \begin{bmatrix} Y^+ \\ Y^- \end{bmatrix} \qquad \text{one-multiplier configuration}$$

$$\begin{bmatrix} X^+ \\ X^- \end{bmatrix} = \dfrac{1}{(1-k^2)^{1/2}} \begin{bmatrix} 1 & -kz^{-1} \\ -k & z^{-1} \end{bmatrix} \begin{bmatrix} Y^+ \\ Y^- \end{bmatrix} \qquad \text{four-multiplier configuration.}$$

Each of the three has the same frequency-domain response, although a different constant factor is involved in each case. The effect of this can be annulled by performing a single multiply operation on the output of a complete lattice chain. The multiplier has the form

$$\left[\frac{1-k_p}{1+k_p} \cdot \frac{1-k_{p-1}}{1+k_{p-1}} \cdot \ldots \cdot \frac{1-k_1}{1+k_1} \right]^{1/2}$$

for single-multiplier lattices, and

$$\left[\frac{1}{1-k_p^2} \cdot \frac{1}{1-k_{p-1}^2} \cdot \ldots \cdot \frac{1}{1-k_1^2} \right]^{1/2}$$

for four-multiplier lattices, where the reflection coefficients in the lattice are k_p, k_{p-1}, ..., k_1.

There are important differences between these three configurations. If multiplication is time-consuming, the one-multiplier model has obvious computational advantages over the other two methods. However, the four-multiplier structure behaves substantially better in finite word-length implementations. It is easy to show that, with this configuration,

$$(X^-)^2 + (Y^+)^2 = (X^+)^2 + (z^{-1}Y^-)^2,$$

a relationship which suggests that the "energy" in the input signals, namely X^+ and Y^-, is preserved in the output signals, X^- and Y^+. Notice that care must be taken with the z-transforms, since squaring is a non-linear operation. $(z^{-1}Y^-)^2$ means the square of the previous value of Y^-, which is not the same as $z^{-2}(Y^-)^2$.

It has been shown (Gray and Markel, 1975) that the four-multiplier configuration has some stability properties which are not shared by other digital filter structures. When a linear predictive filter is used for synthesis, the parameters of the filter (the k-parameters in the case of lattice filters, and the a-parameters in the case of direct ones) change with time. It is usually rather difficult to guarantee stability in the case of time-varying filter parameters, but some guarantees can be made for a chain of four-multiplier lattices. Furthermore, if the input is a discrete delta function, the cumulative energies at each stage of the lattice are the same, and so maximum dynamic range will be achieved for the whole filter if each section is implemented with the same word size.

Lattice Analysis

It is quite easy to construct a filter which is inverse to a single-stage lattice. The structure of Fig. 6.12(a) does the job (ignore for a moment the dashed lines connecting Fig. 6.12(a) and (b). Its matrix transfer function is

$$\begin{bmatrix} Y^+ \\ Y^- \end{bmatrix} = \begin{bmatrix} 1 & -kz^{-1} \\ -k & z^{-1} \end{bmatrix} \begin{bmatrix} X^+ \\ X^- \end{bmatrix} \qquad \text{analysis lattice (Fig. 6.12(a)).}$$

Notice that this is exactly the same as the transfer function of the synthesis lattice of Fig. 6.9, which is reproduced in Fig. 6.12(b), except that the X's and Y's are reversed:

$$\begin{bmatrix} X^+ \\ X^- \end{bmatrix} = \begin{bmatrix} 1 & -kz^{-1} \\ -k & z^{-1} \end{bmatrix} \begin{bmatrix} Y^+ \\ Y^- \end{bmatrix} \qquad \text{synthesis lattice (Fig. 6.12(b)),}$$

or, in other words,

$$\begin{bmatrix} Y^+ \\ Y^- \end{bmatrix} = \begin{bmatrix} 1 & -kz^{-1} \\ -k & z^{-1} \end{bmatrix}^{-1} \begin{bmatrix} X^+ \\ X^- \end{bmatrix} \qquad \text{synthesis lattice (Fig. 6.12(b)).}$$

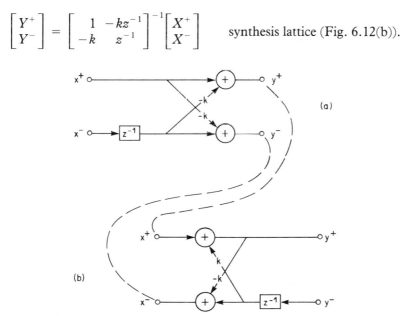

Fig. 6.12. (a) Single stage of an analysis lattice, (b) Single stage of a synthesis lattice.

Hence if the filters of Figs 6.12(a) and (b) were connected together as shown by the dashed lines, they would cancel each other out, and the overall transfer would be unity:

$$
\begin{bmatrix} 1 & -kz^{-1} \\ -k & z^{-1} \end{bmatrix}
\begin{bmatrix} 1 & -kz^{-1} \\ -k & z^{-1} \end{bmatrix}^{-1}
= \begin{bmatrix} 1 & 0 \\ 0 & 1 \end{bmatrix}.
$$

Actually, such a connection is not possible in physical terms, for although the upper paths can be joined together, the lower ones cannot. The right-hand lower point of Fig. 6.12(a) is an *output* terminal, and so is the left-hand lower one of Fig. 6.12(b): However, there is no need to envisage a physical connection of the lower paths. It is sufficient for cancellation just to assume that the signals at both of the points turn out to be the same.

And they do. The general case of a p-stage analysis lattice connected to a p-stage synthesis lattice is shown in Fig. 6.13. Notice that the forward and backward paths are connected together at both of the extreme ends of the system. It is not difficult to show that under these conditions the signal at the lower right-hand terminal of the analysis chain will equal that at the lower left-hand terminal of the synthesis chain, even though they are not connected, provided the upper terminals are connected together as shown by the dashed line. Of course, the reflection coefficients k_1, k_2, ..., k_p in the analysis lattice must equal those in the synthesis lattice, and as Fig. 6.13 shows, the order is reversed in the synthesis lattice. Successive analysis and synthesis sections pair off, working from the middle outwards. At each stage the sections cancel each other out, giving a unit transfer function as demonstrated above.

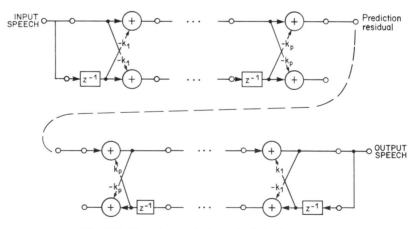

Fig. 6.13. Complete analysis-synthesis lattice structure.

Estimating Reflection Coefficients

As stated earlier in this chapter, the key problem in linear prediction is to determine the values of the predictive coefficients: in this case, the reflection coefficients. If this is done correctly, we have shown using Procedure 6.3 that the synthesis part of Fig. 6.13 performs the same calculation that a conventional direct-form linear predictive synthesizer would, and hence the signal that excites it (that is, the signal represented by the dashed line) must be the prediction residual, or error signal, discussed earlier. The system is effectively the same as the high-order adaptive differential pulse code modulation one of Fig. 6.1.

One of the most interesting features of the lattice structure for analysis filters is that calculation of suitable values for the reflection coefficients can be done locally at each stage of the lattice. For example, consider the i'th section of the analysis lattice in Fig. 6.13. It is possible to determine a suitable value of k_i simply by performing a calculation on the inputs to the i'th section (i.e. X^+ and X^- in Fig. 6.12). No longer need the complicated global optimization technique of matrix inversion be used, as in the autocorrelation and covariance methods discussed earlier.

A suitable value for k in the single lattice section of Fig. 6.12 is

$$k = \frac{E[x^+(n)x^-(n-1)]}{(E[x^+(n)^2]E[x^-(n-1)^2])^{1/2}};$$

that is, the statistical correlation between $x^+(n)$ and $x^-(n-1)$. Here, $x^+(n)$ and $x^-(n)$ represent the input signals to the upper and lower paths (recall that X^+ and X^- are their z-transforms). $x^-(n-1)$ is just $x^-(n)$ delayed by one time unit, that is, the output of the z^{-1} box in the figure.

The criterion of optimality for the autocorrelation and covariance methods was that the prediction error, that is, the signal which emerges from the right-hand end of the upper path of a lattice analysis filter, should be minimized in a mean-square sense. The reflection coefficients obtained from the above formula do not necessarily satisfy any such global minimization criterion. Nevertheless, they do keep the error signal small, and have been used with success in speech analysis systems.

It is easy to minimize the output from either the upper or the lower path of the lattice filter at each stage. For example, the z-transform of the upper output is given by

$$Y^+ = X^+ - kz^{-1}X^-,$$

or

$$y^+(n) = x^+(n) - kx^-(n-1).$$

Hence

$$E[y^+(n)^2] = E[x^+(n)^2] - 2kE[x^+(n)x^-(n - 1)] + k^2E[x^-(n - 1)^2],$$

where E stands for expected value, and this reaches a minimum when the derivative with respect to k becomes zero:

$$-2E[x^+(n)x^-(n - 1)] + 2kE[x^-(n - 1)^2] = 0,$$

that is, when

$$k = \frac{E[x^+(n)x^-(n - 1)]}{E[x^-(n - 1)^2]}.$$

A similar calculation shows that the output of the lower path is minimized when

$$k = \frac{E[x^+(n)x^-(n - 1)]}{E[x^+(n - 1)^2]}.$$

Unfortunately, either of these expressions can exceed 1, leading to an unstable filter. The value of k cited earlier is the geometric mean of these two expressions, and since it is a correlation coefficient, must be less than 1.

Another possibility is to minimize the expected value of the sum of the squares of the upper and lower outputs:

$$y^+(n)^2 + y^-(n)^2 = (1 + k^2)x^+(n)^2 - 2kx^+(n)x^-(n - 1) + (1 + k^2)x^-(n)^2.$$

Taking expected values and setting the derivative with respect to k to zero leads to

$$k = \frac{E[x^+(n)x^-(n - 1)]}{\frac{1}{2}E[x^+(n)^2 + x^-(n - 1)^2]}.$$

This also is guaranteed to be less than 1, and has given good results in speech analysis systems.

Figure 6.14 shows the implementation of a single section of an analysis lattice. The signals $x^+(n)$ and $x^-(n - 1)$ are fed to a correlator, which produces a suitable value for k. This value is used to calculate the output of the lattice section, and hence the input to the next lattice section. The reflection coefficient needs to be low-pass filtered, because it will only be

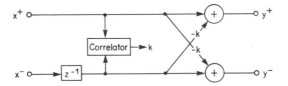

Fig. 6.14. Single stage of an analysis lattice, including calculation of the reflection coefficient.

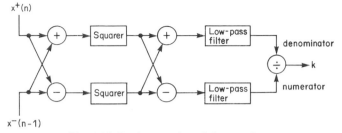

Fig. 6.15. Implementation of the correlator.

transmitted to the synthesizer occasionally (say every 20 msec) and so a short-term average is required.

One implementation of the correlator is shown in Fig. 6.15 (Kang, 1974). This calculates the value of k given by the last equation above, and does it by summing and differencing the two signals $x^+(n)$ and $x^-(n-1)$, squaring the results to give

$$x^+(n)^2 + 2x^+(n)x^-(n-1) + x^-(n-1)^2$$
$$x^+(n)^2 - 2x^+(n)x^-(n-1) + x^-(n-1)^2,$$

and summing and differencing these, to yield

$$2x^+(n)^2 + 2x^-(n-1)^2$$
$$4x^+(n)x^-(n-1).$$

Before these are divided to give the final coefficient k, they are individually low-pass filtered. While some rather complex schemes have been proposed, based upon Kalman filter theory (e.g. Matsui *et al.*, 1972), a simple exponential weighted past average has been found to be satisfactory. This has z-transform

$$\frac{Y(z)}{U(z)} = \frac{1}{64 - 63z^{-1}},$$

that is, in the time domain,

$$y(n) = \frac{63}{64}y(n-1) + \frac{1}{64}u(n).$$

This filter exponentially averages past sample values with a time-constant of 64 sampling intervals: that is, 8 msec at an 8 kHz sampling rate.

6.4 Pitch Estimation

It is sometimes useful to think of linear prediction as a kind of curve-fitting technique. Figure 6.16 illustrates how four samples of a speech signal can

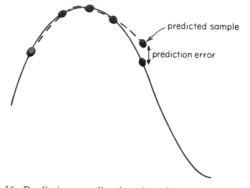

Fig. 6.16. Predictive encoding based on four past sample values.

predict the next one. In essence, a curve is drawn through four points to predict the position of the fifth, and only the prediction error is actually transmitted. Now if the order of linear prediction is high enough (at least 10), and if the coefficients are chosen correctly, the prediction will closely model the resonances of the vocal tract. Thus the error will actually be zero, except at pitch pulses.

Figure 6.17 shows a segment of voiced speech together with the prediction error (often called the prediction residual). It is apparent that the error is indeed small, except at pitch pulses. This suggests that a good way to determine the pitch period is to examine the error signal, perhaps by looking at its autocorrelation function. As with all pitch detection methods, one must be careful: spurious peaks can occur, especially in nasal sounds when the all-pole model provided by linear prediction fails. Continuity constraints, which use previous values of pitch period when determining which peak to accept as a new pitch impulse, can eliminate many of these spurious

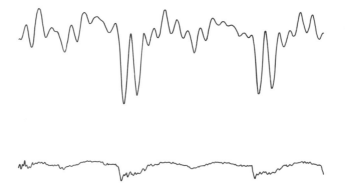

Fig. 6.17. Segment of voiced speech, together with prediction error.

peaks. Unvoiced speech should produce an error signal with no prominent peaks, and this needs to be detected. Voiced fricatives are a difficult case: peaks should be present, but the general noise level of the error signal will be greater than it is in purely voiced speech. Such considerations have been taken into account in a practical pitch estimation system based upon this technique (Markel, 1972).

This method of pitch detection highlights another advantage of the lattice analysis technique. When using autocorrelation or covariance analysis to determine the filter (or reflection) coefficients, the error signal is not normally produced. It can, of course, be found by taking the speech samples which constitute the current frame and running them through an analysis filter whose parameters are those determined by the analysis, but this is a computationally demanding exercise, for the filter must run at the speech sampling rate (say 8 kHz) instead of at the frame rate (say 50 Hz). Usually, pitch is estimated by other methods, like those discussed in Chapter 4, when using autocorrelation or covariance linear prediction. However, we have seen above that with the lattice method, the error signal is produced as a by-product: it appears at the right-hand end of the upper path of the lattice chain. Thus it is already available for use in determining pitch periods.

6.5 Parameter Coding for Linear Predictive Storage or Transmission

In this section, the coding requirements of linear predictive parameters will be examined. The parameters that need to be stored or transmitted are:

—pitch
—voiced-unvoiced flag
—overall amplitude level
—filter coefficients or reflection coefficients.

The first three are parameters of the excitation source. They can be derived directly from the error signal as indicated above, if it is generated (as it is in lattice implementations); or by other methods if no error signal is calculated. The filter or reflection coefficients are, of course, the main product of linear predictive analysis.

It is generally agreed that around 60 levels, logarithmically spaced, are needed to represent pitch for telephone quality speech. The voiced-unvoiced indication requires one bit, but since pitch is irrelevant in unvoiced speech, it can be coded as one of the pitch levels. For example, with 6-bit coding of pitch, the value 0 can be reserved to indicate unvoiced speech, with values 1–63 indicating the pitch of voiced speech. The overall gain has not been discussed above: it is simply the average amplitude of the error signal. Five bits on a logarithmic scale are sufficient to represent it.

Filter coefficients are not very amenable to quantization. At least 8–10 bits are required for each one. However, reflection coefficients are better behaved, and 5–6 bits each seems adequate. The number of coefficients that must be stored or transmitted is the same as the order of the linear prediction: 10 is commonly used for low-quality speech, with as many as 15 for higher qualities.

These figures give around 100 bits/frame for a 10'th order system using filter coefficients, and around 65 bits/frame for a 10'th order system using reflection coefficients. Frame lengths vary between 10 msec and 25 msec, depending on the quality desired. Thus for 20 msec frames, the data rates work out at around 5000 bit/s using filter coefficients, and 3250 bit/s using reflection coefficients.

Substantially lower data rates can be achieved by more careful coding of parameters. In 1976, the US Government defined a standard coding scheme for 10-pole linear prediction with a data rate of 2400 bit/s: conveniently chosen as one of the commonly-used rates for serial data transmission. This standard, called LPC-10, tackles the difficult problem of protection against transmission errors (Fussell *et al.*, 1978).

Whenever data rates are reduced, redundancy inherent in the signal is necessarily lost and so the effect of transmission errors becomes greatly magnified. For example, a single corrupted sample in PCM transmission of speech will probably not be noticed, and even a short burst of errors will be perceived as a click which can readily be distinguished from the speech. However, any error in LPC transmission will last for one entire frame (say 20 msec) and worse still, it will be integrated into the speech signal and will not be easily discriminated from it by the listener's brain. A single corruption may, for example, change a voiced frame into an unvoiced one, or vice versa. Even if it affects only a reflection coefficient, it will change the resonance characteristics of that frame, and will change them in a way that does not simply sound like superimposed noise.

Table 6.1 shows the LPC-10 coding scheme. Different coding is used for voiced and unvoiced frames. Only four reflection coefficients are transmitted for unvoiced frames, because it has been determined that no perceptible increase in speech quality occurs when more are used. The bits saved are more fruitfully employed to provide error detection and correction for the other parameters. Seven bits are used for pitch and the voiced-unvoiced flag, and they are redundant in that only 60 possible pitch values are allowed. Most transmission errors in this field will be detected by the receiver; which can then use an estimate of pitch based on previous values and discard the erroneous one. Pitch values are also Gray coded so that even if errors are

Table 6.1. Bit requirements for each parameter in LPC-10 coding scheme.

	Voiced sounds	Unvoiced sounds	
Pitch/voicing	7	7	60 pitch levels, Hamming and Gray coded
Energy	5	5	logarithmically coded
k_1	5	5	coded by table lookup
k_2	5	5	coded by table lookup
k_3	5	5	
k_4	5	5	
k_5	4	—	
k_6	4	—	
k_7	4	—	
k_8	4	—	
k_9	3	—	
k_{10}	2	—	
Synchronization	1	1	alternating 1, 0 pattern
Error detection/ correction		21	
	54	54	

frame rate: 44.4 Hz (22.5 msec frames)

not detected, there is a good chance that an adjacent pitch value is read instead. Different numbers of bits are allocated to the various reflection coefficients: experience shows that the lower-numbered ones contribute most highly to intelligibility and so these are quantized most finely. In addition, a table lookup operation is performed on the code generated for the first two, providing a non-linear quantization which is chosen to minimize the error on a statistical basis.

With 54 bits/frame and 22.5 msec frames, LPC-10 requires a 2400 bit/s data rate. Even lower rates have been used successfully for lower-quality speech. The *Speak 'n Spell* toy, described in Chapter 11, has an average data rate of 1200 bit/s. Rates as low as 600 bit/s have been achieved (Kang and Coulter, 1976) by pattern recognition techniques operating on the reflection coefficients: however, the speech quality is not good.

6.6 References

Blankinship, W.A. (1974). Note on computing autocorrelations. *IEEE Trans Acoustics, Speech and Signal Processing*, **ASSP-22(1)**76–77, February.
Fussell, J.W., Boudra, P.W., Abzug, B.M. and Cowing, M.D. (1978). Providing channel error protection for a 2400 bps linear predictive coded voice system. *Proc International Conference on Acoustics, Speech and Signal Processing*, 462–465.

Gray, A.H. and Markel, J.D. (1975). A normalized digital filter structure. *IEEE Trans Acoustics, Speech and Signal Processing*, **ASSP-23**(3)268–277, June.

Kang. G.S. (1974). Application of linear prediction encoding to a narrowband voice digitizer. Report 7774, Naval Research Laboratory, Washington DC, October.

Kang, G.S. and Coulter, D.C. (1976). 600 bit-per-second voice digitizer. Report 8043, Naval Research Laboratory, Washington, DC.

Markel, J.D. (1972). The SIFT algorithm for fundamental frequency estimation. *IEEE Trans Audio and Electroacoustics*, **AU-20**(5)367–377, December.

Martin, R.S., Peters, G. and Wilkinson, J.H. (1965). Symmetric decomposition of a positive definite matrix. *Numerische Mathematik*, **7**, 362–383.

Matsui, E., Nakajima, T., Suzuki, T. and Omura, H. (1972). An adaptive method of speech analysis based on Kalman filtering. *Electrotechnical Institute Report*, **36**(3)210–219 (in Japanese).

Witten, I.H. (1980). Algorithms for adaptive linear prediction. *Computer J.*, **23**, 78–84, January.

6.7 Further Reading

Most recent books on digital signal processing contain some information on linear prediction (see Oppenheim and Schafer, 1975; Rabiner and Gold, 1975; and Rabiner and Schafer, 1978; all referenced at the end of Chapter 4).

Atal, B.S. and Hanauer, S.L. (1971). Speech analysis and synthesis by linear prediction of the acoustic wave. *J. Acoustical Society of America*, **50**, 637–655, August.
    This paper is of historical importance because it introduced the idea of linear prediction to the speech processing community.

Makhoul, J.I. (1975). Linear prediction: a tutorial review. *Proc Institute of Electrical and Electronic Engineers*, **63**(4)561–580, April.
    An interesting, informative, and readable survey of linear prediction.

Markel, J.D. and Gray, A.H. (1976). "Linear prediction of speech", Springer Verlag, Berlin.
    This is the only book which is entirely devoted to linear prediction of speech. It is an essential reference work for those interested in the subject.

Wiener, N. (1947). *Extrapolation, interpolation and smoothing of stationary time series*. MIT Press, Cambridge, Massachusetts.
    Linear prediction is often thought of as a relatively new technique, but it is only its application to speech processing that is novel. Wiener develops all of the basic mathematics used in linear prediction of speech, except the lattice filter structure.

7

JOINING SEGMENTS OF SPEECH

The obvious way to provide speech output from computers is to select the basic acoustic units to be used, record them, and generate utterances by concatenating together appropriate segments from this pre-stored inventory. The crucial question then becomes, what are the basic units? Should they be whole sentences, words, syllables or phonemes?

There are several trade-offs to be considered here. The larger the units, the more utterances have to be stored. It is not so much the length of individual utterances that is of concern, but rather their variety, which tends to increase exponentially instead of linearly with the size of the basic unit. Numbers provide an easy example: there are 10^7 7-digit telephone numbers, and it is certainly infeasible to record each one individually. Note that as storage technology improves, the limitation is becoming more and more one of recording the utterances in the first place rather than finding somewhere to store them. At a PCM data rate of 50 Kbit/s, a 100 Mbyte disk can hold over 4 hours of continuous speech. With linear predictive coding at 1 Kbit/s, it holds 0.8 of a megasecond: well over a week. And this is a 24-hour 7-day week, which corresponds to a working month; and continuous speech, without pauses, which probably requires another factor of five for production by a person. Setting up a recording session to fill the disk would be a formidable task indeed! Furthermore, the use of videodisks, which will be common domestic items by the end of the decade, could increase these figures by a factor of 50.

The word seems to be a sensibly-sized basic unit. Many applications use a rather limited vocabulary: 190 words for the airline reservation system described in Chapter 1. Even at PCM data rates, this will consume less than 0.5 Mbyte of storage. Unfortunately, coarticulation and prosodic factors now come into play.

Real speech is connected; there are few gaps between words. Coarticulation, where sounds are affected by those on either side, naturally operates across word boundaries. And the time constants of coarticulation are associated with the mechanics of the vocal tract and hence measure tens or hundreds of msec. Thus the effects straddle several pitch periods (100 Hz pitch has 10 msec period) and cannot be simulated by simple interpolation of the speech waveform.

Prosodic features, notably pitch and rhythm, span much longer stretches of speech than single words. As far as most speech output applications are concerned, they operate at the utterance level of a single, sentence-sized, information unit. They cannot be accommodated if speech waveforms of individual words of the utterance are stored, for it is rarely feasible to alter the fundamental frequency or duration of a time waveform without changing all the formant resonances as well. However, both word-to-word coarticulation and the essential features of rhythm and intonation can be incorporated if the stored words are coded in source-filter form.

For more general applications of speech output, the limitations of word storage soon become apparent. Although people's daily vocabularies are not large, most words have a variety of inflected forms which need to be treated separately if a strict policy is adopted of word storage. For instance, in this book there are 84 000 words, and 6500 (8%) different ones (counting inflected forms). In Chapter 1 alone, there are 6800 words and 1700 (25%) different ones.

It seems crazy to treat a simple inflection like "–s" or its voiced counterpart, "–z" (as in "inflections"), as a totally different word from the base form. But once you consider storing roots and endings separately, it becomes apparent that there is a vast number of different endings, and it is difficult to know where to draw the line. It is natural to think instead of simply using the syllable as the basic unit.

A generous estimate of the number of different syllables in English is 10 000. At three a second, only about an hour's storage is required for them all. But waveform storage will certainly not do. Although coarticulation effects between words are needed to make speech sound fluent, coarticulation between syllables is necessary for it even to be *comprehensible*. Adopting a source-filter form of representation is essential, as is some scheme of interpolation between syllables which simulates coarticulation. Unfortunately, a great deal of acoustic action occurs at syllable boundaries: stops are exploded, the sound source changes between voicing and frication, and so on. It may be more appropriate to consider inverse syllables, comprising a vowel-consonant-vowel sequence instead of consonant-vowel-consonant. (These have jokingly been dubbed "lisibles"!)

There is again some considerable practical difficulty in creating an inventory of syllables, or lisibles. Now it is not so much the recording that is impractical, but the editing needed to ensure that the cuts between syllables are made at exactly the right point. As units get smaller, the exact placement of the boundaries becomes ever more critical, and several thousand sensitive editing jobs is no easy task.

Since quite general effects of coarticulation must be accommodated with syllable synthesis, there will not necessarily be significant deterioration if smaller, demisyllable, units are employed. This reduces the segment inventory to an estimated 1000–2000 entries, and the tedious job of editing each one individually becomes at least feasible, if not enviable. Alternatively, the segment inventory could be created by artificial means involving cut-and-try experiments with resonance parameters.

The ultimate in economy of inventory size, of course, is to use phonemes as the basic unit. This makes the most critical part of the task interpolation between units, rather than their construction or recording. With only about 40 phonemes in English, each one can be examined in many different contexts to ascertain the best data to store. There is no need to record them directly from a human voice: it would be difficult anyway for most cannot be produced in isolation. In fact, a phoneme is an abstract unit, not a particular sound (recall the discussion of phonology in Chapter 2), and so it is most appropriate that data be abstracted from several different realizations rather than an exact record made of any one.

If information is stored about phonological units of speech, phonemes, the difficult task of phonological-to-phonetic conversion must necessarily be performed automatically. Allophones are created by altering the transitions between units, and to a lesser extent by modifying the central parts of the units themselves. The rules for making transitions will have a big effect on the quality of the resulting speech. Instead of trying to perform this task automatically by a computer program, the allophones themselves could be stored. This will ease the job of generating transitions between segments, but will certainly not eliminate it. The total number of allophones will depend on the narrowness of the transcription system: 60–80 is typical, and it is unlikely to exceed one or two hundred. In any case there will not be a storage problem. However, now the burden of producing an allophonic transcription has been transferred to the person who codes the utterance prior to synthesizing it. If he is skilful and patient, he should be able to coax the system into producing fairly understandable speech, but the effort required for this on a per-utterance basis should not be underestimated.

Table 7.1 summarizes in broad brush-strokes the issues which relate to the choice of basic unit for concatenation. The sections which follow provide more detail about the different methods of joining segments of speech together. Only segmental aspects are considered, for the important problems of prosody will be treated in the next chapter. All of the methods rely to some extent on the acoustic properties of speech, and as smaller basic units are considered, the role of speech acoustics becomes more important. It is impossible in a book like this to give a detailed account of acoustic phonetics, for it would take several volumes! What I aim to do in the following pages is to highlight some salient features which are relevant to segment concatenation, without attempting to be complete.

Table 7.1. Some issues relevant to choice of basic unit.

	Size of utterance inventory	Storage method	Source of utterance inventory	Principal burden is placed on
sentences	depends on application	waveform or source-filter parameters	natural speech	recording artist, storage medium
words	depends on application	source-filter parameters	natural speech	recording artist and editor, storage medium
syllables/ lisibles	10 000	source-filter parameters	natural speech	recording editor
demisyllables	1000	source-filter parameters	natural speech or artificially generated	recording editor or inventory compiler
phonemes	40	generalized parameters	artificially generated	author of segment concatenation program
allophones	50–100	generalized or source-filter parameters	artificially generated or natural speech	coder of synthesized utterances

7.1 Word Concatenation

For general speech output, word concatenation is an inherently limited technique because of the large number of phonetically different words. Despite this fact, it is at present the most widely-used synthesis method, and is likely to remain so for several years. We have seen that the primary problems are word-to-word coarticulation and prosody; and both can be overcome, at least to a useful approximation, by coding the words in source-filter form.

Time-domain Techniques

Nevertheless, a surprising number of applications simply store the time waveform, coded, usually, by one of the techniques described in Chapter 3. From an implementation point of view there are many advantages to this.

Speech quality can easily be controlled by selecting a suitable sampling rate and coding scheme. A natural-sounding voice is guaranteed; male or female as desired. The equipment required is minimal: a digital-to-analogue converter and post-sampling filter will do for synthesis if PCM coding is used, and DPCM, ADPCM, and delta modulation decoders are not much more complicated.

From a speech point of view, the resulting utterances can never be made convincingly fluent. We discussed the early experiments of Stowe and Hampton (1961) at the beginning of Chapter 3. A major drawback to word concatenation in the analogue domain is the introduction of clicks and other interference between words: it is difficult to prevent the time waveform transitions from adding extraneous sounds. This poses no problem with digital storage, however, for the waveforms can be edited accurately prior to storage so that they start and finish at an exactly zero level. Rather, the lack of fluency stems from the absence of proper control of coarticulation and prosody.

But this is not necessarily a serious drawback if the application is a sufficiently limited one. Complete, invariant utterances can be stored as one unit. Often they must contain data-dependent slot-fillers, as in

This flight makes __ stops

and

Flight number __ leaves __ at __, arrives in __ at __

(taken from the airline reservation system of Chapter 1 (Levinson and Shipley, 1980)). Then, each slot-filling word is recorded in an intonation consistent both with its position in the template utterance and with the intonation of that utterance. This could be done by embedding the word in the utterance for recording, and excising it by digital editing before storage. It would be dangerous to try to take into account coarticulation effects, for the coarticulation could not be made consistent with both the several slot-fillers and the single template. This could be overcome if several versions of the template were stored, but then the scheme becomes subject to combinatorial explosion if there is more than one slot in a single utterance. But it is not really necessary, for the lack of fluency will probably be interpreted by a benevolent listener as an attempt to convey the information as clearly as possible.

Difficulties will occur if the same slot-filler is used in different contexts. For instance, the first gap in each of the sentences above contains a number; yet the intonation of that number is different. Many systems simply ignore this problem. Then one does notice anomalies, if one is attentive: the words come, as it were, from different mouths, without fluency. However, the problem is not necessarily acute. If it is, two or more versions of each slot-filler can be recorded, one for each context.

As an example, consider the synthesis of 7-digit telephone numbers, like 289–5371. If one version only of each digit is stored, it should be recorded in a level tone of voice. A pause should be inserted after the third digit of the synthetic number, to accord with common elocution. The result will certainly be unnatural, although it should be clear and intelligible. Any pitch errors in the recordings will make certain numbers audibly anomalous. At the other extreme, 70 single digits could be stored, one version of each digit for each position in the number. The recording will be tedious and error-prone, and the synthetic utterances will still not be fluent (for coarticulation is ignored) but instead unnaturally clearly enunciated. A compromise is to record only three versions of each digit, one for any of the five positions xx –xxx, another one for the third position x–   , and the last for the final position   – x. The first version will be in a level voice, the second an incomplete, rising tone; and the third a final, dropping pitch.

Joining Formant-coded Words

The limitations of the time-domain method are lack of fluency caused by unnatural transitions between words, and the combinatorial explosion created by recording slot-fillers several times in different contexts. Both of these problems can be alleviated by storing formant tracks, concatenating them with suitable interpolation, and applying a complete pitch contour suitable for the whole utterance. But one can still not generate conversational speech, for natural speech rhythms cause non-linear warpings of the time axis which cannot reasonably be imitated by this method.

Solving problems often creates others. As we saw in Chapter 4, it is not easy to obtain reliable formant tracks automatically. Yet hand-editing of formant parameters adds a whole new dimension to the problem of vocabulary construction, for it is an exceedingly tiresome and time-consuming task. Even after such tweaking, resynthesized utterances will be degraded considerably from the original, for the source-filter model is by no means a perfect one. A hardware or real-time software formant synthesizer must be added to the system, presenting design problems and creating extra cost. Should a serial or parallel synthesizer be used?: the latter offers potentially better speech (especially in nasal sounds), but requires additional parameters, namely formant amplitudes, to be estimated. Finally, as we will see in the next chapter, it is not an easy matter to generate a suitable pitch contour and apply it to the utterance.

Strangely enough, the interpolation itself does not present any great difficulty, for there is not enough information in the formant-coded words to make possible sophisticated coarticulation. The need for interpolation is most pressing when one word ends with a voiced sound and the next begins with one. If either the end of the first or the beginning of the second word (or both) is unvoiced, unnatural formant transitions do not matter for they will not be heard. Actually, this is only strictly true for fricative transitions: if the juncture is aspirated then formants will be perceived in the aspiration. However, *h* is the only fully aspirated sound in English, and it is relatively uncommon. It is not absolutely necessary to interpolate the fricative filter resonance, because smooth transitions from one fricative sound to another are rare in natural speech.

Hence unless both sides of the junction are voiced, no interpolation is needed: simple abuttal of the stored parameter tracks will do. Note that this is *not* the same as joining time waveforms, for the synthesizer will automatically ensure a relatively smooth transition from one segment to another because of energy storage in the filters. A new set of resonance parameters for the formant-coded words will be stored every 10 or 20 msec (see Chapter 5), and so the transition will automatically be smoothed over this time period.

For voiced-to-voiced transitions, some interpolation is needed. An overlap period of duration, say, 50 msec, is established, and the resonance parameters in the final 50 msec of the first word are averaged with those in the first 50 msec of the second. The average is weighted, with the first word's formants dominating at the beginning and their effect progressively dying out in favour of the second word.

More sophisticated than a simple average is to weight the components according to how rapidly they are changing. If the spectral change in one word is much greater than that in the other, we might expect that this will dominate the transition. A simple measure of spectral derivative at any given time can be found by adding the magnitude of the discrepancies in each formant frequency between one sample and the next. The spectral change in the transition region can be obtained by summing the spectral derivatives at each sample in the region. Such a measure can perhaps be made more accurate by taking into account the relative importance of the formants, but will probably never be more than a rough and ready yardstick. At any rate, it can be used to load the average in favour of the dominant side of the junction.

Much more important for naturalness of the speech are the effects of rhythm and intonation, discussed in the next chapter.

Such a scheme has been implemented and tested on (guess what!) 7-digit telephone numbers (Rabiner *et al.*, 1971). Significant improvement (at the 5% level of statistical significance) in people's ability to recall numbers was found for this method over direct abuttal of either natural or synthetic versions of the digits. Although the method seemed, on balance, to produce utterances that were recalled less accurately than completely natural spoken telephone numbers, the difference was not significant (at the 5% level). The system was also used to generate wiring instructions by computer directly from the connection list, as described in Chapter 1. As noted there, synthetic speech was actually preferred to natural speech in the noisy environment of the production line.

Joining Linear Predictive Coded Words

Because obtaining accurate formant tracks for natural utterances by Fourier transform methods is difficult, it is worth considering the use of linear prediction as the source-filter model. Actually, formant resonances can be extracted from linear predictive coefficients quite easily, but there is no need to do this because the reflection coefficients themselves are quite suitable for interpolation.

A slightly different interpolation scheme from that described in the previous section has been reported (Olive, 1975). The reflection coefficients were spliced during an overlap region of only 20 msec. More interestingly, attempts were made to suppress the plosive bursts of stop sounds in cases where they were followed by another stop at the beginning of the next word. This is a common coarticulation, occurring, for instance, in the phrase "stop burst". In running speech, the plosion on the p of "stop" is normally suppressed because it is followed by another stop. This is a particularly striking case because the place of articulation of the two stops p and b is the same: complete suppression is not as likely to happen in "stop gap", for example (although it may occur). Here is an instance of how extra information could improve the quality of the synthetic transitions considerably. However, automatically identifying the place of articulation of stops is a difficult job, of a complexity far above what is appropriate for simply joining words stored in source-filter form.

Another innovation was introduced into the transition between two vowel sounds, when the second word began with an accented syllable. A glottal stop was placed at the juncture. Although the glottal stop was not described in Chapter 2, it is a sound used in many dialects of English. It frequently occurs in the utterance "uh-uh", meaning "no". Here it *is* used to separate two vowel sounds, but in fact this is not particularly common in most dialects. One could say "the apple", "the orange", "the onion" with a neutral vowel in "the" (to rhyme with "*a*bove") and a glottal stop as separator, but it is much more usual to rhyme "the" with "he" and introduce a y between the words. Similarly, even speakers who do not normally pronounce an *r* at the end of words will introduce one in "bigger apple", rather than using a glottal stop. Note that it would be wrong to put an *r* in "the apple", even for speakers who usually terminate "the" and "bigger" with the same sound. Such effects occur at a high level of processing, and are practically impossible to simulate with word-interpolation rules. Hence the expedient of introducing a glottal stop is a good one, although it is certainly unnatural.

7.2 Concatenating Whole or Partial Syllables

The use of segments larger than a single phoneme or allophone but smaller than a word as the basic unit for speech synthesis has an interesting history. It has long been realized that transitions between phonemes are extremely sensitive and critical components of speech, and thus are essential for successful synthesis. Consider the unvoiced stop sounds *p*, *t* and *k*. Their central portion is actually silence! (Try saying a word like "butter" with a very long *t*.) Hence in this case it is *only* the transitional information which can distinguish these sounds from each other.

Sound segments which comprise the transition from the centre of one phoneme to the centre of the next are called *dyads* or *diphones*. The possibility of using them as the basic units for concatenation was first mooted in the mid 1950s. The idea is attractive because there is relatively little spectral movement in the central, so-called "steady-state", portion of many phonemes; in the extreme case of unvoiced stops there is not only no spectral movement, but no spectrum at all in the steady state! At that time, the resonance synthesizer was in its infancy, and so recorded segments of live speech were used. The early experiments met with little success because of the technical difficulties of joining analogue waveforms and inevitable discrepancies between the steady-state parts of a phoneme recorded in different contexts, not to mention the problems of coarticulation and prosody which effectively preclude the use of waveform concatenation at such a low level.

In the mid 1960s, with the growing use of resonance synthesizers, it became possible to generate diphones by copying resonance parameters manually from a spectrogram, and improving the result by trial and error. It was not feasible to extract formant frequencies automatically from real speech, though, because the fast Fourier transform was not yet widely known and the computational burden of slow Fourier transformation was prohibitive. For example, a project at IBM stored manually-derived parameter tracks for diphones, identified by pairs of phoneme names (Dixon and Maxey, 1968). To generate a synthetic utterance it was coded in phonetic form and used to access the diphone table to give a set of parameter tracks for the complete utterance. Note that this is the first system we have encountered whose input is a phonetic transcription which relates to an inventory of truly synthetic character: all previous schemes used recordings of live speech, albeit processed in some form. Since the inventory was synthetic, there was no difficulty in ensuring that discontinuities did not arise between segments beginning and ending with the same phoneme. Thus interpolation was irrelevant, and the synthesis procedure concentrated on prosodic questions. The resulting speech was reported to be quite impressive.

Strictly speaking, diphones are not demisyllables but phoneme pairs. In the simplest case they happen to be similar, for two primary diphones characterize a consonant-vowel-consonant syllable. There is an advantage to using demisyllables rather than diphones as the basic unit, for many syllables begin or end with complicated consonant clusters which are not easy to produce convincingly by diphone concatenation. But they are not easy to produce by hand-editing resonance parameters either! Now that speech analysis methods have been developed and refined, resonance parameters or linear predictive coefficients can be extracted automatically from natural utterances, and there has been a resurgence of interest in syllabic and demisyllabic synthesis methods. The wheel has turned full circle, from segments of natural speech to hand-tailored parameters and back again!

The advantage of storing demisyllables over syllables (or lisibles) from the point of view of storage capacity has already been pointed out (perhaps 1000–2000 demisyllables as opposed to 4000–10 000 syllables), but it is probably not too significant with the continuing decline of storage costs. The requirements are of the order of 25 Kbyte vs 0.5 Mbyte for 1200 bit/s linear predictive coding, and the latter could almost be accommodated today (1981) on a state-of-the-art read-only memory chip. A bigger advantage comes from rhythmic considerations. As we will see in the next chapter, the rhythms of fluent speech cause dramatic variations in syllable duration, but these seem to affect the vowel and closing consonant cluster much more than the initial consonant cluster. Thus if a demisyllable is deemed to begin shortly (say 60 msec) after onset of the vowel, when the formant structure has settled down, the bulk of the vowel and the closing consonant cluster will form a single demisyllable. The opening cluster of the next syllable will lie in the next demisyllable. Then differential lengthening can be applied to that part of the syllable which tends to be stretched in live speech.

One system for demisyllable concatenation has produced excellent results for monosyllabic English words (Lovins and Fujimura, 1976). Complex word-final consonant clusters are excluded from the inventory by using syllable affixes s, z, t and d; these are attached to the syllabic core as a separate exercise (Macchi and Nigro, 1977). Prosodic rather than segmental considerations are likely to prove the major limiting factor when this scheme is extended to running speech.

Monosyllabic words spoken in isolation are coded as linear predictive reflection coefficients, and segmented by digital editing into the initial consonant cluster and the vocalic nucleus plus final cluster. The cut is made 60 msec into the vowel, as suggested above. This minimizes the difficulty of interpolation when concatenating segments, for there is ample voicing on either side of the juncture. The reflection coefficients should not differ radically because the vowel is the same in each demisyllable. A 40 msec overlap is used, with the usual linear interpolation. An alternative smoothing rule applies when the second segment has a nasal or glide after the vowel. In this case anticipatory coarticulation occurs, affecting even the early part of the vowel. For example, a vowel is frequently nasalized when followed by a nasal sound, even in English where nasalization is not a distinctive feature in vowels (see Chapter 2). Under these circumstances the overlap area is moved forward in time so that the coloration applies throughout almost the whole vowel.

7.3 Phoneme Synthesis

Acoustic phonetics is the study of how the acoustic signal relates to the phonetic sequence which was spoken or heard: People (especially engineers) often ask, how could phonetics not be acoustic? In fact it can be articulatory, auditory or linguistic (phonological), for example, and we have touched on the first and last in Chapter 2. The invention of the sound spectrograph in the late 1940s was an event of colossal significance for acoustic phonetics, for it somehow seemed to make the intricacies of speech visible. (This was thought to be a greater advance than actually turned out: historically-minded readers should refer to Potter *et al.*, 1947, for an enthusiastic contemporary appraisal of the invention.) A result of several years of research at Haskins Laboratories in New York during the 1950s was a set of "minimal rules for synthesizing speech", which showed how stylized formant patterns could generate cues for identifying vowels and, particularly, consonants (Liberman, 1957; Liberman *et al.*, 1959).

These were to form the basis of many speech synthesis-by-rule computer programs in the ensuing decades. Such programs take as input a phonetic transcription of the utterance and generate a spoken version of it. The transcription may be broad or narrow, depending on the system. Experience has shown that the Haskins rules really are minimal, and the success of a synthesis-by-rule program depends on a vast collection of minutia, each seemingly insignificant in isolation but whose effects combine to influence the speech quality dramatically. The best current systems produce clearly understandable speech which is nevertheless something of a strain to listen to for long periods. However many are not good, and some are execrable. In recent times commercial influences have unfortunately restricted the free exchange of results and programs between academic researchers, thus slowing down progress. Research attention has turned to prosodic factors, which are certainly less well understood than segmental ones, and to synthesis from plain English text rather than from phonetic transcriptions.

The remainder of this chapter describes the techniques of segmental synthesis. First it is necessary to introduce some elements of acoustic phonetics. It may be worth re-reading Chapter 2 at this point, to refresh your memory about the classification of speech sounds.

7.4 Acoustic Characterization of Phonemes

Shortly after the invention of the sound spectrograph, an inverse instrument was developed, called the "pattern playback" synthesizer. This took as input a spectrogram, either in its original form or painted by hand. An optical arrangement was used to modulate the amplitude of some fifty harmonically-related oscillators by the lightness or darkness of each point on the frequency axis of the spectrogram. As it was drawn past the playing head, sound was produced which had approximately the frequency components shown on the spectrogram, although the fundamental frequency was constant.

This device allowed the complicated acoustic effects seen on a spectrogram (see for example Figs 2.3 and 2.4) to be replayed in either original or simplified form. Hence the features which are important for perception of the different sounds could be isolated. The procedure was to copy from an actual spectrogram the features which were most prominent visually, and then to make further changes by trial and error until the result was judged to have reasonable intelligibility when replayed.

For the purpose of acoustic characterization of particular phonemes, it is useful to consider the central, steady-state part separately from transitions into and out of the segment. The steady-state part is that sound which is heard when the phoneme is prolonged. The term "phoneme" is being used in a rather loose sense here: it is more appropriate to think of a "sound segment" rather than the abstract unit which forms the basis of phonological classification, and this is the terminology I will adopt.

The essential auditory characteristics of some sound segments are inherent in their steady states. If a vowel, for example, is spoken and prolonged, it can readily be identified by listening to any part of the utterance. This is not true for diphthongs: if you say "I" very slowly and freeze your vocal tract posture at any time, the resulting steady-state sound will not be sufficient to identify the diphthong. Rather, it will be a vowel somewhere between *aa* (in "had") or *ar* (in "hard") and *ee* (in "heed"). Neither is it true for glides, for prolonging *w* (in "want") or *y* (in "you") results in vowels resembling respectively *u* ("hood") or *ee* ("heed"). Fricatives, voiced or unvoiced, can be identified from the steady state; but stops can not, for theirs is silent (or, in the case of voiced stops, something close to it).

Segments which are identifiable from their steady state are easy to synthesize. The difficulty lies with the others, for it must be the transitions which carry the information. Thus "transitions" are an essential part of speech, and perhaps the term is unfortunate for it calls to mind an unimportant bridge between one segment and the next. It is tempting to use the words "continuant" and "non-continuant" to distinguish the two categories; unfortunately they are used by phoneticians in a different sense. We will call them "steady-state" and "transient" segments. The latter term is not particularly appropriate, for even sounds in this class *can* be prolonged; the point is that the identifying information is in the transitions rather than the steady state.

Steady-state Segments

Table 7.2 shows appropriate values for the resonance parameters and excitation sources of a resonance synthesizer, for steady-state segments only. There are several points to note about it. First, all the frequencies involved obviously depend upon the speaker: the size of his vocal tract, his accent and speaking habits. The values given are nominal ones for a male speaker with a dialect of British English called "received pronunciation" (RP), for it is what used to be "received" on the wireless in the old days before the British Broadcasting Corporation adopted a policy of more informal, more regional, speech. Female speakers have formant frequencies approximately 15% higher than male ones. Secondly, the third formant is relatively unimportant for vowel identification; it is the first and second that give the vowels their character. Thirdly, formant values for *h* are not given, for they would be meaningless. Although it is certainly a steady-state sound, *h* changes radically in context. If you say "had", "heed", "hud", and so on, and freeze your vocal tract posture on the initial *h*, you will find it already configured for the following vowel: an excellent example of anticipatory coarticulation. Fourthly, amplitude values do play some part in identification, particularly for fricatives. *th* is the weakest sound, closely followed by *f*, with *s* and *sh* the strongest. It is necessary to get a reasonable mix of excitation in the voiced fricatives; the voicing amplitude is considerably less than in vowels. Finally, there are other sounds that might be considered

Table 7.2. Resonance synthesizer parameters for steady-state sounds.

		Excitation	Formant resonance frequencies (Hz)			Fricative resonance (Hz)
uh	(the)	voicing	500	1500	2500	
a	(bud)	voicing	700	1250	2550	
e	(head)	voicing	550	1950	2650	
i	(hid)	voicing	350	2100	2700	
o	(hod)	voicing	600	900	2600	
u	(hood)	voicing	400	950	2450	
aa	(had)	voicing	750	1750	2600	
ee	(heed)	voicing	300	2250	3100	
er	(heard)	voicing	600	1400	2450	
ar	(hard)	voicing	700	1100	2550	
aw	(hoard)	voicing	450	750	2650	
uu	(food)	voicing	300	950	2300	
h	(he)	aspiration				
s	(sin)	frication				6000
z	(zed)	frication and voicing				6000
sh	(shin)	frication				2300
zh	(vision)	frication and voicing				2300
f	(fin)	frication				4000
v	(vat)	frication and voicing				4000
th	(thin)	frication				5000
dh	(that)	frication and voicing				5000

steady state ones. You can probably identify *m, n,* and *ng* just by their steady states. However, the difference is not particularly strong; it is the transitional parts which discriminate most effectively between these sounds. The steady state of *r* is quite distinctive, too, for most speakers, because the top of the tongue is curled back in a so-called "retroflex" action and this causes a radical change in the third formant resonance.

Transient Segments

Transient sounds include diphthongs, glides, nasals, voiced and unvoiced stops and affricates. The first two are relatively easy to characterize, for they are basically continuous, gradual transitions from one vocal tract posture to another: sort of dynamic vowels. Diphthongs and glides are similar to each other. In fact "you" could be transcribed as a triphthong, *i e uu,* except that in the initial posture the tongue is even higher, and the vocal tract correspondingly more constricted, than in *i* ("hid"); though not as constricted as in *sh.* Both categories can be represented in terms of target formant values, on the understanding that these are not to be interpreted as steady state configurations but strictly as extreme values at the beginning or end of the formant motion (for transitions out of and into the segment, respectively).

Nasals have a steady-state portion comprising a strong nasal formant at a fairly low frequency, on account of the large size of the combined nasal and oral cavity which is resonating. Higher formants are relatively weak, because of attenuation effects. Transitions into and out of nasals are strongly nasalized, as indeed are adjacent vocalic segments, with the oral and nasal tract operating in parallel. As discussed in Chapter 5, this cannot be simulated on a series synthesizer. However, extremely fast motions of the formants occur on account of the binary switching action of the velum, and it turns out that fast formant transitions are sufficient to simulate nasals because the speech perception mechanism is accustomed to hearing them only in that context! Contrast this with the extremely slow transitions in diphthongs and glides.

Stops form the most interesting category, and research using the pattern playback synthesizer was instrumental in providing adequate acoustic characterizations for them. Consider unvoiced stops. They each have three phases: transition in, silent central portion, and transition out. There is a lot of action on the transition out (and many phoneticians would divide this part alone into several "phases"). First, as the release occurs, there is a small burst of fricative noise. Say "t t t ..." as in "tut-tut", without producing any voicing. Actually, when used as an admonishment this is accompanied by an ingressive, inhaling air-stream instead of the normal egressive, exhaling one used in English speech (although some languages do have ingressive sounds). In any case, a short fricative somewhat resembling a tiny s can be heard as the tongue leaves the roof of the mouth. Frication is produced when the gap is very narrow, and ceases rapidly as it becomes wider. Next, when an unvoiced stop is released, a significant amount of aspiration follows the release. Say "pot", "tot", "cot" with force and you will hear the h-like aspiration quite clearly. It doesn't always occur, though: for example you will hear little aspiration when a fricative like s precedes the stop in the same syllable, as in "spot", "scot". The aspiration is a distinguishing feature between "white spot" and the rather unlikely "White's pot". It tends to increase as the emphasis on the syllable increases, and this is an example of a prosodic feature influencing segmental characteristics. Finally, at the end of the segment, the aspiration (if any) will turn to voicing.

What has been described applies to all unvoiced stops. What distinguishes one from another? The tiny fricative burst will be different because the noise is produced at different places in the vocal tract: at the lips for p, tongue and front of palate for t, and tongue and back of palate for k. The most important difference, however, is the formant motion illuminated by the last vestiges of voicing at closure and by both aspiration and the onset of voicing at opening. Each stop has target formant values which, although they cannot be heard during the stopped portion (for there is no sound there), do affect the transitions in and out. An added complexity is that the target positions themselves vary to some extent depending on the adjacent segments. If the stop is heavily aspirated, the vocal posture will have almost attained that for the following vowel before voicing begins, but the formant transitions will be perceived because they affect the sound quality of aspiration.

The voiced stops *b*, *d* and *g* are quite similar to their unvoiced analogues *p*, *t* and *k*. What distinguishes them from each other are the formant transitions to target positions, heard during closure and opening. They are distinguished from their unvoiced counterparts by the fact that more voicing is present: it lingers on longer at closure and begins earlier on opening. Thus little or no aspiration appears during the opening phase. If an unvoiced stop is uttered in a context where aspiration is suppressed, as in "spot", it is almost identical to the corresponding voiced stop, "sbot". Luckily no words in English require us to make a distinction in such contexts. Voicing sometimes pervades the entire stopped portion of a voiced stop, especially when it is surrounded by other voiced segments. When saying a word like "baby" slowly you can choose whether or not to prolong voicing throughout the second *b*. If you do, creating what is called a "voice bar" in spectrograms, the sound escapes through the cheeks, for the lips are closed: try doing it for a very long time and your cheeks will fill up with air! This severely attenuates high-frequency components, and can be simulated with a weak first formant at a low resonant frequency.

Table 7.3 summarizes some of the acoustic phases of voiced and unvoiced stops. There are many variations that have not been mentioned. Nasal plosion ("good news") occurs (at the word boundary, in this case) when

Table 7.3. Acoustic phases of stop consonants.

unvoiced stops:	closure (early cessation of voicing)
	silent steady state
	opening, comprising
	   short fricative burst
	   aspiration burst (context- and emphasis-dependent)
	   onset of voicing

voiced stops:	closure (late cessation of voicing)
	steady state (possibility of voice bar)
	opening, comprising
	   pre-voicing
	   short fricative burst

the nasal formant pervades the opening phase. Stop bursts are suppressed when the next sound is a stop too (the burst on the p of "apt", for example). It is difficult to distinguish a voiced stop from an unvoiced one at the end of a word ("cab" and "cap"); if the speaker is trying to make himself particularly clear, he will put a short neutral vowel after the voiced stop to emphasize its early onset of voicing. (If he is Italian he will probably do this anyway, for it is the norm in his own language.)

Finally we turn to affricates, of which there are only two in English: *ch* ("chin") and *j* ("djinn"). They are very similar to the stops *t* and *d* followed by the fricatives *sh* and *zh* respectively, and their acoustic characterization is similar to that of the phoneme pair. *ch* has a closing phase, a stopped phase, and a long fricative burst. There is no aspiration, for the vocal cords are not involved. *j* is the same except that voicing extends further into the stopped portion, and the terminating fricative is also voiced. It may be pronounced with a voice bar if the preceding segment is voiced ("adjunct").

7.5 Speech Synthesis by Rule

Generation of speech by rules acting upon a phonetic transcription was first investigated in the early 1960s (Kelly and Gerstman, 1961). Most systems employ a hardware resonance synthesizer, analogue or digital, series or parallel, to reduce the load on the computer which operates the rules. The speech-by-rule program, rather than the synthesizer, inevitably contributes by far the greater part of the degradation in the resulting speech. Although parallel synthesizers offer greater potential control over the spectrum, it is not clear to what extent a synthesis program can take advantage of this. Parameter tracks for a series synthesizer can easily be converted into linear predictive coefficients, and systems which use a linear predictive synthesizer will probably become popular in the near future.

The phrase "synthesis by rule", which is in common use, does not make it clear just what sort of features the rules are supposed to accommodate, and what information must be included explicitly in the input transcription. Early systems made no attempt to simulate prosodics. Pitch and rhythm could be controlled, but only by inserting pitch specifiers and duration markers in the input. Some kind of prosodic control was often incorporated later, but usually as a completely separate phase from segmental synthesis. This does not allow interaction effects (such as the extra aspiration for voiceless stops in accented syllables) to be taken into account easily. Even systems which perform prosodic operations invariably need to have prosodic specifications embedded explicitly in the input.

Generating parameter tracks for a synthesizer from a phonetic transcrip-

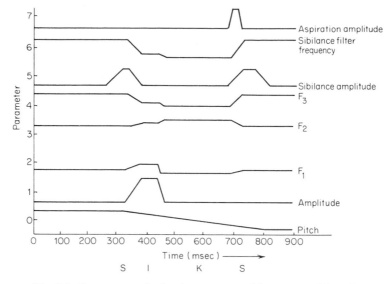

Fig. 7.1. Parameter tracks for the utterance *s i k s,* generated by rule.

tion is a process of data *expansion.* Six bits are ample to specify a phoneme, and a speaking rate of 12 phonemes/sec leads to an input data rate of 72 bit/s. The data rate required to control the synthesizer will depend upon the number of parameters and the rate at which they are sampled, but a typical figure is 6 Kbit/s (Chapter 5). Hence there is something like a hundredfold data expansion.

Figure 7.1 shows the parameter tracks for a series synthesizer's rendering of the utterance *s i k s.* There are eight parameters. You can see the onset of frication at the beginning and end (parameter 5), and the amplitude of voicing (parameter 1) come on for the *i* and off again before the *k.* The pitch (parameter 0) is falling slowly throughout the utterance. These tracks are stylized: they come from a computer synthesis-by-rule program and not from a human utterance. With a parameter update rate of 10 msec, the graphs can be represented by 90 sets of eight parameter values, a total of 720 values or 4320 bits if a 6-bit representation is used for each value. Contrast this with the input of only four phoneme segments, or say 24 bits.

A Segment-by-segment System

A seminal paper appearing in 1964 was the first comprehensive description of a computer-based synthesis-by-rule system (Holmes *et al.,* 1964). The same system is still in use and has been reimplemented in a more portable form (Wright, 1976). The inventory of sound segments includes the phonemes listed in Table 2.1, as well as diphthongs and a second allophone of *l*. (Many British speakers use quite a different vocal posture for pre- and post-vocalic *l*'s, called clear and dark *l*'s respectively.) Some phonemes are expanded into sub-phonemic "phases" by the program. Stops have three phases, corresponding to the closure, silent steady state, and opening. Diphthongs have two phases. We will call individual phases and single-phase phonemes "segments", for they are subject to exactly the same transition rules.

Parameter tracks are constructed out of linear pieces. Consider a pair of adjacent segments in an utterance to be synthesized. Each one has a steady-state portion and an internal transition. The internal transition of one phoneme is dubbed "external" as far as the other is concerned. This is important because instead of each segment being responsible for its own internal transition, one of the pair is identified as "dominant", and it controls the duration of both transitions: its internal one and its external (the other's internal) one. For example, in Fig. 7.2 the segment *sh* dominates *ee*, and so it governs the duration of both transitions shown. Note that each segment contributes as many as three linear pieces to the parameter track.

The notion of domination is similar to that discussed earlier for word concatenation. The difference is that for word concatenation, the dominant segment was determined by computing the spectral derivative over the transition region, whereas for synthesis-by-rule segments are ranked according to a static precedence, and the higher-ranking segment dominates. Segments of stop consonants have the highest rank (and also the greatest spectral derivative), while fricatives, nasals, glides, and vowels follow in that order.

The concatenation procedure is controlled by a table which associates 25 quantities with each segment. They are:

rank
2 overall durations (for stressed and unstressed occurrences)

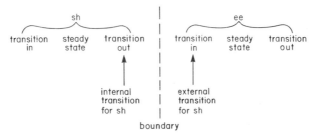

Fig. 7.2. Internal and external transitions between two segments.

4 transition durations (for internal and external transitions of formant frequencies and amplitudes)
8 target parameter values (amplitudes and frequencies of three formant resonances, plus fricative information)
5 quantities which specify how to calculate boundary values for formant frequencies (two for each formant except the third, which has only one)
5 quantities which specify how to calculate boundary values for amplitudes.

This table is rather large. There are 80 segments in all (remember that many phonemes are represented by more than one segment), and so it has 2000 entries. The system was an offline one which ran on what was then (1964) a large computer.

The advantage of such a large table of "rules" is the flexibility it affords. Notice that transition durations are specified independently for formant frequency and amplitude parameters; this permits fine control which is particularly useful for stops. For each parameter, the boundary value between segments is calculated using a fixed contribution from the dominant one and a proportion of the steady state value of the other.

It is possible that the two transition durations which are calculated for a segment actually exceed the overall duration specified for it. In this case, the steady-state target values will be approached but not actually attained, simulating a situation where coarticulation effects prevent a target value from being reached.

An Event-based System

The synthesis system described above, in common with many others, takes an uncompromisingly segment-by-segment view of speech. The next phoneme is read, perhaps split into a few segments, and these are synthesized one by one with due attention being paid to transitions between them. Some later work has taken a more syllabic view. Mattingly (1976) urges a return to syllables for both practical and theoretical reasons. Transitional effects are particularly strong within a syllable and comparatively weak (but by no means negligible) from one syllable to the next. From a theoretical viewpoint, there are much stronger phonetic restrictions on phoneme sequences than there are on syllable sequences: pretty well any syllable can follow another (although whether the pair makes sense is a different matter), but the linguistically acceptable phoneme sequences are only a fraction of those formed by combining phonemes in all possible ways. Hill (1978) argues against what he calls the "segmental assumption", that progress through the utterance should be made one segment at a time, and recommends a description of speech based upon perceptually relevant "events". This framework is interesting because it provides an opportunity for prosodic considerations to be treated as an integral part of the synthesis process.

The phonetic segments and other information that specify an utterance can be regarded as a list of events which describes it at a relatively high level. Synthesis-by-rule is the act of taking this list and elaborating on it to produce lower-level events which are realized by the vocal tract, or acoustically simulated by a resonance synthesizer, to give a speech waveform. In articulatory terms, an event might be "begin tongue motion towards upper teeth with a given effort", while in resonance terms it could be "begin second formant transition towards 1500 Hz at a given rate". (These two examples are *not* intended to describe the same event: a tongue motion causes much more than the transition of a single formant.) Coarticulation issues such as stop burst suppression and nasal plosion should be easier to imitate within an event-based scheme than a segment-to-segment one.

The ISP system (Witten and Abbess, 1979) is event-based. The key to its operation is the *synthesis list*. To prepare an utterance for synthesis, the lexical items which specify it are joined into a linked list. Figure 7.3 shows the start of the list created for

1 *dhis iz /*dzhaaks /haaus*

(this is Jack's house); the "1 ... /* ... / ..." are prosodic markers which will be discussed in the next chapter. Next, the rhythm and pitch assignment routines augment the list with syllable boundaries, phoneme cluster identifiers, and duration and pitch specifications. Then it is passed to the segmental synthesis routine which chains events into the appropriate places

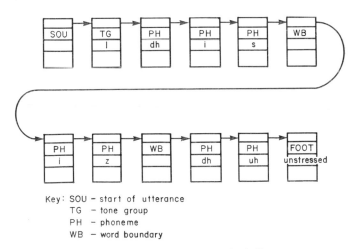

Key: SOU – start of utterance
     TG – tone group
     PH – phoneme
     WB – word boundary

Fig. 7.3. Start of an ISP synthesis list.

and, as it proceeds, removes the no longer useful elements (phoneme names, pitch specifiers, etc.) which originally constituted the synthesis list. Finally, an interrupt-driven speech synthesizer handler removes events from the list as they become due and uses them to control the hardware synthesizer.

By adopting the synthesis list as a uniform data structure for holding utterances at every stage of processing, the problems of storage allocation and garbage collection are minimized. Each list element has a forward pointer and five data words, the first indicating what type of element it is. Lexical items which may appear in the input are

end of utterance (".", "!", ",", ";")
intonation indicator ("1", ...)
rhythm indicator ("/", "/*")
word boundary (" ")
syllable boundary ("'")
phoneme segment (*ar*, *b*, *ng*, ...)
explicit duration or pitch information.

Several of these have to do with prosodic features: a prime advantage of the structure is that it does not create an artificial division between segmentals and prosody. Syllable boundaries and duration and pitch information are optional. They will normally be computed by ISP, but the user can override them in the input in a natural way. The actual characters which identify lexical items are not fixed but are taken from the rule table.

As synthesis proceeds, new elements are chained in to the synthesis list. For segmental purposes, three types of event are defined: target events, increment events and aspiration events. With each event is associated a time at which the event becomes due. For a target event, a parameter number, target parameter value and time-increment are specified. When it becomes due, motion of the parameter towards the target is begun. If no other event for that parameter intervenes, the target value will be reached after the given time-increment. However, another target event for the parameter may change its motion before the target has been attained. Increment events contain a parameter number, a parameter increment and a time-increment. The fixed increment is added to the parameter value throughout the time specified. This provides an easy way to make a fricative burst during the opening phase of a stop consonant. Aspiration events switch the mode of excitation from voicing to aspiration for a given period of time. Thus the aspirated part of unvoiced stops can be accommodated in a natural manner, by changing the mode of excitation for the duration of the aspiration.

Now the rule table, which is shown in Table 7.4, holds simple target positions for each phoneme segment, as well as the segment type. The latter is used to trigger events by computer procedures which have access to the

Table 7.4. Rule table for an event-based synthesis-by-rule program.

	Excitation	Formant resonance frequencies (Hz)			Fricative resonance (Hz)	Type
uh	voicing	490	1480	2500		vowel
a	voicing	720	1240	2540		vowel
e	voicing	560	1970	2640		vowel
i	voicing	360	2100	2700		vowel
o	voicing	600	890	2600		vowel
u	voicing	380	950	2440		vowel
aa	voicing	750	1750	2600		vowel
ee	voicing	290	2270	3090		long vowel
er	voicing	580	1380	2440		long vowel
ar	voicing	680	1080	2540		long vowel
aw	voicing	450	740	2640		long vowel
uu	voicing	310	940	2320		long vowel
h	aspiration					h
r	voicing	240	1190	1550		glide
w	voicing	240	650			glide
l	voicing	380	1190			glide
y	voicing	240	2270			glide
m	voicing	190	690	2000		nasal
b	none	100	690	2000		stop
p	none	100	690	2000		stop
n	voicing	190	1780	3300		nasal
d	none	100	1780	3300		stop
t	none	100	1780	3300		stop
ng	voicing	190	2300	2500		nasal
g	none	100	2300	2500		stop
k	none	100	2300	2500		stop
s	frication				6000	fricative
z	voice + fric	190	1780	3300	6000	fricative
sh	frication				2300	fricative
zh	voice + fric	190	2120	2700	2300	fricative
f	frication				4000	fricative
v	voice + fric	190	690	3300	4000	fricative
th	frication				5000	fricative
dh	voice + fric	190	1780	3300	5000	fricative

context of the segment. In principle, this allows considerably more sophistication to be introduced than does a simple segment-by-segment approach.

For example, Table 7.5 summarizes some of the subtleties of the speech production process which have been mentioned earlier in this chapter. Most of them are context-dependent, with the prosodic context (whether two segments are in the same syllable; whether a syllable is stressed) playing a significant role. A scheme where data-dependent "demons" fire on par-

Table 7.5. Some coarticulation effects.

---

fricative bursts on stops
aspiration bursts on unvoiced stops, affected by
   preceding consonant in this syllable (suppress burst if fricative)
   following consonant (suppress burst if another stop; introduce nasal plosion if a
     nasal)
   prosodics (increase burst if syllable is stressed)
voice bar on voiced stops (in intervocalic position)
post-voicing on terminating voiced stops, if syllable is stressed
anticipatory coarticulation for *h*
vowel colouring when a nasal or glide follows

---

ticular patterns in a linked list seems to be a sensible approach towards incorporating such rules.

Discussion

There are two opposing trends in speech synthesis by rule. On the one hand, larger and larger segment inventories can be used, containing more and more allophones explicitly. This is the approach of the Votrax sound-segment synthesizer discussed in Chapter 11. It puts an increasing burden on the person who codes the utterances for synthesis, although as we shall see, computer programs can assist with this task. On the other hand, the segment inventory can be kept small, perhaps comprising just the logical phonemes as in the ISP system. This places the onus on the computer program to accommodate allophonic variations, and to do so it must take account of the segmental and prosodic context of each phoneme. An event-based approach seems to give the best chance of incorporating contextual modification while avoiding undesired interactions.

The second trend brings synthesis closer to the articulatory process of speech production. In fact an event-based system would be an ideal way of implementing an articulatory model for speech synthesis by rule. It would be much more satisfying to have the rule table contain articulatory target positions instead of resonance ones, with events like "begin tongue motion towards upper teeth with a given effort". The problem is that hard data on articulatory postures and constraints is much more difficult to gather than resonance information.

An interesting question that relates to articulation is whether formant motion can be simulated adequately by a small number of linear pieces. The segment-by-segment system described above had as many as nine pieces for a single phoneme, for some phonemes had three phrases and each one contributes up to three pieces (transition in, steady state, and transition out). Another system used curves of decaying exponential form which ensured that all transitions started rapidly towards the target position but slowed down as it was approached (Rabiner, 1968, 1969). The time-constant of decay was stored with each segment in the rule table. The rhythm of the synthetic speech was controlled at this level, for the next segment was begun when all the formants had attained values sufficiently close to the current targets. This is a poor model of the human speech production process, where rhythm is dictated at a relatively high level and the next phoneme is not simply started when the current one happens to end. Nevertheless, the algorithm produced smooth, continuous formant motions not unlike those found in spectrograms.

There is, however, by no means universal agreement on decaying exponential formant motions. Lawrence (1974) divided segments into "checked" and "free" categories, corresponding roughly to consonants and vowels; and postulated *increasing* exponential transitions into checked segments, and decaying transitions into free ones. This is a reasonable supposition if you consider the mechanics of articulation. The speed of movement of the tongue (for example) is likely to increase until it is physically stopped by reaching the roof of the mouth. When moving away from a checked posture into a free one, the transition will be rapid at first but slow down to approach the target asymptotically, governed by proprioceptive feedback.

The only thing that seems to be agreed is that the formant tracks should certainly *not* be piecewise linear. However, in the face of conflicting opinions as to whether exponentials should be decaying or increasing, piecewise linear motions seem to be a reasonable compromise! It is likely that the precise shape of formant tracks is unimportant so long as the gross features are imitated correctly. Nevertheless, this is a question which an articulatory model could help to answer.

7.6 References

Dixon, N.R. and Maxey, H.D. (1968). Terminal analogue synthesis of continuous speech using the diphone method of segment assembly. *IEEE Trans Audio and Electroacoustics*, **AU-16**(1) 40–50, March.

Hill, D.R. (1978). A program structure for event-based speech synthesis by rules within a flexible segmental framework *Int J Man-Machine Studies*, **10**(3) 285–294, May.

Holmes, J.N., Mattingly, I.G. and Shearme, J.N. (1964). Speech synthesis by rule. *Language and Speech* **7**(3) 127–143, July–September.

Kelly, J.L. and Gerstman, J.L. (1961). An artificial talker driven from a phonetic input. *J Acoustical Society of America*, **33**, 835 (abstract).

Lawrence, W. (1974). The phoneme, the syllable, and the parameter track. *Proc Speech Communication Seminar*, Stockholm, August 1–3.

Levinson, S.E. and Shipley, K.L. (1980). A conversational-mode airline information and reservation system using speech input and output. *Bell System Technical J*, **59**(1) 119–137, January.

Liberman, A.M. (1957). Some results of research on speech perception. *J Acoustical Society of America* **29**(1) 117–123.

Liberman, A.M., Ingemann, F., Lisker, L., Delattre, P. and Cooper, F.S. (1959). Minimal rules for synthesising speech. *J Acoustical Society of America*, **31**(11) 1490–1499, November.

Lovins, J.B. and Fujimura, O. (1976). Synthesis of English monosyllables by demi-syllable concatenation. Presented at 92nd meeting of Acoustical Society of America, San Diego, California, November.

Macchi, M.J. and Nigro, G. (1977). Syllable affixes in speech synthesis. Presented at 93rd meeting of Acoustical Society of America, Pennsylvania State University, June.

Mattingly, I.G. (1976). Syllable synthesis. Presented at 92nd meeting of Acoustical Society of America, San Diego, California, November.

Olive, J. (1975). Fundamental frequency rules for the synthesis of simple declarative English sentences. *J Acoustical Society of America*, **57**(2) 476–482, February.

Potter, R.K., Kopp, G. A. and Green, H.C. (1947). Visible speech, Van Nostrand, New York.

Rabiner, L.R. (1968). Speech synthesis by rule: an acoustic domain approach. *Bell System Technical J*, **47**(1) 17–37, January.

Rabiner, L.R. (1969). A model for synthesizing speech by rule. *IEEE Trans Audio and Electroacoustics*, **AU-17**, 7–13, March.

Rabiner, L.R., Schafer, R.W. and Flanagan, J.L. (1971). Computer synthesis of speech by concatenation of formant-coded words. *Bell System Technical J*, **50**(5) 1541–1558, May–June.

Stowe, A.N. and Hampton, D.B. (1961). Speech synthesis with pre-recorded syllables and words. *J Acoustical Society of America*, **33**(6) 810–811, June.

Witten, I.H. and Abbess, J. (1979). "A microcomputer-based real-time speech synthesis-by-rule system" *Int J Man-Machine Studies*, **11**(5) 585–620, September.

Wright, R.D. (1976). "A system for implementing rule synthesis of speech" *Proc Institute of Acoustics Autumn Conference*, 2/20/1–2/20/4, Edinburgh.

7.7 Further Reading

There are unfortunately few books to recommend on the subject of joining segments of speech. The references form a representative and moderately comprehensive bibliography. Here is some relevant background reading in linguistics.

Fry, D.B. (Editor) (1976). "Acoustic phonetics". Cambridge Univ Press, Cambridge, England.
> This book of readings contains many classic papers on acoustic phonetics published from 1922–1965. It covers much of the history of the subject, and is intended primarily for students of linguistics.

Lehiste, I. (Editor) (1967). "Readings in acoustic phonetics", MIT Press, Cambridge, Massachusetts.
> Another basic collection of references which covers much the same ground as Fry (1976), above.

Sivertsen, E. (1961). Segment inventories for speech synthesis. *Language and Speech*, **4**, 27–89.
   This is a careful early study of the quantitative implications of using phonemes, demisyllables, syllables, and words as the basic building blocks for speech synthesis.

8

PROSODIC FEATURES IN SPEECH SYNTHESIS

Prosodic features are those which characterize an utterance as a whole, rather than having a local influence on individual sound segments. For speech output from computers, an "utterance" usually comprises a single unit of information which stretches over several words: a clause or sentence. In natural speech an utterance can be very much longer, but it will be broken into prosodic units which are again roughly the size of a clause or sentence. These prosodic units are certainly closely related to each other. For example, the pitch contour used when introducing a new topic is usually different from those employed to develop it subsequently. However, for the purposes of synthesis, the successive prosodic units can be treated independently, and information about pitch contours to be used will have to be specified in the input for each one. The independence between them is not complete, however, and lower-level contextual effects, such as interpolation of pitch between the end of one prosodic unit and the start of the next, must still be imitated.

Prosodic features were introduced briefly in Chapter 2. Variations in voice dynamics occur in three dimensions: pitch of the voice, time and amplitude. These dimensions are inextricably twined together in living speech. Variations in voice quality are much less important for the factual kind of speech usually sought in voice response applications, although they can play a considerable role in conveying emotions (for a discussion of the acoustic manifestations of emotion in speech, see Williams and Stevens, 1972).

The distinction between prosodic and segmental effects is a traditional one, but it becomes rather fuzzy when examined in detail. It is analogous to the distinction between hardware and software in computer science: although useful from some points of view, the borderline becomes blurred as one gets closer to actual systems: with microcode, interrupts, memory management and the like. At a trivial level, prosodics cannot exist without segmentals, for there must be some vehicle to carry the prosodic contrasts. Timing, a prosodic feature, is actually realized by the durations of individual segments. Pauses are tantamount to silent segments.

While pitch may seem to be relatively independent of segmentals (and this view is reinforced by the success of the source-filter model which separates the frequency of the excitation source from the filter characteristics), there are some subtle phonetic effects of pitch. It has been observed that it drops on the transition into certain consonants, and rises again on the transition out (Haggard *et al.*, 1970). This can be explained in terms of variations in pressure from the lungs on the vocal cords (Ladefoged, 1967). Briefly, the increase in mouth pressure which occurs during some consonants causes a reduction in the pressure difference across the vocal cords and in the rate of flow of air between them. This results in a decrease in their frequency of vibration. When the constriction is released, there is a temporary increase in the air flow which increases the pitch again. The phenomenon is called "microintonation". It is particularly noticeable in voiced stops, but also occurs in voiced fricatives and unvoiced stops. Simulation of the effect in synthesis-by-rule has often been found to give noticeable improvements in the speech quality.

Loudness also has a segmental role. For example, we noted in the last chapter that amplitude values play a small part in identification of fricatives. In fact loudness is a very *weak* prosodic feature. It contributes little to the perception of stress. Even for shouting, the distinction from normal speech is as much in the voice quality as in amplitude *per se*. It is not necessary to consider varying loudness on a prosodic basis in most speech synthesis systems.

The above examples show how prosodic features have segmental influences as well. The converse is also true: some segmental features have a prosodic effect. The last chapter described how stress is associated with increased aspiration of syllable-initial unvoiced stops. Furthermore, stressed syllables are articulated with greater effort than unstressed ones, and hence the formant transitions are more likely to attain their target values under circumstances which would otherwise cause them to fall short. In unstressed syllables, extreme vowels (like *ee, aa, uu*) tend to more centralized sounds (like *i, uh, u* respectively). Although all British English vowels *can* appear in unstressed syllables, they often become "reduced" into a centralized form. Consider the following examples:

diplomat   *dipluhmaat*
diplomacy *dipluhumuhsi*
diplomatic *dipluhmaatik.*

The vowel of the second syllable is reduced to *uh* in "diplomat" and "diplomatic", whereas the root form "diploma", and also "diplomacy", has a diphthong (*uhu*) there. The third syllable has an *aa* in "diplomat" and "diplomatic" which is reduced to *uh* in "diplomacy". In these cases, the reduction is shown explicitly in the phonetic transcription; but in more marginal examples where it is less extreme it will not be.

I have tried to emphasize in previous chapters that prosodic features are important in speech synthesis. There is something very basic about them. Rhythm is an essential part of all bodily activity, of breathing, walking, working and playing, and so it pervades speech too. Mothers and babies communicate effectively using intonation alone. Some experiments have indicated that the language environment of an infant affects his babbling at an early age, before he has effective segmental control. There is no doubt that "tone of voice" plays a large part in human communication.

However, early attempts at synthesis did not pay too much attention to prosodics, perhaps because it was thought sufficient to get the meaning across by providing clear segmentals. As artificial speech grows more widespread, however, it is becoming apparent that its acceptability to users, and hence its ultimate success, depends to a large extent on incorporating natural-sounding prosodics. Flat, arhythmic speech may be comprehensible in short stretches, but it strains the concentration in significant discourse, and people are not usually prepared to listen to it. Unfortunately, current commercial speech output systems do not really tackle prosodic questions, which indicates our present rather inadequate state of knowledge.

The importance of prosodics for automatic speech *recognition* is beginning to be appreciated too. Some research projects have attended to the automatic identification of points of stress, in the hope that the clear articulation of stressed syllables can be used to provide anchor points in an unknown utterance (for example, see Lea *et al.*, 1975).

But prosodics and segmentals are closely intertwined. I have chosen to treat them in separate chapters in order to split the material up into manageable chunks rather than to enforce a deep division between them. It is also true that synthesis of prosodic features is an uncharted and controversial area, which gives this chapter rather a different flavour from the last. It is hard to be as definite about alternative strategies and methods as you can for segment concatenation. In order to make the treatment as concrete and down-to-earth as possible, I will describe in some detail two example projects in prosodic synthesis. The first treats the problem of transferring pitch from one utterance to another, while the second considers how artificial timing and pitch can be assigned to synthetic speech. These examples illustrate quite different problems, and are reasonably representative of current research activity. (Other systems are described by Mattingly, 1966; Rabiner *et al.*, 1969.) Before looking at the two examples, we will discuss a feature which is certainly prosodic but does not appear in the list given earlier: stress.

8.1 Stress

Stress is an everyday notion, and when listening to natural speech people can usually agree on which syllables are stressed. But it is difficult to characterize in acoustic terms. From the speaker's point of view, a stressed syllable is produced by pushing more air out of the lungs. For a listener, the points of stress are "obvious". You may think that stressed syllables are louder than the others: however, instrumental studies show that this is not necessarily (nor even usually) so (e.g. Lehiste and Peterson, 1959). Stressed syllables frequently have a longer vowel than unstressed ones, but this is by no means universally true: if you say "little" or "bigger", you will find that the vowel in the first, stressed, syllable is short and shows little sign of lengthening as you increase the emphasis. Moreover, experiments using bisyllabic nonsense words have indicated that some people consistently judge the *shorter* syllable to be stressed in the absence of other clues (Morton and Jassem, 1965). Pitch often helps to indicate stress. It is not that stressed syllables are always higher- or lower-pitched than neighbouring ones, or even that they are uttered with a rising or falling pitch. It is the *rate of change* of pitch that tends to be greater for stressed syllables: a sharp rise or fall, or a reversal of direction, helps to give emphasis.

Stress is acoustically manifested in timing and pitch, and to a much lesser extent in loudness. However it is a rather subtle feature and does *not* correspond simply to duration increases or pitch rises. It seems that listeners unconsciously put together all the clues that are present in an utterance in order to deduce which syllables are stressed. It may be that speech is perceived by a listener with reference to how he would have produced it himself, and that this is how he detects which syllables were given greater vocal effort.

The situation is confused by the fact that certain syllables in words are often said in ordinary language to be "stressed" on account of their position in the word. For example, the words "diplomat", "diplomacy" and "diplomatic" have stress on the first, second and third syllables respectively. But here we are talking about the word itself rather than any particular utterance of it. The "stress" is really *latent* in the indicated syllables, and only made manifest upon uttering them, and then to a greater or lesser degree depending on exactly how they are uttered.

Some linguists draw a careful distinction between salient syllables, accented syllables and stressed syllables, although the words are sometimes used differently by different authorities. I will not adopt a precise terminology here, but it is as well to be aware of the subtle distinctions involved. The term "salience" is applied to actual utterances, and salient syllables are those that are perceived as being more prominent than their neighbours.

"Accent" is the potential for salience, as marked, for example, in a dictionary or lexicon. Thus, the discussion of the "diplo-" words above is about accent. Stress is an articulatory phenomenon associated with increased muscular activity. Usually, syllables which are perceived as salient were produced with stress; but in shouting, for example, all syllables can be stressed: even non-salient ones. Furthermore, accented syllables may not be salient. For instance, the first syllable of the word "very" is accented, that is, potentially salient, but in a sentence as uttered it may or may not be salient. One can say

"he's very good"

with salience on "he" and possibly "good", or

"he's *very* good"

with salience on the first syllable of "very", and possibly "good".

Nonstandard stress patterns are frequently used to bring out contrasts. Words like "a" and "the" are normally unstressed, but can be stressed in contexts where ambiguity has arisen. Thus factors which operate at a much higher level than the phonetic structure of the utterance must be taken into account when deciding where stress should be assigned. These include syntactic and semantic considerations, as well as the attitude of the speaker and the likely attitude of the listener to the material being spoken. For example, I might say

"Anna *and* Nikki should go".

With emphasis on the "and" purely because I was aware that my listener might quibble about the expense of sending them both. Clearly some notation is needed to communicate to the synthesis process how the utterance is supposed to be rendered.

8.2 Transferring Pitch from One Utterance to Another

For speech stored in source-filter form and concatenated on a slot-filling basis, it would be useful to have stored typical pitch contours which can be applied to the synthetic utterances. From a practical point of view, it is important to be able to generate natural-sounding pitch for high-quality artificial speech. Although several algorithms for creating completely synthetic contours have been proposed (and we will examine one later in this chapter), they are unsuitable for high-quality speech. They are generally designed for use with synthesis-by-rule from phonetics, and the rather poor quality of articulation does not encourage the development of excellent pitch assignment procedures. With speech synthesized by rule there is generally an emphasis on keeping the data storage requirements to a minimum, and so it is not appropriate to store complete contours. Moreover, if speech is entered in textual form as phoneme strings, it is natural to attach pitch information as markers in the text rather than by entering a complete and detailed contour.

The picture is rather different for concatenated segments of natural speech. In the airline reservation system, with utterances formed from templates like

Flight number ___ leaves ___ at ___, arrives in ___ at ___,

it is attractive to store the pitch contour of one complete instance of the utterance and apply it to all synthetic versions.

There is an enormous literature on the anatomy of intonation, and much of it rests upon the notion of a pitch contour as a descriptive aid to analysis. Underlying this is the assumption, usually unstated, that a contour can be discussed independently of the particular stream of words that manifests it; that a single contour can somehow be bound to any sentence (or phrase, or clause) to produce an acceptable utterance. But the contour, and its binding, are generally described only at the grossest level, the details being left unspecified.

There are phonetic influences on pitch (the characteristic lowering during certain consonants was mentioned above) and these are not normally considered as part of intonation. Such effects will certainly spoil attempts to store contours extracted from living speech and apply them to different utterances, but the impairment may not be too great, for pitch is only one of many segmental clues to consonant identification.

In the system mentioned earlier which generated 7-digit telephone numbers by concatenating formant-coded words, a single natural pitch contour was applied to all utterances. It was taken to match as well as possible the general shape of the contours measured in naturally-spoken telephone numbers. However, this is a very restricted environment, for telephone numbers exhibit almost no variety in the configuration of stressed and unstressed syllables: the only digit which is not a monosyllable is "seven". Significant problems arise when more general utterances are considered.

Suppose the pitch contour of one utterance (the "source") is to be transferred to another (the "target"). Assume that the utterances are encoded in source-filter form, either as parameter tracks for a formant synthesizer or as linear predictive coefficients. Then there are no technical obstacles to combining pitch and segmentals. The source must be available as a complete utterance, while the target may be formed by concatenating smaller units such as words.

For definiteness, we will consider utterances of the form

The price is __ dollars and __ cents,

where the slots are filled by numbers less than 100; and of the form

The price is __ cents.

The domain of prices encompasses a wide range of syllable configurations. There are between one and five syllables in each variable part, if the numbers are restricted to be less than 100. The sentences have a constant pragmatic, semantic and syntactic structure. As in the vast majority of real-life situations, minimal phonetic distinctions between utterances do not occur.

Pitch transfer is complicated by the fact that values of the source pitch are only known during the voiced parts of the utterance. Although it would certainly be possible to extrapolate pitch over unvoiced parts, this would introduce some artificiality into the otherwise completely natural contours. Let us assume, therefore, that the pitch contour of the voiced nucleus of each syllable in the source is applied to the corresponding syllable nucleus in the target.

The primary factors which might tend to inhibit successful transfer are

—different numbers of syllables in the utterances,
—variations in the pattern of stressed and unstressed syllables,
—different syllable durations,
—pitch discontinuities,
—phonetic differences between the utterances.

Syllabification

It is essential to take into account the syllable structures of the utterances, so that pitch is transferred between corresponding syllables rather than over the utterance as a whole. Fortunately, syllable boundaries can be detected automatically with a fair degree of accuracy, especially if the speech is carefully enunciated. It is worth considering briefly how this can be done, even though it takes us off the main topic of synthesis and into speech analysis.

A procedure developed by Mermelstein (1975) involves integrating the spectral energy at each point in the utterance. First the low (<500 Hz) and high (>4000 Hz) ends are filtered out with 12 dB/octave cutoffs. The resulting energy signal is smoothed by a 40 Hz lowpass filter, giving a so-called "loudness" function. All this can be accomplished with simple recursive digital filters.

Then, the loudness function is compared with its convex hull. The convex hull is the shape a piece of elastic would assume if stretched over the top of the loudness function and anchored down at both ends, as illustrated in Fig. 8.1. The point of maximum difference between the hull and loudness function is taken to be a tentative syllable boundary. The hull is recomputed, but anchored to the actual loudness function at the tentative boundary, and the points of maximum hull-loudness difference in each of the two halves are selected as further tentative boundaries. The procedure continues recursively until the maximum hull-loudness difference, with the hull anchored at each tentative boundary, falls below a certain minimum (say 4 dB).

At this stage, the number of tentative boundaries will greatly exceed the actual number of syllables (by a factor of around 5). Many of the extraneous boundaries are eliminated by the following constraints:

—if two boundaries lie within a certain time of each other (say 120 msec), one of them is discarded;
—if the maximum loudness within a tentative syllable falls too far short of the overall maximum for the utterance (more than 20 dB), one boundary is discarded.

The question of which boundary to discard can be decided by examining the voicing continuity of the utterance. If possible, voicing across a syllable boundary should be avoided. Otherwise, the boundary with the smallest hull-loudness difference should be rejected.

Table 8.1 illustrates the success of this syllabification procedure, in a particular example. Segmentation is performed with less than 10% of extraneous boundaries being inserted, and much less than 10% of actual boundaries being missed. These figures are rather sensitive to the values of the

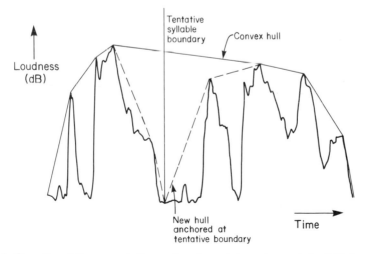

Fig. 8.1. Operation of the convex hull procedure for tentative assignment of syllable boundaries.

Table 8.1. Success of the syllable segmentation procedure.

total syllable count	332	
boundaries missed by algorithm	9	(3%)
extra boundaries inserted by algorithm	29	(9%)
boundaries moved slightly to correspond better with voicing	3	(1%)
total errors	41	(12%)

three thresholds. The values were chosen to err on the side of over-zealous syllabification, because all the boundaries need to be checked by ear and eye, and it is easier to delete a boundary by hand than to insert one at an appropriate place. It may well be that with careful optimization of thresholds, better figures could be achieved.

Stressed and Unstressed Syllables

If the source and target utterances have the same number of syllables, and the same pattern of stressed and unstressed syllables, pitch can simply be transferred from a syllable in the source to the corresponding one in the target. But if the pattern differs (even though the number of syllables may be the same, as in "eleven" and "seventeen") then a one-to-one mapping will conflict with the stress points, and certainly sound unnatural. Hence an attempt should be made to ensure that the pitch is mapped in a plausible way.

The syllables of each utterance can be classified as "stressed" and "unstressed". This distinction could be made automatically by inspection of the pitch contour, within the domain of utterances used, and possibly even in general (Lea *et al.*, 1975). However, in many cases it is expedient to perform the job by hand. In our example, the sentences have fixed "carrier" parts and variable "number" parts. The stressed carrier syllables, namely

"... price ... dol– ... cents",

can be marked as such, by hand, to facilitate proper alignment between the source and target. This marking would be difficult to do automatically because it would be hard to distinguish the carrier from the numbers.

Even after classifying the syllables as "carrier stressed", "stressed" and "unstressed", alignment still presents problems, because the configuration of syllables in the variable parts of the utterances may differ. Syllables in the source which have no correspondence in the target can be ignored. The pitch track of the source syllable can be replicated for each additional syllable in corresponding position in the target. Of course, a stressed syllable should be selected for copying if the unmatched target syllable is stressed, and

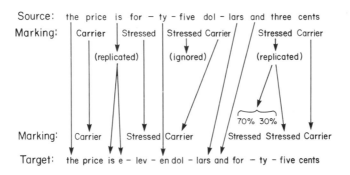

Fig. 8.2. Example of the pitch transfer procedure.

similarly for unstressed ones. It is rather dangerous to copy exactly a part of a pitch contour, for the ear is very sensitive to the juxtaposition of identically intoned segments of speech, especially when the segment is stressed. To avoid this, whenever a stressed syllable is replicated the pitch values should be decreased by, say, 20%, on the second copy. It sometimes happens that a single stressed syllable in the source needs to cover a stressed-unstressed pair in the target; in this case the first part of the source pitch track can be used for the stressed syllable, and the remainder for the unstressed one.

The example of Fig. 8.2 will help to make these rules clear. Note that the marking alone is done by hand. The detailed mapping decisions can be left to the computer. The rules were derived intuitively, and do not have any sound theoretical basis. They are intended to give reasonable results in the majority of cases.

Figure 8.3 shows the result of transferring the pitch from "the price is ten cents" to "the price is seventy-seven cents". The syllable boundaries which are marked were determined automatically. The use of the last 30% of the "ten" contour to cover the first "-en" syllable, and its replication to serve the "-ty" syllable, can be seen. However, the 70%–30% proportion is applied to the source contour, and the linear distortion (described next) upsets the proportion in the target utterance. The contour of the second "seven" can be seen to be a replication of that of the first one, lowered by 20%. Notice that the pitch extraction procedure has introduced an artifact into the final part of one of the "cents" contours by doubling the pitch.

Stretching and Squashing

The pitch contour over a source syllable nucleus must be stretched or squashed to match the duration of the target nucleus. It is difficult to see

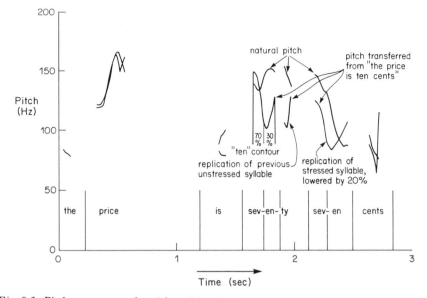

Fig. 8.3. Pitch contour transferred from "the price is ten cents" to "the price is seventy-seven cents".

how anything other than linear stretching and squashing could be done without considerably increasing the complexity of the procedure. The gross non-linearities will have been accounted for by the syllable alignment process, and so simple linear time-distortion should not cause too much degradation.

Pitch Discontinuities

Sudden jumps in pitch during voiced speech sound peculiar, although they can in fact be produced naturally (by yodelling). People frequently burst into laughter on hearing them in synthetic speech. It is particularly important to avoid this diverting effect in voice response applications, for the listener's attention is instantly directed away from what is said to the voice that speaks.

Discontinuities can arise in the pitch-transfer procedure either by a voiced-unvoiced-voiced transition between syllables mapping on to a voiced-voiced transition in the target, or by voicing continuity being broken when the syllable alignment procedure drops or replicates a syllable. There are several ways in which at least some of the possibilities can be avoided. For example, one could hold unstressed syllables at a constant pitch whose value coincides with either the end of the previous syllable's contour or the beginning of the next syllable's contour, depending on which transition is voiced. Alternatively, the policy of reserving the trailing part of a stressed syllable in the source to cover an unmatched following unstressed syllable in the target could be generalized to allow use of the leading 30% of the next stressed syllable's contour instead, if that maintained voicing continuity. A third solution is simply to merge the pitch contours at a discontinuity by mixing the average pitch value at the break with the pitch contour on either side of it in a proportion which increases linearly from the edges of the domain of influence to the discontinuity. Figure 8.4 shows the effect of this merging, when the pitch contour of "the price is seven cents" is transferred to "the price is eleven cents". Of course, the interpolated part will not necessarily be linear.

Results of an Experiment on Pitch Transfer

Some experiments have been conducted to evaluate the performance of this pitch transfer method on the kind of utterances discussed above (Witten, 1979). First, the source and target sentences were chosen to be lexically identical, that is, the same words were spoken. For this experiment alone, expert judges were employed. Each sentence was recorded twice (by the same person), and pitch was transferred from copy A to copy B and vice versa. Also, the originals were resynthesized from their linear predictive

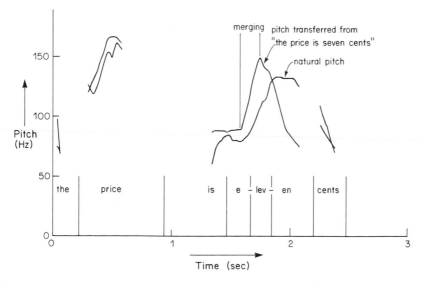

Fig. 8.4. Pitch contour transferred from "the price is seven cents" to "the price is eleven cents".

coefficients with their own pitch contours. Although all four often sounded extremely similar, sometimes the pitch contours of originals A and B were quite different, and in these cases it was immediately obvious to the ear that two of the four utterances shared the same intonation, which was different to that shared by the other two.

Experienced researchers in speech analysis-synthesis served as judges. In order to make the test as stringent as possible, it was explained to them exactly what had been done, except that the order of the utterances in each quadruple was kept secret. They were asked to identify which two of the four sentences did not have their original contours, and were allowed to listen to each quadruple as often as they liked. On occasion they were prepared to identify only one, or even none, of the sentences as artificial.

The result was that an utterance with pitch transferred from another, lexically identical, one is indistinguishable from a resynthesized version of the original, even to a skilled ear. (To be more precise, this hypothesis could not be rejected even at the 1% level of statistical significance.) This gave confidence in the transfer procedure. However, one particular judge was quite successful at identifying the bogus contours, and he attributed his success to the fact that on occasion, the segmental durations did not accord with the pitch contour. This casts a shadow of suspicion on the linear stretching and squashing mechanism.

The second experiment examined pitch transfers between utterances having only one variable part each ("the price is ... cents") to test the transfer method under relatively controlled conditions. Ten sentences of the form

"The price is ____ cents"

were selected to cover a wide range of syllable structures. Each one was regenerated with pitch transferred from each of the other nine, and these nine versions were paired with the original resynthesized with its natural pitch. The $10 \times 9 = 90$ resulting pairs were recorded on tape in random order.

Five males and five females, with widely differing occupations (secretaries, teachers, academics and students), served as judges. Written instructions explained that the tape contained pairs of sentences which were lexically identical but had a slight difference in "tone of voice", and that the subjects were to judge which of each pair sounded "most natural and intelligible". The response form gave the price associated with each pair (a preliminary experiment had shown that there was never any difficulty in identifying this) and a column for decision. With each decision, the subjects recorded their confidence in the decision. Subjects could rest at any time during the test, which lasted for about 30 minutes, but they were not permitted to hear any pair a second time.

Defining a "success" to be a choice of the utterance with natural pitch as the best of a pair, the overall success rate was about 60%. If choices were random, one would of course expect only a 50% success rate, and the figure obtained was significantly different from this. Almost half the choices were correct and made with high confidence; high-confidence but incorrect choices accounted for a quarter of the judgements.

To investigate structural effects in the pitch transfer process, low confidence decisions were ignored to eliminate noise, and the others lumped together and tabulated by source and target utterance. The number of stressed and unstressed syllables does not appear to play an important part in determining whether a particular utterance is an easy target. For example, it proved to be particularly difficult to tell natural from transferred contours with utterances $0.37 and $0.77. In fact, the results showed no better than random discrimination for them, even though the decisions in which listeners expressed little confidence had been discarded. Hence it seems that the syllable alignment procedure and the policy of replication were successful.

The worst target scores were for utterances $0.11 and $0.79. Both of these contained large unbroken voiced periods in the "variable" part: almost twice as long as the next longest voiced period. The first has an unstressed syllable followed by a stressed one with no break in voicing, involving, in a natural contour, a fast but continuous climb in pitch over the juncture, and it is not surprising that it proved to be the most difficult target. A more sophisticated "smoothing" algorithm than the one used may be worth investigating.

In a third experiment, sentences with two variable parts were used to check that the results of the second experiment extended to more complex utterances. The overall success rate was 75%, significantly different from chance. However, a breakdown of the results by source and target utterance showed that there was one contour (for the utterance "the price is 19 dollars and 8 cents") which exhibited very successful transfer, subjects identifying the transferred-pitch utterances at only a chance level.

Finally, transfers of pitch from utterances with two variable parts to those with one variable part were tested. Pitch contours were transferred to sentences with the same "cents" figure but no "dollars" part; for example, "the price is five dollars and thirteen cents", to "the price is thirteen cents". The contour was simply copied between the corresponding syllables, so that no adjustment needed to be made for different syllable structures. The overall score was 60 successes in 100 judgements: the same percentage as in the second experiment.

To summarize the results of these four experiments:

—even accomplished linguists cannot distinguish an utterance from one with pitch transferred from a different recording of it;

—when the utterance contained only one variable part embedded in a carrier sentence, lay listeners identified the original correctly in 60% of cases, over a wide variety of syllable structures: this figure differs significantly from the chance value of 50%;

—lay listeners identified the original confidently and correctly in 50% of cases; confidently but incorrectly in 25% of cases;

—the greatest hindrance to successful transfer was the presence of a long uninterrupted period of voicing in the target utterance;

—the performance of the method deteriorates as the number of variable parts in the utterances increases;

—some utterances seemed to serve better than others as the pitch source for transfer, although this was not correlated with complexity of syllable structure;

—even when the utterance contained two variable parts, there was one source utterance whose pitch contour was transferred to all the others so successfully that listeners could not identify the original.

The fact that only 60% of originals in the second experiment were spotted by lay listeners in a stringent paired-comparison test (many of them being identified without confidence) does encourage the use of the procedure for generating stereotyped, but different, utterances of high quality in voice-response systems. The experiments indicate that although different syllable patterns can be handled satisfactorily by this procedure, long voiced periods should be avoided if possible when designing the message set, and that if individual utterances must contain multiple variable parts the source utterance should be chosen with the aid of listening tests.

8.3 Assigning Timing and Pitch to Synthetic Speech

The pitch transfer method can give good results within a fairly narrow domain of application. But like any speech output technique which treats complete utterances as a single unit, with provision for a small number of slot-fillers to accomodate data-dependent messages, it becomes unmanageable in more general situations with a large variety of utterances. As with segmental synthesis, it becomes necessary to consider methods which use a textual rather than an acoustically-based representation of the prosodic features.

This raises a problem with prosodics that was not there for segmentals: how *can* prosodic features be written in text form? The standard phonetic transcription method does not give much help with notation for prosodics. It does provide a diacritical mark to indicate stress, but this is by no means enough information for synthesis. Furthermore, text-to-speech procedures (described in the next chapter) promise to allow segmentals to be specified by an ordinary orthographic representation of the utterance; but we have seen that considerable intelligence is required to derive prosodic features from text. (More than mere intelligence may be needed: this is underlined by a paper (Bolinger, 1972) delightfully entitled "Accent is predictable— if you're a mind reader"!)

If synthetic speech is to be used as a computer output medium rather than as an experimental tool for linguistic research, it is important that the method of specifying utterances is natural and easy to learn. Prosodic features must be communicated to the computer in a manner considerably simpler than individual duration and pitch specifications for each phoneme, as was required in early synthesis-by-rule systems. Fortunately, a notation has been developed for conveying some of the prosodic features of utterances, as a by-product of the linguistically important task of classifying the intonation contours used in conversational English (Halliday, 1967). This system has even been used to help foreigners speak English (Halliday, 1970), which emphasizes the fact that it was designed for use by laymen, not just linguists!

Here are examples of the way utterances can be conveyed to the ISP speech synthesis system which was described in the previous chapter. The notation is based upon Halliday's.

> *3 ˇ aw tuh/m aa t ik /si n th uh s i s uh v /*s p ee t sh,*
> *1 ˇ f r uh m uh f uh/*n e t ik /re p r uh z e n/t e i sh uhn.*

(Automatic synthesis of speech, from a phonetic representation.) Three levels of stress are distinguished: tonic or "sentence" stress, marked by "*" before the syllable; foot stress (marked by "/"); and unstressed syllables. The notion of a "foot" controls the rhythm of the speech in a way that will be described shortly. A fourth level of stress is indicated on a segmental basis when a syllable contains a reduced vowel.

Utterances are divided by punctuation into *tone groups*, which are the basic prosodic unit: there are two in the example. The shape of the pitch contour is governed by a numeral at the start of each tone group. Crude control over pauses is achieved by punctuation marks: full stop (period), for example, signals a pause while comma does not. (Longer pauses can be obtained by several full stops as in "...".) The "ˇ" character stands for a so-called "silent stress" or breath point. Word boundaries are marked by two spaces between phonemes. As mentioned in the previous chapter, syllable boundaries and explicit pitch and duration specifiers can also be included in the input. If they are not, the ISP system will attempt to compute them.

Rhythm

Our understanding of speech rhythm knows many laws but little order. In the mid 1970s there was a spate of publications reporting new data on segmental duration in various contexts, and there is a growing awareness that segmental duration is influenced by a great many factors, ranging from the structure of a discourse, through semantic and syntactic attributes of the utterances, their phonemic and phonetic make-up, right down to physiological constraints (these multifarious influences are ably documented and reviewed by Klatt, 1976). What seems to be lacking in this work is a conceptual framework on to which new information about segmental duration can be nailed.

One starting-point for imitating the rhythm of English speech is the hypothesis of regularly recurring stresses. These stresses are primarily *rhythmic* ones, and should be distinguished from the tonic stress mentioned above which is primarily an *intonational* one. Rhythmic stresses are marked in the transcription by a "/". The stretch between one and the next is called a "foot", and the hypothesis above is often referred to as that of isochronous feet ("isochronous" means "of equal time"). There is considerable controversy about this hypothesis. It is most popular among British linguists and, it must be admitted, among those who work by introspection and intuition and do not actually *measure* things. Although the question of isochrony of feet has long been debated, there seems to be general agreement (even among American linguists) that there is at least a tendency towards equal spacing of foot boundaries. However, little is known about the strength of this tendency and the extent of deviations from it (see Hill *et al.*, 1979, for an attempt to quantify it), and there is even evidence to suggest that it may in part be a *perceptual* phenomenon (Lehiste, 1973). On this basic point, as on many others, the designer of a prosodic synthesis strategy must needs make assumptions which cannot be properly justified.

From a pragmatic point of view, there are two advantages to basing a synthesis strategy on this hypothesis. First, it provides a way to represent the many influences of higher-level processes (like syntax and semantics) on rhythm using a simple notation which fits naturally into the phonetic utterance representation, and which people find quite easy to understand and generate. Secondly, it tends to produce a heavily accentuated, but not unnatural, speech rhythm which can easily be moderated into a more acceptable rhythm by departing from isochrony in a controlled manner.

The ISP procedure does not make feet exactly isochronous. It starts with a standard foot time and attempts to fit the syllables of the foot into this time. If doing so would result in certain syllables having less than a preset minimum duration, the isochrony constraint is relaxed and the foot is expanded. There is no preset *maximum* syllable length. However, when the durations of individual phoneme postures are adjusted to realize the calculated syllable durations, limits are imposed on the amount by which individual phonemes can be expanded or contracted. Thus a hierarchy of limits exists.

The rate of talking is determined by the standard foot time. If this time is short, many feet will be forced to have durations longer than the standard, and the speech will be "less isochronous". This seems to accord with common human experience. If the standard time is longer, however, the minimum syllable limit will always be exceeded and the speech will be completely isochronous. If it is too long, the above-mentioned limits to phoneme expansion will come into play and again partially destroy the isochrony.

It has often been observed that the final foot of an utterance tends to be longer than others; as does the tonic foot: that which bears the major stress This is easy to accomodate, simply by making the target duration longer for these feet.

From Feet to Syllables

A foot is a succession of syllables, one or more. And it is obvious that since there are more syllables in some feet than others, some syllables must occupy less time than others in order to preserve the tendency towards isochrony of feet.

However, the duration of a foot is not divided evenly between its constituent syllables. The syllables have a definite rhythm of their own, which seems to be governed by

—the nature of the salient (that is, the first) syllable of the foot
—the presence of word boundaries within the foot.

A salient syllable tends to be long either if it contains one of a class of so-called "long" vowels, or if there is a cluster of two or more consonants following the vowel. The pattern of syllables and word boundaries governs the rhythm of the foot, and Table 8.2 shows the possibilities for one-, two-, and three-syllable feet. This theory of speech rhythm is due to Abercrombie (1964).

A foot may have the rhythmical characteristics of a two-syllable foot while having only one syllable, if the first place in it is filled by a silent stress (marked by " ^ "). This is shown in the second one-syllable example of Table 8.2. A similar effect may occur with two- and three-syllable feet, although examples are not given in the table. Feet of four and five syllables, with or without a silent stress, are considerably rarer.

Table 8.2. Syllable patterns and rhythms.

	Syllable pattern			Example	Syllable rhythm
One-syllable feet	salient			/*good* /show	1
	ˆ	weak		/ˆ*good*/bye	2:1
Two-syllable feet	sal-long	weak		/*centre* /forward	1:1
	sal-short	weak		/*atom* /bomb	1:2
	salient #	weak		/*tea for* /two	2:1
Three-syllable feet	salient #	weak [#]	weak	/*one for the* /road	2:1:1
				/*it's incon*/ceivable	
	sal-long	weak #	weak	/*after the* /war	2:3:1
	sal-short	weak #	weak	/*middle to* /top	1:3:2
	sal-long	weak	weak	/*nobody* /knows	3:1:2
	sal-short	weak	weak	/*anything* /more	1:1:1

# denotes a word boundary;
[#] is an optional word boundary

Syllabification (splitting an utterance into syllables) is a job which had to be done for the pitch-transfer procedure described earlier, and the nature of syllable rhythms calls for it here too. Even though the utterance is now specified phonetically instead of acoustically, the same basic principle applies. Syllables normally coincide with peaks of sonority, where "sonority" measures the inherent loudness of a sound relative to other sounds of the same duration and pitch. However, difficult cases exist where it seems to be unclear how many syllables there are in a word. (Ladefoged, 1975, discusses this problem with examples such as "real", "realistic" and "reality".) Furthermore, care must be taken to avoid counting two syllables in a word like "sky" because of its two peaks of sonority: for the stop *k* has lower sonority than the fricative *s*.

Three levels of notional sonority are enough for syllabification. Dividing phoneme segments into *sonorants* (glides and nasals), *obstruents* (stops and fricatives), and vowels; a general syllable has the form

⟨obstruent⟩* ⟨sonorant⟩* ⟨vowel⟩* ⟨sonorant⟩* ⟨obstruent⟩*

where "*" means repetition, that is, occurrence zero or more times. This sidesteps the "sky" problem by giving fricatives the same sonority as stops. It is easy to use the above structure to count the number of syllables in a given utterance by counting the sonority peaks.

However, what is required is an indication of syllable *boundaries* as well as a syllable count. For slow conversational speech, these can be approximated as follows. Word divisions obviously form syllable boundaries, as should foot markers, but it may be wise not to assume that the latter do if the utterance has been prepared by someone with little knowledge of linguistics. Syllable boundaries should be made to coincide with sonority minima. As an *ad hoc* pragmatic rule, if only one segment has the minimum sonority the boundary is placed before it. If there are two segments, each with the minimum sonority, it is placed between them, while for three or more it is placed after the first two.

These rules produce obviously acceptable divisions in many cases (to'day, ash'tray, tax'free), with perhaps unexpected positioning of the boundary in others (ins'pire, de'par'tment). Actually, people do differ in placement of syllable boundaries (Abercrombie, 1967).

From Syllables to Segments

The theory of isochronous feet (with the caveats noted earlier) and that of syllable rhythms provide a way of producing durations for individual syllables. But where are these durations supposed to be measured? There is a beat point, or tapping point, near the beginning of each syllable. This is the place where a listener will tap if asked to give one tap to each syllable; it has been investigated experimentally by Allen (1972). It is not necessarily at the very beginning of the syllable. For example, in "straight", the tapping point is certainly after the *s* and the stopped part of the *t*.

Another factor which relates to the division of the syllable duration among phonetic segments is the often-observed fact that the length of the vocalic nucleus is a strong clue to the degree of voicing of the terminating cluster (Lehiste, 1970). If you say in pairs words like "cap", "cab"; "cat", "cad"; "tack", "tag"; you will find that the vowel in the first word of each pair is significantly shorter than that in the second. In fact, the major difference between such pairs is the vowel length, not the final consonant.

Such effects can be taken into account by considering a syllable to comprise an initial consonant cluster, followed by a vocalic nucleus and a final consonant cluster. Any of these elements can be missing: the most unusual case where the nucleus is absent occurs, for example, in so-called syllabic *n*'s (as in renderings of "button", "pudding" which might be written "butt'n", "pudd'n"). However, it is convenient to modify the definition of the nucleus so as to rule out the possibility of it being empty. Using the characterization of the syllable given above, the clusters can be defined as:

initial cluster = ⟨obstruent⟩* ⟨sonorant⟩*
nucleus   = ⟨vowel⟩* ⟨sonorant⟩*
final cluster = ⟨obstruent⟩*.

Sonorants are included in the nucleus so that it is always present, even in the case of a syllabic consonant.

Then, rules can be used to divide the syllable duration between the initial cluster, nucleus, and final cluster. These must distinguish between situations where the terminating cluster is voiced or unvoiced so that the characteristic differences in vowel lengths can be accommodated.

Finally, the cluster durations must be apportioned among their constituent phonetic segments. There is little published data on which to base this. Two simple schemes which have been used in ISP are described in Witten (1977) and Witten and Smith (1977).

Pitch

There are two basically different ways of looking at the pitch of an utterance. One is to imagine pitch *levels* attached to individual syllables. This has been popular among American linguists, and some people have even gone so far as to associate pitch levels with levels of stress. The second approach is to consider pitch *contours*, as we did earlier when examining how to transfer pitch from one utterance to another. This seems to be easier for the person who transcribes the utterances to produce, for the information required is much less detailed than levels attached to each syllable. Some indication needs to be given of how the contour is to be bound to the utterance, and in the notation introduced above the most prominent, or "tonic", syllable is indicated in the transcription.

Halliday's (1970) classification identifies five different primary intonation contours, each hinging on the tonic syllable. These are sketched in Fig. 8.5, in the style of Halliday. Several secondary contours, which are variations on the primary ones, are defined as well. However, this classification scheme is intended for consumption by people, who bring to the problem a wealth of prior knowledge of speech and years of experience with it! It captures only the gross features of the infinite variety of pitch contours found in living speech. In a sense, the classification is *phonological* rather than *phonetic*, for it attempts to distinguish the features which make a logical difference to the listener instead of the acoustic details of the pitch contours.

It is necessary to take these contours and subject them to a sort of phonological-to-phonetic embellishment before applying them in synthetic speech. For example, the stretches with constant pitch which precede the tonic syllable in tone groups 1, 2, and 3 sound most unnatural when synthesized, for pitch is hardly ever exactly constant in living speech. Some pretonic pitch variation is necessary, and this can be made to emphasize the salient syllable of each foot. A "lilting" effect which reaches a peak at each foot boundary, and drops rather faster at the beginning of the foot

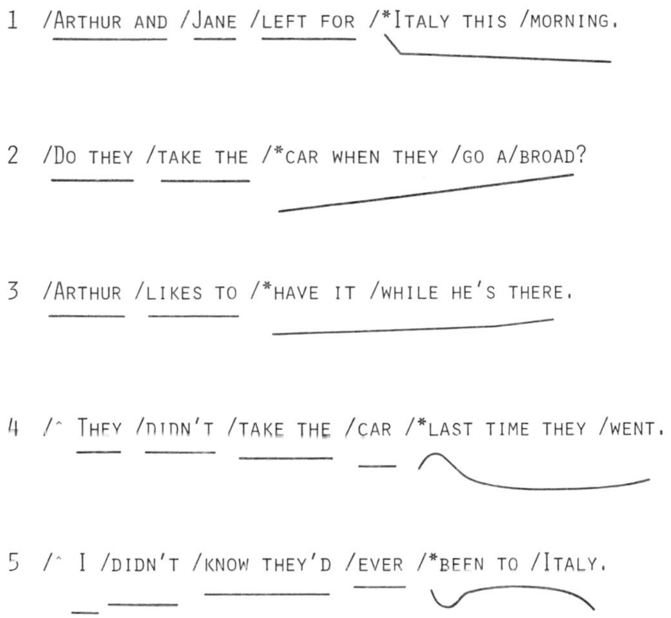

1 /ᴀʀᴛʜᴜʀ ᴀɴᴅ /ᴊᴀɴᴇ /ʟᴇғᴛ ғᴏʀ /*ɪᴛᴀʟʏ ᴛʜɪs /ᴍᴏʀɴɪɴɢ.

2 /ᴅᴏ ᴛʜᴇʏ /ᴛᴀᴋᴇ ᴛʜᴇ /*ᴄᴀʀ ᴡʜᴇɴ ᴛʜᴇʏ /ɢᴏ ᴀ/ʙʀᴏᴀᴅ?

3 /ᴀʀᴛʜᴜʀ /ʟɪᴋᴇs ᴛᴏ /*ʜᴀᴠᴇ ɪᴛ /ᴡʜɪʟᴇ ʜᴇ's ᴛʜᴇʀᴇ.

4 /^ ᴛʜᴇʏ /ᴅɪᴅɴ'ᴛ /ᴛᴀᴋᴇ ᴛʜᴇ /ᴄᴀʀ /*ʟᴀsᴛ ᴛɪᴍᴇ ᴛʜᴇʏ /ᴡᴇɴᴛ.

5 /^ ɪ /ᴅɪᴅɴ'ᴛ /ᴋɴᴏᴡ ᴛʜᴇʏ'ᴅ /ᴇᴠᴇʀ /*ʙᴇᴇɴ ᴛᴏ /ɪᴛᴀʟʏ.

Fig. 8.5. The five primary intonation contours (after Halliday, 1970)

than it rises at the end, sounds more natural. The magnitude of this inflection can be altered slightly to add interest, but a considerable increase in it produces a semantic change by making the utterance sound more emphatic. It is a major problem to pin down exactly the turning points of pitch in the falling-rising and rising-falling contours (4 and 5 in Fig. 8.5). And even deciding on precise values for the pitch frequencies involved is not always easy.

The aim of the pitch assignment method of ISP is to allow the person (or program) which originates a spoken message to exercise a great deal of control over its intonation, without having to concern himself with foot or syllable structure. The message to be spoken must be broken down into tone groups, which correspond roughly to Halliday's tone groups. Each one comprises a *tonic* of one or more feet, which is optionally preceded by a *pretonic*, also with a number of feet. It is advantageous to allow a tone group boundary to occur in the middle of a foot (whereas Halliday's scheme insists that it occurs at a foot boundary). The first foot of the tonic, the *tonic foot*, is marked by an asterisk at the beginning. It is on the first syllable of this foot (the "tonic" or "nuclear" syllable) that the major stress of the tone group occurs. If there is no asterisk in a tone group, ISP takes the final foot as the tonic (since this is the most common case).

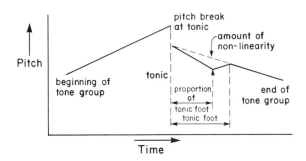

Fig. 8.6. Basic shape of synthetic pitch contour.

The pitch contour on a tone group is specified by an array of ten numbers. Of course, the system cannot generate all conceivable contours for a tone group, but the definitions of the ten specifiable quantities have been chosen to give a useful range of contours. If necessary, more precise control over the pitch of an utterance can be achieved by making the tone groups smaller.

The overall pitch movement is controlled by specifying the pitch at three places: the beginning of the tone group, the beginning of the tonic syllable, and the end of the tone group. Provision is made for an abrupt pitch break at the start of the tonic syllable in order to simulate tone groups 2 and 3, and to a lesser extent, tone groups 4 and 5. The pitch is interpolated linearly over the first part of the tone group (up to the tonic syllable) and over the last part (from there to the end), except that it is possible to specify a non-linearity on the tonic syllable, for emphasis, as shown in Fig. 8.6.

On the basic shape are superimposed two finer pitch patterns. One of these is an initialization-continuation option which allows the pitch to rise (or fall) independently on the initial and final feet to specified values, without affecting the contour on the rest of the tone group (Fig. 8.7). The other

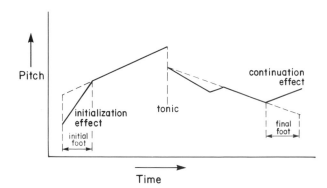

Fig. 8.7. Initialization and continuation effects.

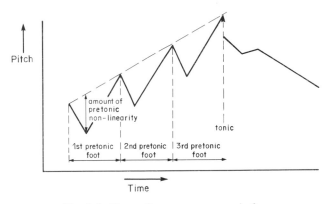

Fig. 8.8. Shape of contour on pretonic feet.

is a foot pattern which is superimposed on each pretonic foot, to give the stressed syllables of the pretonic added prominence and avoid the monotony of constant pitch. This is specified by a *non-linearity* parameter which distorts the contour on the foot at a pre-determined point along it. Fig. 8.8 shows the effect.

The ten quantities that define a pitch contour are summarized in Table 8.3, and shown diagrammatically in Fig. 8.9.

The intention of this parametric method of specifying contours is that the parameters should be easily derivable from semantic variables like emphasis, novelty of idea, surprise, uncertainty, incompleteness. Here we really are getting into controversial, unresearched areas. Roughly speaking, parameters D and G control emphasis, G by itself controls novelty and surprise, and H and the relative sizes of E and F control uncertainty and incom-

Table 8.3. The quantities that define a pitch contour.

A:	continuation from previous tone group
	zero gives no continuation
	non-zero gives pitch at start of tone group
B:	notional pitch at start
C:	pitch range on whole of pretonic
D:	departure from linearity on each foot of pretonic
E:	pitch change at start of tonic
F:	pitch range on tonic
G:	departure from linearity on tonic
H:	continuation to next tone group
	zero gives no continuation
	non-zero gives pitch at end of tone group
I:	fraction along foot of the non-linearity position, for pretonic feet
J:	fraction along foot of the non-linearity position, for the tonic foot

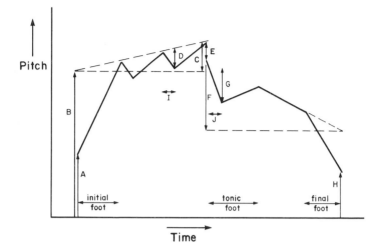

Fig. 8.9. The quantities that define a pitch contour.

pleteness. Certain parameters (notably I and J) are defined because although they do not appear to correspond to semantic distinctions, we do not yet know how to generate them automatically.

One basic requirement of the pitch assignment scheme was the ability to generate contours which approximate Halliday's five primary tone groups. Values of the ten specifiable quantities are given in Table 8.4, for each tone group. All pitches are given in Hz. A distinctly dipping pitch movement has been given to each pretonic foot (parameter D), to lend prominence to the salient syllables.

8.4 Evaluating Prosodic Synthesis

It is extraordinarily difficult to evaluate schemes for prosodic synthesis, and this is surely a large part of the reason why prosodics are among the least

Table 8.4. Pitch contour table for Halliday's primary tone groups.

Halliday's tone group	A	B	C	D	E	F	G	H	I	J
1	0	175	0	−40	0	−100	−40	0	0.33	0.5
2	0	280	0	−40	−190	100	0	0	0.33	0.5
3	0	175	0	−40	−70	45	−10	0	0.33	0.5
4	0	280	−100	−40	20	45	−45	0	0.33	0.5
5	0	175	60	−40	−20	−45	45	0	0.33	0.5

advanced aspects of artificial speech. Segmental synthesis can be tested by playing people minimal pairs of words which differ in just one feature that is being investigated. For example, one might experiment with "pit", "bit"; "tot", "dot"; "cot", "got"; to test the rules which discriminate unvoiced from voiced stops. There are standard word-lists for intelligibility tests which can be used to compare systems, too. No equivalent of such micro-level evaluation exists for prosodics, for they by definition have a holistic effect on utterances. They are most noticeable, and most important, in longish stretches of speech. Even monotonous, arhythmic speech will be intelligible in sufficiently short samples provided the segmentals are good enough, but it is quite impossible to concentrate on such speech in quantity. Some attempts at evaluation appear in Ainsworth (1974) and McHugh (1976), but these are primarily directed at assessing the success of pronunciation rules, which are discussed in the next chapter.

One evaluation technique is to compare synthetic with natural versions of utterances, as was done in the pitch transfer experiment. The method described earlier used a sensitive paired-comparison test, where subjects heard both versions in quick succession and were asked to judge which was "most natural and intelligible". This is quite a stringent test, and one that may not be so useful for inferior, completely synthetic, contours. It is essential to degrade the "natural" utterance so that it is comparable seg-mentally to the synthetic one: this was done in the experiment described by extracting its pitch and resynthesizing it from linear predictive coefficients.

Several other experiments could be undertaken to evaluate artificial pros-ody. For example, one could compare:

—natural and artificial rhythms, using artificial segmental synthesis in both cases;
—natural and artificial pitch contours, using artificial segmental synthesis in both cases;
—natural and artificial pitch contours, using segmentals extracted from natural utterances.

There are many other topics which have not yet been fully investigated. It would be interesting, for example, to define rules for generating speech at different tempos. Elisions, where phonemes or even whole syllables are suppressed, occur in fast speech; these have been analysed by linguists but not yet incorporated into synthetic models. It should be possible to simulate emotion by altering parameters such as pitch range and mean pitch level, but this seems exceptionally difficult to evaluate. One situation where it would perhaps be possible to measure emotion is in the reading of sports results: in fact a study has already been made of intonation in soccer results (Bonnet, 1980)! Even the synthesis of voices with different pitch ranges requires investigation, for as noted earlier, it is difficult to place precise frequency specifications on phonological contours such as those sketched in Fig. 8.5. Clearly the topic of prosodic synthesis is a rich and potentially rewarding area of research.

8.5 References

Abercrombie, D. (1964). Syllable quantity and enclitics in English. *In* "In honour of Daniel Jones," (D. Abercrombie *et al.*, eds) pp. 216–222. Longmans, London.

Abercrombie, D. (1967). "Elements of general phonetics," Edinburgh University Press.

Ainsworth, W.A. (1974). Performance of a speech synthesis system. *Int J Man-Machine Studies*, **6**(5) 493–511, September.

Allen, G.D. (1972). The location of rhythmic stress beats in English: an experimental study Part One. *Language and Speech*, **15**(1) 72–100, January–March.

Bolinger, D. (1972). Accent is predictable (if you're a mind reader). *Language*, **48**(3) 633–644, July–September.

Bonnet, G. (1980). A study of intonation in the soccer results. *J Phonetics*, **8**, 21–38.

Haggard, M.P., Ambler, S. and Callow, M. (1970). Pitch as a voicing cue. *J Acoustical Society of America*, **47**, 613–617.

Halliday, M.A.K. (1967). "Intonation and grammar in British English," Mouton, The Hague.

Halliday, M.A.K. (1970). "A course in spoken English: Intonation," Oxford University Press, London.

Hill, D.R., Jassem, W. and Witten, I.H. (1979). A statistical approach to the problems of isochronicity. *In* "Current issues in linguistic theory Vol 9: Current issues in the phonetic sciences," (H. Hollien and P. Hollien, eds), pp. 285–294. John Benjamins, Amsterdam.

Klatt, D.H. (1976). Linguistic uses of segmental duration in English: acoustic and perceptual evidence. *J Acoustical Society of America*, **59**(5) 1208–1221, May.

Ladefoged, P. (1967). "Three areas of experimental phonetics," Oxford University Press, London.

Ladefoged, P. (1975). "A course in phonetics," Harcourt Brace and Jovanovich, New York.

Lea, W.A., Medress, M.F. and Skinner, T.E. (1975). A prosodically guided speech understanding strategy. *IEEE Trans Acoustics, Speech and Signal Processing*, **ASSP-23**(1) 30–38, February.

Lehiste, I. and Peterson, G.E. (1959). Vowel amplitudes and phonemic stress in American English. *J Acoustical Society of America*, **54**, 1228–1234.

Lehiste, I. (1970). "Suprasegmentals," MIT Press, Cambridge, Massachusetts.

Lehiste, I. (1973). Rhythmic units and syntactic units in production and perception. *J Acoustical Society of America*, **54**(5) 1228–1234, November.

Mattingly, I.G. (1966). Synthesis by rule of prosodic features. *Language and Speech*, **9**(1) 1–13, January–March.

McHugh, A. (1976). Listener preference and comprehension tests of stress algorithms for a text-to-phonetic speech synthesis program. Report 8015, Naval Research Lab, Washington, DC, September.

Mermelstein, P. (1975). Automatic segmentation of speech into syllabic units. *J Acoustical Society of America*, **58**(4) 880–883, October.

Morton, J. and Jassem, W. (1965). Acoustic correlates of stress. *Language and Speech*, **8**, 159–181.

Rabiner, L.R., Levitt, H. and Rosenberg, A.E. (1969). Investigation of stress patterns for speech synthesis by rule. *J Acoustical Society of America*, **45**(1) 92–101, January.

Williams, C. and Stevens, K. (1972). Functions and speech: some acoustical correlates. *J Acoustical Society of America*, **52**(4:2) 1238–1250, October.

Witten, I.H. (1977). A flexible scheme for assigning timing and pitch to synthetic speech. *Language and Speech*, **20**(3) 240–260, July–September.

Witten, I.H. and Smith, A. (1977). Synthesizing British English rhythm—a structured approach. *Proc Canadian Man-Computer Communication Conference*, 175–185, Calgary, May.

Witten, I.H. (1979). On transferring pitch from one utterance to another. *J Acoustical Society of America*, **65**(6) 1576–1579, June.

8.6 Further Reading

There are quite a lot of books in the field of linguistics which describe prosodic features. Here is a small but representative sample from both sides of the Atlantic.

Abercrombie, D. (1965). "Studies in phonetics and linguistics," Oxford Univ Press, London.

> Abercrombie is one of the leading English authorities on phonetics, and this is a collection of essays which he has written over the years. Some of them treat prosodics explicitly, and others show the influence of verse structure on Abercrombie's thinking.

Bolinger, D. (Editor) (1972). "Intonation," Penguin, Middlesex, England.

> A collection of papers that treat a wide variety of different aspects of intonation in living speech.

Crystal, D. (1969). "Prosodic systems and intonation in English," Cambridge Univ Press.

> This book attempts to develop a theoretical basis for the study of British English intonation.

Gimson, A.C. (1966). The linguistic relevance of stress in English. *In* "Phonetics and linguistics," (W.E. Jones and J. Laver, eds), pp. 94–102. Longmans, London.

> Here is a careful discussion of what is meant by "stress", with much more detail than has been possible in this chapter.

Lehiste, I. (1970). "Suprasegmentals," MIT Press, Cambridge, Massachusetts.

> This is a comprehensive study of suprasegmental phenomena in natural speech. It is divided into three major sections: quantity (timing), tonal features (pitch) and stress.

Pike, K.L. (1945). "The intonation of American English," University of Michigan Press, Ann Arbor, Michigan.

> A classic, although somewhat dated, study. Notice that it deals specifically with American English.

9

GENERATING SPEECH FROM TEXT

In the preceding two chapters I have described how artificial speech can be produced from a written phonetic representation with additional markers indicating intonation contours, points of major stress, rhythm and pauses. This representation is substantially the same as that used by linguists when recording natural utterances. What we will discuss now are techniques for generating this information, or at least some of it, from text.

Figure 9.1 shows various levels of the speech synthesis process. Starting from the top with plain text, the first box splits it into intonation units (tone groups), decides where the major emphases (tonic stresses) should be placed, and further subdivides the tone group into rhythmic units (feet). For intonation analysis it is necessary to decide on an "interpretation" of the text, which in turn, as was emphasized at the beginning of the previous chapter, depends both on the semantics of what is being said and on the attitude of the speaker to his material. The resulting representation will be at the level of Halliday's notation for utterances, with the words still in English rather than phonetics. Table 9.1 illustrates the utterance representation at the various levels of the Figure.

The next job is to translate the plain text into a broad phonetic transcription. This requires knowledge of letter-to-sound pronunciation rules for the language under consideration. But much more is needed. The structure of each word must be examined for prefixes and suffixes, because they (especially the latter) have a strong influence on pronunciation. This is called "morphological" analysis. Actually it is also required for rhythmical purposes, because prefixes are frequently unstressed (note that the word "prefix" is itself an exception to this!). Thus the appealing segmentation of the overall problem shown in Fig. 9.1 is not very accurate, for the individual processes cannot be rigidly separated as it implies. In fact, we saw earlier how this intermixing of levels occurs with prosodic and segmental features. Nevertheless, it is helpful to structure discussion of the problem by separating levels as a first approximation. Further influences on pronunciation come from the semantics and syntax of the utterance, and both also play a part in intonation and rhythm analysis. The result of this second process is a phonetic representation, still adorned with prosodic markers.

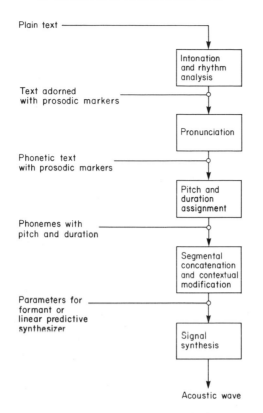

Plain text

Intonation and rhythm analysis

Text adorned with prosodic markers

Pronunciation

Phonetic text with prosodic markers

Pitch and duration assignment

Phonemes with pitch and duration

Segmental concatenation and contextual modification

Parameters for formant or linear predictive synthesizer

Signal synthesis

Acoustic wave

Fig. 9.1. Levels in speech synthesis.

Now we move down from higher-level intonation and rhythm considerations to the details of the pitch contour and segment durations. This process was the subject of the previous chapter. The problems are twofold: to map an appropriate acoustic pitch contour on to the utterance, using tonic stress point and foot boundaries as anchor points; and to assign durations to segments using the foot-syllable-cluster-segment hierarchy. If it is accepted that the overall rhythm can be captured adequately by foot markers, this process does not interact with earlier ones. However, many researchers do not, believing instead that rhythm is syntactically determined at a very detailed level. This will, of course, introduce strong interaction between the duration assignment process and the levels above. (Klatt, 1975, puts it into his title "Vowel lengthening is syntactically determined in a connected discourse". Contrast this with the paper cited earlier (Bolinger, 1972) entitled "Accent is predictable (if you're a mind reader)". No one would disagree that "accent" is an influential factor in vowel length!)

Table 9.1. Utterance representations at various levels in speech synthesis.

Representation	Example
plain text	Automatic synthesis of speech from a phonetic representation.
text adorned with prosodic markers	3 ˆ auto/matic /synthesis of /*speech, 1 ˆ from a pho/*netic /represen/tation.
phonetic text with prosodic markers	3 ˆ *aw t uh/m a a t i k /s i n t h uh s i s uh v /*s p ee t sh,* 1 ˆ *f r uh m uh f uh/*n e t i k /r e p r uh z e n/t e i sh uh n.*
phonemes with pitch and duration	pause 80 msec *aw* 70 msec 105 Hz *t* 40 msec 136 Hz *uh* 50 msec 148 Hz *m* 70 msec 175 Hz *aa* 90 msec 140 Hz ... ...
parameters for formant or linear predictive synthesizer	10 parameters, each updated at a frame rate of 10 msec (4 second utterance gives 400 frames, or 4000 data values)
acoustic wave	at 8 kHz sampling rate a 4-second utterance has 32 000 samples

Notice incidentally that the representation of the result of the pitch and duration assignment process in Table 9.1 is inadequate, for each segment is shown as having just one pitch. In practice the pitch varies considerably throughout every segment, and can easily rise and fall on a single one. For example,

"he's *very* good"

may have a rise-fall on the vowel of "very". The linked event-list data-structure of ISP is much more suitable than a textual string for utterance representation at this level.

The fourth and fifth processes of Fig. 9.1 have little interaction with the first two, which are the subject of this chapter. Segmental concatenation, which was treated in Chapter 7, is affected by prosodic features like stress; but a notation which indicates stressed syllables (like Halliday's) is sufficient to capture this influence. Contextual modification of segments, by which I mean the coarticulation effects which govern allophones of phonemes, is included explicitly in the fourth process to emphasize that the upper levels need only provide a broad phonemic transcription rather than a detailed phonetic one. Signal synthesis can be performed by either a formant synthesizer or a linear predictive one (discussed in Chapters 5 and 6). This will affect the details of the segmental concatenation process but should have no impact at all on the upper levels.

Figure 9.1 performs a useful function by summarizing where we have been in earlier chapters (the lower three boxes) and introducing the remaining problems that must be faced by a full text-to-speech system. It also serves to illustrate an important point: that a speech output system can demand that its utterances be entered in any of a wide range of representations. Thus one can enter at a low level with a digitized waveform or linear predictive parameters; or higher up with a phonetic representation that includes detailed pitch and duration specification at the phoneme level; or with a phonetic text or plain text adorned with prosodic markers; or at the very top with plain text as it would appear in a book. A heavy price in naturalness and intelligibility is paid by moving up *any* of these levels, and this is just as true at the top of the Figure as at the bottom.

9.1 Deriving Prosodic Features

If you really need to start with plain text, some very difficult problems present themselves. The text should be understood, first of all, and then decisions need to be made about how it is to be interpreted. For an excellent speaker (like an actor), these decisions will be artistic, at least in part. They should certainly depend upon the opinion and attitude of the speaker, and his perception of the structure and progress of the dialogue. Very little is known about this upper level of speech synthesis from text. In practice it is almost completely ignored, and the speech is at most barely intelligible, and certainly uncomfortable to listen to. Hence anybody contemplating building or using a speech output system which starts from something close to plain text should consider carefully whether some extra semantic information can be coded into the initial utterances to help with prosodic interpretation. Only rarely is this impossible, and reading machines for the blind are a prime example of a situation where arbitrary, unannotated, texts must be read.

Intonation Analysis

One distinction which a program can usefully try to make is between basically rising and basically falling pitch contours. It is often said that pitch rises on a question and falls on a statement, but if you listen to speech you will find this to be a gross oversimplification. It normally falls on statements, certainly; but it falls as often as it rises on questions. It is more accurate to say that pitch rises on "yes–no" questions and falls on other utterances, although this rule is still only a rough guide. A simple test which operates lexically on the input text is to determine whether a sentence is a question by looking at the punctuation mark at its end, and then to examine the first word. If it is a "wh"-word like "what", "which", "when", "why" (and also "how"), a falling contour is likely to fit. If not, the question is probably a yes–no one, and the contour should rise. Such a crude rule will certainly not be very accurate (it fails, for example, when the "wh"-word is embedded in a phrase as in "at what time are you going?"), but at least it provides a starting-point.

An air of finality is given to an utterance when it bears a definite fall in pitch, dropping to a rather low value at the end. This should accompany the last intonation unit in an utterance (unless it is a yes–no question). However, a rise-fall contour such as Halliday's tone group 5 (Fig. 8.5) can easily be used in utterance-final position by one person in a conversation, although it would be unlikely to terminate the dialogue altogether. A new topic is frequently introduced by a fall–rise contour (such as Halliday's tone group 4) and this often begins a paragraph.

Determining the type of pitch contour is only one part of intonation assignment. There are really three separate problems:

—dividing the utterance into tone groups;
—choosing the tonic syllable, or major stress point, of each one;
—assigning a pitch contour to each tone group.

Let us continue to use the Halliday notation for intonation, which was introduced in simplified form in the previous chapter. Moreover, assume that the foot boundaries can be placed correctly; this problem will be discussed in the next sub-section. Then a scheme which considers only the lexical form of the utterance and does not attempt to "understand" it (whatever that means) is as follows:

—place a tone group boundary at every punctuation mark;
—place the tonic at the first syllable of the last foot in a tone group;
—use contour 4 for the first tone group in a paragraph and contour 1 elsewhere, except for a yes-no question which receives contour 2.

These extremely crude and simplistic rules are really the most that one can do without subjecting the utterance to a complicated semantic analysis. In statistical terms, they are actually remarkably effective. Table 9.2 shows part of a spontaneous monologue which was transcribed by Halliday and

Table 9.2. Example of intonation and rhythm analysis (from Halliday, 1970).

Plain text	Text adorned with prosodic markers
From Scarborough to Whitby is a very pleasant journey, with very beautiful countryside. In fact the Yorkshire coast is lovely,	4 ˆ from /Scarborough to /*Whitby is a 1 – very /pleasant /*journey with 1 – very /beautiful /*country side... 1+ ˆ in /fact the /Yorkshire /coast is /*lovely
all along, ex-cept the parts that are covered in caravans of course; and if you go in spring, when the gorse is out, or in summer, when the heather's out, it's really one of the most delightful areas in the whole country.	1+ all a/*long ex __4 cept the /parts that are /covered in /*caravans of /course and 4 if you /go in /*spring 4 ˆ when the /*gorse is /out 4 ˆ or in /*summer 4 ˆ when the /*heather's /out 13 ˆ it's /really /one of the /most de/*lightful /*areas in the 1 whole /*country
The moorland is rather high up, and fairly flat—a sort of plateau. At least, it isn't really flat, when you get up on the top; it's rolling moorland cut across by steep valleys. But seen from the coast it's "up there on the moors," and you always think of it as a kind of tableland.	4 ˆ the /*moorland is 1 rather /high /*up and 1 fairly /ˮflat a 1 sort of /*plateau... 1 ˆ at /*least 13 ˆ it /*isn't /really /*flat – 3 ˆ when you /get up on the /*top 1 ˆ it's /rolling /ˮmoorland 1 cut across by /steep /*valleys but 4 seen from the /*coast it's... 1 up there on the /*moors and you – 4 always /*think of it as a 1 kind of /*tableland

appears in his teaching text on intonation (Halliday, 1970, p. 133). Among the prosodic markers are some that were not introduced in Chapter 8. First, each tone group has secondary contours which are identified by "1+", "1–" (for tone group 1), and so on. Secondly, the mark "..." is used to indicate a pause which disrupts the speech rhythm. Notice that its positioning belies the advice of the old elocutionists:

> A comma stops the Voice while we may privately tell *one*, a Semi-colon *two*; a Colon *three*: and a Period *four*.
>
> (Mason, 1748)

Thirdly, compound tone groups such as "13" appear which contain *two* tonic syllables. This differs from a simple concatenation of tone groups (with contours 1 and 3 in this case) because the second is in some sense subsidiary to the first. Typically it forms an adjunct clause, while the first clause gives the main information. Halliday provides many examples, such as

/Jane goes /shopping in /*town /every /*Friday
/ˆ I /met /*Arthur on the /*train.

But he does not comment on the *acoustic* difference between a compound tone group and a concatenation of simple ones; which is, after all, the information needed for synthesis. A final, minor, difference between Halliday's scheme and that outlined earlier is that he compels tone group boundaries to occur at the beginning of a foot.

Applying the simple rules given above to the text of Table 9.2 leads to the results in the first column of Table 9.3. Three-quarters of the tone group boundaries are flagged by punctuation marks, with no extraneous ones being included. Of tone groups, 88% have a tonic syllable at the start of the final foot. However, the compound tone groups each have two tonic syllables, and of course only the second one is predicted by the final-foot rule. Assigning intonation contours on the extremely simple basis of using contour 4 for the first tone group in a paragraph, and contour 1 thereafter, also seems to work quite well. Secondary contours such as "1+" and "1−" have been mapped into the appropriate primary contour (1, in this case) for the present purpose, and compound tone groups have been assigned the first contour of the pair. The result is that 68% of contours are given correctly.

Table 9.3. Success of simple intonation assignment rules.

	Excerpt in Table 9.2	Complete passage
number of tone groups	25	74
number of boundaries correctly placed	19 (76%)	47 (64%)
number of boundaries incorrectly placed	0	1 (1%)
number of tone groups having a tonic syllable at the beginning of the final foot	22 (88%)	60 (81%)
number of tone groups whose contours are correctly assigned	17 (68%)	51 (69%)
number of compound tone groups	2 (8%)	6 (8%)
number of secondary intonation contours	7 (28%)	13 (17%)

In order to give some idea of the reliability of these figures, the results for the whole passage transcribed by Halliday (of which Table 9.2 is an excerpt) are shown in the second column of Table 9.3. Although it looks as though the rules may have been slightly lucky with the excerpt, the general trends are the same, with 65% to 80% of features being assigned correctly. It could be argued, though, that the complete text is punctuated fairly liberally by present-day standards, so that the tone-group boundary rule is unusually successful.

These results are really astonishingly good, considering the crudeness of the rules. However, they should be interpreted with caution. What is missed by the rules, although appearing to comprise only 20%–35% of the features, is certain to include the important, information-bearing, and variety-producing features that give the utterance its liveliness and interest. It would be rash to assume that all tone-group boundaries, all tonic positions, and all intonation contours, are equally important for intelligibility and naturalness. It is much more likely that the rules predict a default pattern, while most information is borne by deviations from them. To give an engineering analogy, it may be as though the carrier waveform of a modulated transmission is being simulated, instead of the information-bearing signal! Certainly the utterance will, if synthesized with intonation given by these rules, sound extremely dull and repetitive, mainly because of the overwhelming predominance of tone group 1 and the universal placement of tonic stress on the final foot.

There are certainly many different ways to orate any particular text, and that given by Halliday and reproduced in Table 9.2 is only one possible version. However, it is fair to say that the default intonation discussed above could only occur naturally under very unusual circumstances, such as a petulant child, unwilling and sulky, having been forced to read aloud. This is hardly how we want our computers to speak!

Rhythm Analysis

Consider now how to decide where foot boundaries should be placed in English text. Clearly semantic considerations sometimes play a part in this: one could say.

/^ is /this /train /going /*to /London

instead of the more usual

/^ is /this /train /going to /*London

in circumstances where the train might be going *to* or *from* London. Such effects are ignored here, although it is worth noting in passing that the rogue words will often be marked by underscoring or italicizing (as in the previous sentence). If the text is liberally underlined, semantic analysis may be unnecessary for the purposes of rhythm.

A rough and ready rule for placing foot boundaries is to insert one before each word which is not in a small closed set of "function words". The set includes, for example, "a", "and", "but", "for", "is", "the", "to". If a verb or adjective begins with a prefix, the boundary should be moved between it and the root; but not for a noun. This will give the distinction between *con*vert (noun) and con*vert* (verb), *ex*tract and ex*tract*, and for many North American speakers, will help to distinguish *in*quiry from in*quire*. However, detecting prefixes by a simple splitting algorithm is dangerous. For example, "predate" is a verb with stress on what appears to be a prefix, contrary to the rule; while the "pre" in "predator" is not a prefix: at least, it is not pronounced as the prefix "pre" normally is. Moreover, polysyllabic words like "/diplomat", "dip/lomacy", "diplo/matic"; or "/telegraph", "te/legraphy", "tele/graphic" cannot be handled on such a simple basis.

In 1968, a remarkable work on English sound structure was published (Chomsky and Halle, 1968) which proposes a system of rules to transform English text into a phonetic representation in terms of distinctive features, with the aid of a lexicon. A great deal of attention is paid to stress, and rules are given which perform well in many tricky cases.

It uses the American system of levels of stress, marking so-called primary stress with a superscript 1, secondary stress with a superscript 2, and so on. The superscripts are written on the vowel of the stressed syllable; completely unstressed syllables receive no annotation. For example, the sentence "take John's blackboard eraser" is written

$$ta^2ke \ Jo^3hn's \ bla^1ckboa^5rd \ era^4ser.$$

In foot notation this utterance is

/take /John's /*blackboard e/raser.

It undoubtedly contains less information than the stress-level version. For example, the second syllable of "blackboard" and the first one of "erase" are both unstressed, although the rhythm rules given in Chapter 8 will cause them to be treated differently because they occupy different places in the syllable pattern of the foot. "Take", "John's", and the second syllable of "erase" are all non-tonic foot-initial syllables and hence are not distinguished in the notation; although the pitch contours schematized in Fig. 8.9 will give them different intonations.

An indefinite number of levels of stress can be used. For example, according to the rules given by Chomsky and Halle, the word "sad" in my friend can't help being shocked at anyone who would fail to consider his sad plight

has level-8 stress, the final two words being annotated as "sa^{8}d pli^{1}ght". However, only the first few levels are used regularly, and it is doubtful whether acoustic distinctions are made in speech between the weaker ones.

Chomsky and Halle are concerned to distinguish between such utterances as

bla^{2}ck boa^{1}rd-era^{3}ser ("board eraser that is black")
bla^{1}ckboa^{3}rd era^{2}ser ("eraser for a blackboard")
bla^{3}ck boa^{1}rd era^{2}ser ("eraser of a black board"),

and their stress assignment rules do indeed produce each version when appropriate. In foot notation the distinctions can still be made:

/black /*board-eraser/
/*blackboard e/raser/
/black /*board e/raser/

The rules operate on a grammatical derivation tree of the text. For instance, input for the three examples would be written

[$_{NP}$[$_A$ black]$_A$ [$_N$[$_N$ board]$_N$ [$_N$ eraser]$_N$]$_N$]$_{NP}$
[$_N$[$_N$[$_A$ black]$_A$ [$_N$ board]$_N$]$_N$ [$_N$ eraser]$_N$]$_N$
[$_N$[$_{NP}$[$_A$ black]$_A$ [$_N$ board]$_N$]$_{NP}$ [$_N$ eraser]$_N$]$_N$,

representing the trees shown in Fig. 9.2. Here, N stands for a noun, NP for a noun phrase, and A for an adjective. These categories appear explicitly as nodes in the tree. In the linearized textual representation they are used to label brackets which represent the tree structure. An additional piece of information which is needed is the lexical entry for "eraser", which would show that it has only one accented (that is, potentially stressed) syllable, namely, the second.

Consider now how to account for stress in prefixed and suffixed words, and those polysyllabic ones with more than one potential stress point. For these, the morphological structure must appear in the input.

Now *morphemes* are well-defined minimal units of grammatical analysis from which a word may be composed. For example, [went] = [go] + [ed] is a morphemic decomposition, where "[ed]" denotes the past-tense morpheme. This representation is not particularly suitable for speech synthesis for the obvious reason that the result bears no phonetic resemblance to the input. What is needed is a decomposition into *morphs*, which occur only when the lexical or phonetic representation of a word may easily be seg-

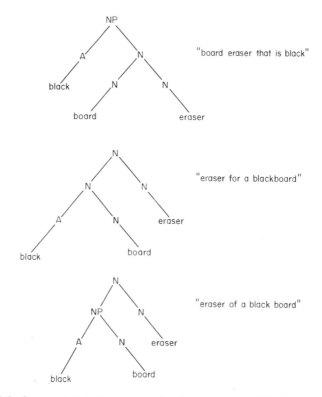

Fig. 9.2. Grammatical derivation trees for three versions of "black board eraser".

mented into parts. Thus [wanting] = [want] + [ing] and [bigger] = [big] + [er] are simultaneously morphic and morphemic decompositions. Notice that in the second example, a rule about final consonant doubling has been applied at the lexical level (although it is not needed in a phonetic representation): this comes into the sphere of "easy" segmentation. Contrast this with [went] = [go] + [ed] which is certainly not an easy segmentation and hence a morphemic but not a morphic decomposition. But between these extremes there are some difficult cases: [specific] = [specify] + [ic] is probably morphic as well as morphemic, but it is not clear that [galactic] = [galaxy] + [ic] is.

Assuming that the input is given as a derivation tree with morphological structure made explicit, Chomsky and Halle present rules which assign stress correctly in nearly all cases. For example, their rules give

$$[_A[_N \text{ incident }]_N + \text{al}]_A \rightarrow \text{i}^2\text{ncide}^1\text{ntal};$$

and if the stem is marked by $[_S \dots]_S$ in prefixed words, they can deduce

$$[_N \text{ tele } [_S \text{ graph }]_S]_N \quad \rightarrow \text{te}^1\text{legra}^3\text{ph}$$
$$[_N[_N \text{ tele } [_S \text{ graph }]_S]_N\text{y }]_N \quad \rightarrow \text{tele}^1\text{graphy}$$
$$[_A[_N \text{ tele } [_S \text{ graph }]_S]_N\text{ic }]_A \rightarrow \text{te}^3\text{legra}^1\text{phi}^2\text{c}.$$

There are two rules which account for the word-level stress on such examples: the "main stress" rule and the "alternating stress" rule. In essence, the main stress rule emphasizes the last strong syllable of a stem. A syllable is "strong" either if it contains one of a class of so-called "long" vowels, or if there is a cluster of two or more consonants following the vowel; otherwise it is "weak". (If you are exceptionally observant you will notice that this strong–weak distinction has been used before, when discussing the rhythm of feet in syllables.) Thus the verb "torment" receives stress on the second syllable, for it is a strong one. A noun like "torment" is treated as being derived from the corresponding verb, and the rule assigns stress to the verb first and then modifies it for the noun. The second, "alternating stress", rule gives some stress to alternate syllables of polysyllabic words like "formaldehyde".

It is quite easy to incorporate the word-level rules into a computer program which uses feet rather than stress levels as the basis for prosodic description. A foot boundary is simply placed before the primary-stressed (level-1) syllable, except for function words, which do not begin a foot. The other stress levels should be ignored, except that for slow, deliberate speech, secondary (level-2) stress is mapped into a foot boundary too, if it precedes the primary stress. There is also a rule which reduces vowels in unstressed syllables.

The stress assignment rules can work on phonemic script, as well as English. For example, starting from the phonetic form $[_V \textit{ aastonish}]_V$, the stress assignment rules produce $aasto^1nish$; the vowel reduction rule generates $uhsto^1nish$; and the foot conversion process gives $uhs/tonish$. This appears to provide a fairly reliable algorithm for foot boundary placement.

Speech Synthesis from Concept

I argued earlier that in order to derive prosodic features of an utterance from text it is necessary to understand its role in the dialogue, its semantics, its syntax, and (as we have just seen) its morphological structure. This is a very tall order, and the problem of natural language comprehension by machine is a vast research area in its own right. However, in many applications requiring speech output, utterances are generated by the computer from internally stored data rather than being read aloud from pre-prepared text. Then the problem of comprehending text may be evaded, for presumably the language-generation module can provide a semantic, syntactic, and even morphological decomposition of the utterance, as well as some indication of its role in the dialogue (that is, why it is necessary to say it).

This forms the basis of the appealing notion of "speech synthesis from concept". It has some advantages over speech generation from text, and in principle should provide more natural-sounding speech. Every word produced by the system can have a complete lexical entry which shows its morphological decomposition and potential stress points. The full syntactic history of each utterance is known. The Chomsky-Halle rules described above can therefore be used to place foot boundaries accurately, without the need for a complex parsing program and without the risk of having to make guesses about unknown words.

However, it is not clear how to take advantage of any semantic information which is available. Ideally, it should be possible to place tone group boundaries and tonic stress points, and assign intonation contours, in a natural-sounding way. But look again at the example text of Table 9.2 and imagine that you have at your disposal as much semantic information as is needed. It is *still* far from obvious how the intonation features could be assigned! It is, in the ultimate analysis, interpretive and stylistic *choices* that add variety and interest to speech.

Take the problem of determining pitch contours, for instance. Some of them may be explicable. Contour 4 on

except the parts that are covered in caravans of course

is due to its being a contrastive clause, for it presents essentially new information. Similarly, the succession

if you go in spring
when the gorse is out
or in summer
when the heather's out

could be considered contrastive, being in the subjunctive voice, and this could explain why contour 4's were used. But this is all conjecture, and it is difficult to apply throughout the passage. Halliday (1970) explains the contexts in which each tone group is typically used, but in an extremely high-level manner which would be impossible to embody directly in a computer program. At the other end of the spectrum, computer systems for written discourse production do not seem to provide the subtle information needed to make intonation decisions (see, for example, Davey, 1978, for a fairly complete description of such a system).

One project which uses such a method for generating speech has been described (Young and Fallside, 1980). Although some attention is paid to rhythm, the intonation contours which are generated are disappointingly repetitive and lacking in richness. In fact, very little semantic information is used to assign contours; really just that inferred by the crude punctuation-driven method described earlier.

The higher-level semantic problems associated with speech output were studied some years ago under the title "synthetic elocution" (Vanderslice, 1968). A set of rules was generated and tested by hand on a sample passage, the first part of which is shown in Table 9.4. However, no attempt was made to formalize the rules in a computer program, and indeed it was recognized that a number of important questions, such as the form of the semantic information assumed at the input, had been left unanswered.

The comments in the table, which are selected and slightly edited versions

Table 9.4. Sample passage and comments pertinent to synthetic elocution.

Human experience and human behaviour are accessible to observation by everyone. The psychologist tries to bring them under systematic study. What he perceives, however, anyone can perceive; for his task he requires no microscope or electronic gear.

Word	Comments
1 Human	special treatment because paragraph-initial
4 human	accent deleted because it echoes word 1
13 psychologist	emphasis assigned because of antithesis with "everyone"
17 them	anaphoric to "Human experience and human behaviour"
19 systematic	emphasis assigned because of contrast with "observation"
20 study	emphasis?—text is ambiguous whether "observation" is a kind of study that is nonsystematic, or an activity contrasting with the entire concept of "systematic study"
21 What	increase in pitch for "What he perceives" because it is not the subject
22 he	accented although anaphoric to word 13 because of antithesis with word 25
24 however	decrease in pitch because it is parenthetical
25 anyone	emphasized by antithesis with word 22
27 perceive	unaccented because it echoes word 23, "perceives"
;	semicolon assigns falling intonation
30 task	unaccented because it is anaphoric with "tries to bring them under systematic study"

of those appearing in the original work (Vanderslice, 1968), are intended as examples of the nature and subtlety of the prosodic influences which were examined. The concepts of "accent" and "emphasis" are used; these relate to stress but are not easy to define precisely in our tone-group terminology. Fortunately we do not need an exact characterization of them for the present purpose. Roughly speaking, "accent" encompasses both foot-initial stress and tonic stress, whereas "emphasis" is something more than this, typically being realized by the fall-rise or rise-fall contours of Halliday's tone groups 4 and 5 (Fig. 8.5).

Particular attention is paid to anaphora and antithesis (among other things). The first term means the repetition of a word or phrase in the text, and is often applied to pronoun references. In the example, the word "human" is repeated in the first few words; "them" in the second sentence refers to "human experience and human behaviour"; "he" in the third sentence is the previously-mentioned psychologist; and "task" is anaphoric with "tries to bring them under systematic study". Other things being equal, anaphoric references are unaccented. In our terms this means that they certainly do not receive tonic stress, and may not even receive foot stress.

Antithesis is defined as the contrast of ideas expressed by parallelism of strongly contrasting words or phrases, and the second element taking part in it is generally emphasized. "Psychologist" in the passage is an antithesis of "everyone"; "systematic" and possibly "study" of "observation". Thus

/ˆ the psy/*chologist

would probably receive intonation contour 4, since it is also introducing a new actor; while

/tries to /bring them /under /syste/*matic /study

could receive contour 5. "He" and "everyone" are antithetical; not only does the latter receive emphasis but the former has its accent restored—for otherwise it would have been removed because of anaphora with "psychologist". Hence it will certainly begin a foot, possibly a tonic foot.

A factor that does not affect the sample passage is the accentuation of unusual syllables of similar words to bring out a contrast. For example,

he went *out*side, not *in*side.

Although this may seem to be just another facet of antithesis, Vanderslice points out that it is phonetic rather than structural similarity that is contrasted:

I said *de*plane, not *com*plain.

This introduces an interesting interplay between the phonetic and prosodic levels.

Anaphora and antithesis provide an ideal domain for speech synthesis from concept. Determining them from plain text is a very difficult problem, requiring a great deal of real-world knowledge. The first has received some attention in the field of natural language understanding. Finding pronoun referents is an important problem for language translation, for their gender is frequently distinguished in, say, French where it is not in English. Examples such as

> I bought the wine, sat on a table, and drank it
> I bought the wine, sat on a table, and broke it

have been closely studied (Wilks, 1975); for if they were to be translated into French, the pronoun "it" would be rendered differently in each case (*le* vin, *la* table).

In spoken language, emphasis is used to indicate the referent of a pronoun when it would not otherwise be obvious. Vanderslice gives the example

> Bill saw John across the room and he ran over to him
> Bill saw John across the room and *he* ran over to *him*,

where the emphasis reverses the pronoun referents (so that John did the running). He suggests accenting a personal pronoun whenever the true antecedent is not the same as the "unmarked" or default one. Unfortunately he does not elaborate on what is meant by "unmarked". Does it mean that the referent cannot be predicted from knowledge of the words alone, as in the second example above? If so, this is a clear candidate for speech synthesis from concept, for the distinction cannot be made from text!

9.2 Pronunciation

English pronunciation is notoriously irregular. A poem by Charivarius, the pseudonym of a Dutch high school teacher and linguist G.N. Trenité (1870–1946), surveys the problems in an amusing way and is worth quoting in full.

The Chaos

> Dearest creature in Creation
> Studying English pronunciation,
>   I will teach you in my verse
>   Sounds like corpse, corps, horse and worse.
> It will keep you, Susy, busy,
> Make your head with heat grow dizzy;

Tear in eye your dress you'll tear.
So shall I! Oh, hear my prayer:
Pray, console your loving poet,
Make my coat look new, dear, sew it.
Just compare heart, beard and heard,
Dies and diet, lord and word.
Sword and sward, retain and Britain,
(Mind the latter, how it's written).
Made has not the sound of bade,
Say—said, pay—paid, laid, but plaid.
Now I surely will not plague you
With such words as vague and ague,
But be careful how you speak:
Say break, steak, but bleak and streak,
Previous, precious; fuchsia, via;
Pipe, shipe, recipe and choir;
Cloven, oven; how and low;
Script, receipt; shoe, poem, toe.
Hear me say, devoid of trickery;
Daughter, laughter and Terpsichore;
Typhoid, measles, topsails, aisles;
Exiles, similes, reviles;
Wholly, holly; signal, signing;
Thames, examining, combining;
Scholar, vicar and cigar,
Solar, mica, war and far.
Desire—desirable, admirable—admire;
Lumber, plumber; bier but brier;
Chatham, brougham; renown but known,
Knowledge; done, but gone and tone,
One, anemone; Balmoral,
Kitchen, lichen; laundry, laurel;
Gertrude, German; wind and mind;
Scene, Melpemone, mankind;
Tortoise, turquoise, chamois-leather,
Reading, Reading; heathen, heather.
This phonetic labyrinth
Gives: moss, gross; brook, brooch; ninth, plinth.
Billet does not end like ballet;
Bouquet, wallet, mallet, chalet;
Blood and flood are not like food,
Nor is mould like should and would.
Banquet is not nearly parquet,
Which is said to rime with darky
Viscous, viscount; load and broad;
Toward, to forward, to reward.
And your pronunciation's O.K.
When you say correctly; croquet;
Rounded, wounded; grieve and sieve;
Friend and fiend, alive and live

Liberty, library; heave and heaven;
Rachel, ache, moustache; eleven.
We say hallowed, but allowed;
People, leopard; towed, but vowed.
    Mark the difference moreover
    Between mover, plover, Dover;
Leeches, breeches; wise, precise;
Chalice, but police and lice.
    Camel, constable, unstable,
    Principle, discipline, label;
Petal, penal and canal;
Wait, surmise, plait, promise; pal.
    Suit, suite, ruin; circuit, conduit,
    Rime with: "shirk it" and "beyond it";
But it is not hard to tell
Why it's pall, mall, but Pall Mall.
    Muscle, muscular; goal and iron;
    Timber, climber; bullion, lion;
Worm and storm; chaise, chaos, chair;
Senator, spectator, mayor.
    Ivy, privy; famous, clamour
    and enamour rime with "hammer".
Pussy, hussy and possess,
Desert, but dessert, address.
    Golf, wolf; countenants; lieutenants
    Hoist, in lieu of flags, left pennants.
River, rival; tomb, bomb, comb;
Doll and roll, and some and home.
    Stranger does not rime with anger,
    Neither does devour with clangour.
Soul, but foul; and gaunt, but aunt;
Font, front, won't; want, grand and grant;
    Shoes, goes, does. Now first say: finger,
    And then; singer, ginger, linger.
Real, zeal; mauve, gauze and gauge;
Marriage, foliage, mirage, age.
    Query does not rime with very,
    Nor does fury sound like bury.
Dost, lost, post; and doth, cloth, loth;
Job, Job; blossom, bosom, oath.
    Though the difference seems little
    We say actual, but victual;
Seat, sweat; chaste, caste; Leigh, eight, height;
Put, nut; granite but unite.
    Reefer does not rime with deafer,
    Feoffer does, and zephyr, heifer.
Dull, bull; Geoffrey, George; ate, late;
Hint, pint; senate, but sedate.
    Scenic, Arabic, Pacific;
    Science, conscience, scientific.

Tour, but our, and succour, four;
Gas, alas and Arkansas!
    Sea, idea, guinea, area,
    Psalm, Maria, but malaria.
Youth, south, southern; cleanse and clean;
Doctrine, turpentine, marine.
    Compare alien with Italian.
    Dandelion with battalion,
Sally with ally, Yea, Ye,
Eye, I, ay, aye, whey, key, quay.
Say aver, but ever, fever,
Neither, leisure, skein, receiver.
    Never guess—it is not safe;
    We say calves, valves, half, but Ralf.
Heron, granary, canary;
Crevice and device and eyrie;
    Face, preface, but efface,
    Phlegm, phlegmatic; ass, glass, bass;
Large, but target, gin, give, verging;
Ought, out, joust and scour, but scourging;
    Ear, but earn; and wear and tear
    Do not rime with "here", but "ere".
Seven is right, but so is even;
Hyphen, roughen, nephew, Stephen;
    Monkey, donkey; clerk and jerk;
    Asp, grasp, wasp; and cork and work.
Pronunciation—think of psyche—
Is a paling, stout and spikey;
    Won't it make you lose your wits,
    Writing groats and saying "groats"?
It's a dark abyss or tunnel,
Strewn with stones, like rowlock, gunwale,
    Islington and Isle of Wight,
    Housewife, verdict and indict.
Don't you think so, reader, rather
Saying lather, bather, father?
    Finally: which rimes with "enough",
    Though, through, plough, cough, hough or tough?
Hiccough has the sound of "cup",
My advice is ... give it up!

Letter-to-sound Rules

Despite such irregularities, it is surprising how much can be done with
simple letter-to-sound rules. These specify phonetic equivalents of word
fragments and single letters. The longest stored fragment which matches
the current word is translated, and then the same strategy is adopted on
the remainder of the word. Table 9.5 shows some English fragments and
their pronunciations.

Table 9.5. Word fragments and their pronunciations.

Fragment	Pronunciation
-p-	*p*
-ph-	*f*
-phe|	*fee*
-phe|s	*feez*
-phot-	*fuhut*
-place|-	*pleis*
-plac|i-	*pleisi*
-ple|ment-	*pliment*
-plie|-	*plaaiy*
-post	*puhust*
-pp-	*p*
-pp|ly-	*plee*
-preciou-	*presuh*
-proce|d-	*pruhuseed*
-prope|r-	*propuhr*
-prov-	*pruuv*
purpose-	*perpuhs*
-push-	*push*
-put	*put*
-puts	*puts*

It is sometimes important to specify that a rule applies only when the fragment is matched at the beginning or end of a word. In the Table "-" means that other fragments can precede or follow this one. The "|" sign is used to separate suffixes from a word stem, as will be explained shortly.

An advantage of the longest-string search strategy is that it is easy to account for exceptions simply by incorporating them into the fragment table. If they occur in the input, the complete word will automatically be matched first, before any fragment of it is translated. The exception list of complete words can be surprisingly small for quite respectable performance. Table 9.6 shows the entire dictionary for an excellent early pronunciation system written at Bell Laboratories (McIlroy, 1974). Some of the words are notorious exceptions in English, while others are included simply because the rules would run amok on them. Notice that the exceptions are all quite short, with only a few of them having more than two syllables.

Special action has to be taken with final "e" 's. These lengthen and alter the quality of the preceding vowel, so that "bit" becomes "bite" and so on. Unfortunately, if the word has a suffix, the "e" must be detected even though it is no longer final, as in "lonely", and it is even dropped sometimes ("biting"); otherwise these would be pronounced "lonelly", "bitting". To make matters worse, the suffix may be another word: we do not want

Table 9.6. Exception table for a simple pronunciation program.

a	doesn't	guest	meant	reader	those
alkali	doing	has	moreover	refer	to
always	done	have	mr	says	today
any	dr	having	mrs	seven	tomorrow
april	early	heard	nature	shall	tuesday
are	earn	his	none	someone	two
as	eleven	imply	nothing	something	upon
because	enable	into	nowhere	than	very
been	engine	is	nuisance	that	water
being	etc	island	of	the	wednesday
below	evening	john	on	their	were
body	every	july	once	them	who
both	everyone	live	one	there	whom
busy	february	lived	only	thereby	whose
copy	finally	living	over	these	woman
do	friday	many	people	they	women
does	gas	maybe	read	this	yes

"kiteflying" to have an extra syllable which rhymes with "deaf"! Although simple procedures can be developed to take care of common word endings like "-ly", "-ness", "-d", it is difficult to decompose compound words like "wisecrack" and "bumblebee" reliably, but this must be done if they are not to be articulated with three syllables instead of two. Of course, there are exceptions to the final "e" rule. Many common words ("some", "done", "[live]$_V$") disobey the rule by not lengthening the main vowel, while in other, rarer, ones ("anemone", "catastrophe", "epitome") the final "e" is actually pronounced. There are also some complete anomalies ("fete").

McIlroy's (1974) system is a superb example of a robust program which takes a pragmatic approach to these problems, accepting that they will never be fully solved, and which is careful to degrade gracefully when stumped. The pronunciation of each word is found by a succession of increasingly desperate trials:

  —replace upper- by lower-case letters, strip punctuation, and try again;
  —remove final "-s", replace final "ie" by "y", and try again;
  —reject a word without a vowel;
  —repeatedly mark any suffixes with "|";
  —mark with "|" probable morph divisions in compound words;
  —mark potential long vowels indicated by "e|", and long vowels elsewhere in the word;
  —mark voiced medial "s" as in "busy", "usual"; replace final "-s" if stripped;
  —scanning the word from left to right, apply letter-to-sound rules to word fragments;

—when all else fails spell the word, punctuation and all (burp on letters for which no spelling rule exists).

Table 9.7 shows the suffixes which the program recognizes, with some comments on their processing. Multiple suffixes are detected and marked in words like "force|ful|ly" and "spite|ful|ness". This allows silent "e"s to be spotted even when they occur far back in a word. Notice that the suffix marks are available to the word-fragment rules of Table 9.5, and are frequently used by them.

The program has some *ad hoc* rules for dealing with compound words like "race|track", "house|boat"; these are applied as well as normal suffix splitting so that multiple decompositions like "pace|make|r" can be accomplished. The rules look for short letter sequences which do not usually appear in monomorphemic words. It is impossible, however, to detect every morph boundary by such rules, and the program inevitably makes mistakes. Examples of boundaries which go undetected are "edge|ways", "fence|post", "horse|back", "large|mouth", "where|in"; while boundaries are incorrectly inserted into "comple|mentary", "male|volent", "prole|tariat", "Pame|la".

Table 9.7. Rules for detecting suffixes for final "e" processing.

Suffix	Action	Notes and exceptions
s	strip off final s	except in context us
'	strip off final '	
ie	replace final ie by y	
e	replace final e by E (long "e")	when it is the only vowel in a word
|able	place suffix mark as shown	except when no vowel would remain in the rest of the word
|ably		
e | d		
e | n		
e | r		
e | ry		
e | st		
e | y		
| ful		
| ing		
| less		
| ly		
| ment		
| ness		
| or		
| ic	place suffix mark as shown and terminate final e processing	
| ical		
e |		

We now seem to have presented two opposing points of view on the pronunciation problem. Charivarius, the Dutch poet, shows that an enormous number of exceptional words exist; whereas McIlroy's program makes do with a tiny exception dictionary. These views can be reconciled by noting that most of Charivarius' words are relatively uncommon. McIlroy tested his program against the 2000 most frequent words in a large corpus (Kucera and Francis, 1967), and found that 97% were pronounced correctly if word frequencies were taken into account. (The notion of "correctness" is of course a rather subjective one.) However, he estimated that on the remaining words the success rate was only 88%.

The system is particularly impressive in that it is prepared to say anything: if used, for example, on source programs in a high-level computer language it will say the keywords and pronounceable identifiers, spell the other identifiers, and even give the names of special symbols (like $+$, $<$, $=$) correctly!

Morphological Analysis

The use of letter-to-sound rules provides a cheap and fast technique for pronunciation; the fragment table and exception dictionary for the program described above occupy only 11 Kbyte of storage, and can easily be kept in solid-state read-only memory. It produces reasonable results if careful attention is paid to rules for suffix-splitting. However, it is inherently limited because it is not possible in general to detect compound words by simple rules which operate on the lexical structure of the word.

Compounds can only be found reliably by using a morph dictionary. This gives the added advantage that syntactic information can be stored with the morphs to assist with rhythm assignment according to the Chomsky-Halle theory. However, it was noted earlier that morphs, unlike the grammatically-determined morphemes, are not very well defined from a linguistic point of view. Some morphemic decompositions are obviously not morphic because the constituents do not in any way resemble the final word; while others, where the word is simply a concatenation of its components, are clearly morphic. Between these extremes lies a hazy region where what one considers to be a morph depends upon how complex one is prepared to make the concatenation rules. The following description draws on techniques used in a project at MIT in which a morph-based pronunciation system has been implemented (Lee, 1969; Allen, 1976).

Estimates of the number of morphs in English vary from 10 000 to 30 000. Although these seem to be very large numbers, they are considerably less than the number of words in the language. For example, Webster's *New Collegiate Dictionary* (Seventh edition) contains about 100 000 entries. If all forms of the words were included, this number would probably double.

There are several classes of morphs, with restrictions on the combinations that occur. A general word has prefixes, a root, and suffixes, as shown in Fig. 9.3; only the root is mandatory. Suffixes usually perform a grammatical role, affecting the conjugation of a verb or declension of a noun; or transforming one part of speech into another ("-al" can make a noun into an adjective, while "-ness" performs the reverse transformation.) Other suffixes, such as "-dom" or "-ship", only apply to certain parts of speech (nouns, in this case), but do not change the grammatical role of the word. Such suffixes, and all prefixes, alter the meaning of a word.

Some root morphs cannot combine with other morphs but always stand alone, for instance, "this". Others, called free morphs, can either occur on their own or combine with further morphs to form a word. Thus the root "house" can be joined on either side by another root, such as "boat", or by a suffix such as "ing". A third type of root morph is one which *must* combine with another morph, like "crimin-", "-ceive".

Even with a morph dictionary, decomposing a word into a sequence of morphs is not a trivial operation. The process of lexical concatenation often results in a minor change in the constituents. How big this change is allowed to be governs the morph system being used. For example, Allen (1976) gives three concatenation rules: a final "e" can be omitted, as in

$$\text{give} + \text{ing} \rightarrow \text{giving};$$

the last consonant of the root can be doubled, as in

$$\text{bid} + \text{ing} \rightarrow \text{bidding};$$

or a final "y" can change to an "i", as in

$$\text{handy} + \text{cap} \rightarrow \text{handicap}.$$

If these are the only rules permitted, the morph dictionary will have to include multiple versions of some suffixes. For example, the plural morpheme [-s] needs to be represented both by "-s" and "-es", to account for

$$\text{pea} + \text{s} \rightarrow \text{peas}$$

and

$$\text{baby} + \text{es} \rightarrow \text{babies} \quad (\text{using the "y"} \rightarrow \text{"i" rule}).$$

Fig. 9.3. The structure of a word.

This would not be necessary if a "y" → "ie" rule were included too. Similarly, the morpheme [-ic] will include morphs "-ic" and "-c"; the latter to cope with

$$\text{specify} + c \rightarrow \text{specific} \quad \text{(using the "y"} \rightarrow \text{"i" rule).}$$

Furthermore, non-morphemic roots such as "galact" need to be included because the concatenation rules do not capture the transformation

$$\text{galaxy} + \text{ic} \rightarrow \text{galactic.}$$

There is clearly a trade-off between the size of the morph dictionary and the complexity of the concatenation rules.

Since a text-to-speech system is presented with already-concatenated morphs, it must be prepared to reverse the effects of the concatenation rules to deduce the constituents of a word. When two morphs combine with any of the three rules given above, the changes in spelling occur only in the left-hand one. Therefore the word is best scanned in a right-to-left direction to split off the morphs starting with suffixes, as McIlroy's program does. If the procedure fails at any point, one of the three rules is hypothesized, its effect is undone, and splitting continues. For example, consider the word

$$\text{grasshoppers} \leftarrow \text{grass} + \text{hop} + \text{er} + \text{s}$$

(Lee, 1969). The "-s" is detected first, then "-er"; these are both stored in the dictionary as suffixes. The remainder, "grasshopp", cannot be decomposed and does not appear in the dictionary. So each of the rules above is hypothesized in turn, and the result investigated. (The "y" → "i" rule is obviously not applicable.) When the final-consonant-doubling rule is considered, the sequence "grasshop" is investigated. "Shop" could be split off this, but then the unknown morph "gras" would result. The alternative, to remove "hop", leaves a remainder "grass" which *is* a free morph, as desired. Thus a unique and correct decomposition is obtained. Notice that the procedure would fail if, for example, "grass" had been inadvertently omitted from the dictionary.

Sometimes, several seemingly valid decompositions present themselves (Allen, 1976). For example:

scarcity   ← scar + city
           ← scarce + ity (using final-"e" deletion)
           ← scar + cite + y (using final-"e" deletion)
resting   ← rest + ing
           ← re + sting
biding   ← bide + ing (using final-"e" deletion)
           ← bid + ing

$$\text{unionized} \leftarrow \text{un} + \text{ion} + \text{ize} + \text{d}$$
$$\leftarrow \text{union} + \text{ize} + \text{d}$$
$$\text{winding} \quad \leftarrow [\text{wind}]_N + \text{ing}$$
$$\leftarrow [\text{wind}]_V + \text{ing}.$$

The last distinction is important because the pronunciation of "wind" depends on whether it is a noun or a verb.

Several sources of information can be used to resolve these ambiguities. The word structure of Fig. 9.3, together with the division of root morphs into bound and free ones, may eliminate some possibilities. Certain letter sequences (such as "rp") do not appear at the beginning of a word or morph, and others never occur at the end. Knowledge of these sequences can reject some unacceptable decompositions, or perhaps more importantly, can enable intelligent guesses to be made in cases where a constituent morph has been omitted from the dictionary. The grammatical function of suffixes allows suffix sequences to be checked for compatibility. The syntax of the sentence, together with suffix knowledge, can rule out other combinations. Semantic knowledge will occasionally be necessary (as in the "unionized" and "winding" examples above, compare a "winding road" with a "winding blow"). Finally, Allen (1976) suggests that a preference structure on composition rules can be used to resolve ambiguity.

Once the morphological structure has been determined, the rest of the pronunciation process is relatively easy. A phonetic transcription of each morph may be stored in the morph dictionary, or else letter-to-sound rules can be used on individual morphs. These are likely to be quite successful because final-"e" processing can now be done with confidence: there are no hidden final "e"s in the middle of morphs. In either case the resulting phonetic transcriptions of the individual morphs must be concatenated to give the transcription of the complete word. Although some contextual modification has to be accounted for, it is relatively straightforward and easy to predict. For example, the plural morphs "-s" and "-es" can be realized phonetically by uhz, s, or z depending on context. Similarly the past-tense suffix "-ed" may be rendered as uhd, t, or d. The suffixes "-ion" and "-ure" sometimes cause modification of the previous morph: for example

$$\text{act} + \text{ion} \rightarrow akt + \text{ion} \rightarrow akshuhn.$$

The morph dictionary does not remove the need for a lexicon of exceptional words. The irregular final-"e" words mentioned earlier ("done", "anemone", "fete") need to be treated on an individual basis, as do words such as "quadruped" which have misleading endings (it should not be decomposed as "quadrup|ed").

Pronunciation of Languages other than English

Text-to-speech systems for other languages have been reported in the literature. (For example, French, Esperanto, Italian, Russian, Spanish and German are covered by Lesmo *et al.*, 1978; O'Shaughnessy *et al.*, 1981; Sherwood, 1978; Mangold and Stall, 1978). Generally speaking, these present fewer difficulties than does English. Esperanto is particularly easy because each letter in its orthography has only one sound, making the pronunciation problem trivial. Moreover, stress in polysyllabic words always occurs on the penultimate syllable.

It is tempting and often sensible when designing a synthesis system for English to use an utterance representation somewhere between phonetics and ordinary spelling. This may happen in practice even if it is not intended: a user, finding that a given word is pronounced incorrectly, will alter the spelling to make it work. The Word English Spelling alphabet (Dewey, 1971), among others (Haas, 1966), is a simplified and apparently natural scheme which was developed by the spelling reform movement. It maps very simply on to a phonetic representation, just like Esperanto. However, it can provide little help with the crucial problem of stress assignment, except perhaps by explicitly indicating reduced vowels.

9.3 Discussion

This chapter has really only touched the tip of a linguistic iceberg. I have given some examples of representations, rules, algorithms and exceptions, to make the concepts more tangible; but a whole mass of detail has been swept under the carpet.

There are two important messages that are worth reiterating once more. The first is that the representation of the input (that is, whether it be a "concept" in some semantic domain, a syntactic description of an utterance, a decomposition into morphs, plain text or some contrived re-spelling of it) is crucial to the quality of the output. Almost any extra information about the utterance can be taken into account and used to improve the speech. It is difficult to derive such information if it is not provided explicitly, for the process of climbing the tree from text to semantic representation is at least as hard as descending it to a phonetic transcription.

Secondly, simple algorithms perform remarkably well: witness the punctuation-driven intonation assignment scheme, and word fragment rules for pronunciation. However, the combined degradation contributed by several imperfect processes is likely to impair speech quality very seriously. And great complexity is introduced when these simple algorithms are discarded in favour of more sophisticated ones. There is, for example, a world of difference between a pronunciation program that copes with 97% of common words and one that deals correctly with 99% of a random sample from a dictionary.

Some of the options that face the system designer are recapitulated in Fig. 9.4. Starting from text, one can take the simple approach of lexically-based suffix-splitting, letter-to-sound rules, and prosodics derived from punctuation, to generate a phonetic transcription. This will provide a cheap system which is relatively easy to implement but whose speech quality will probably not be acceptable to any but the most dedicated listener (such as a blind person with no other access to reading material).

The biggest improvement in speech quality from such a system would almost certainly come from more intelligent prosodic control, particularly of intonation. This, unfortunately, is also by far the most difficult to make unless intonation contours, tonic stresses, and tone-group boundaries are hand-coded into the input. To generate the appropriate information from text, one has to climb to the upper levels in Fig. 9.4; and even when these are reached, the problems are by no means over. Still, let us climb the tree.

For syntax analysis, part-of speech information is needed; and for this the grammatical roles of individual words in the text must be ascertained. A morph dictionary is the most reliable way to do this. A linguist may prefer to go from morphs to syntax by way of morphemes; but this is not

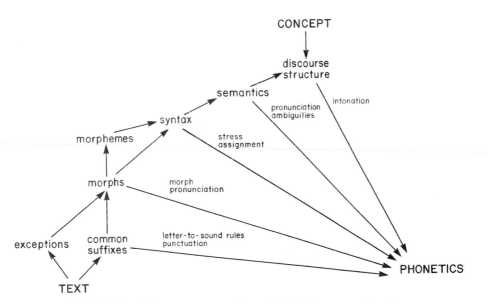

Fig. 9.4. Levels in text understanding and their influence on elocution.

necessary for the present purpose. Just the information that the morph "went" is a verb can be stored in the dictionary, instead of its decomposition [went] = [go] + [ed].

Now that we have the morphological structure of the text, stress assignment rules can be applied to produce more accurate speech rhythms. The morph decomposition will also allow improvements to be made to the pronunciation, particularly in the case of silent "e"s in compound words. But the ability to assign intonation has hardly been improved at all.

Let us proceed upwards. Now the problems become really difficult. A semantic representation of the text is needed; but what exactly does this mean? We certainly must have *morphemic* knowledge, for now the fact that "went" is a derivative of "go" (rather than any other verb) becomes crucial. Very well, let us augment the morph dictionary with morphemic information. But this does not attack the problem of semantic representation. We may wish to resolve pronoun references to help assign stress. Parts of the problem are solved in principle and reported in the artificial intelligence literature, but if such an ability is incorporated into the speech synthesis system, it will become enormously complicated. In addition, we have seen that knowledge of antitheses in the text will greatly assist intonation assignment, but procedures for extracting this information constitute a research topic in their own right.

Now step back and take a top-down approach. What could we do with this semantic understanding and knowledge of the structure of the discourse if we had it? Suppose the input were a "concept" in some as yet undetermined representation. What are the *acoustic* manifestations of such high-level features as anaphoric references or antithetical comparisons, of parenthetical or satirical remarks, of emotions: warmth, sarcasm, sadness and despair? Can we program the art of elocution? These are good questions.

9.4 References

Allen, J. (1976). Synthesis of speech from unrestricted text. *Proc Institute of Electrical and Electronic Engineers,* **64**(4) 433–442, April.

Bolinger, D. (1972). Accent is predictable (if you're a mind reader). *Language,* **48**(3) 633–644, July–September.

Chomsky, N. and Halle, M. (1968). "The sound pattern of English", Harper and Row, New York.

Davey, A. (1978). "Discourse production", Edinburgh University Press.

Dewey, G. (1971). "English spelling: roadblock to reading", Teachers College Press, Columbia University, New York.

Haas, W. (Editor) (1966). "Alphabets for English", Manchester University Press, Manchester, England.

Halliday, M.A.K. (1970). "A course in spoken English: Intonation", Oxford University Press, London.

Klatt, D.H. (1975). Vowel lengthening is syntactically determined in a connected discourse. *J Phonetics*, **3**, 129–140.

Kucera, H. and Francis, W.N. (1967). "Computational analysis of present-day American English", Brown University Press, Providence, Rhode Island.

Lee, F.F. (1969). Reading machine: from text to speech. *IEEE Trans Audio and Electroacoustics*, **AU-17**(4) 275–282, December.

Lesmo, L., Mezzalama, M. and Torasso, P. (1978). A text-to-speech translation system for Italian. *Int J Man-Machine Studies*, **10**(5) 569–591, September.

Mangold, H. and Stall, D.S. (1978). Principles of text-controlled speech synthesis with special application to German. *In* "Speech communication with computers", (L. Bolc, ed.) pp. 139–181. MacMillan, London.

McIlroy, M.D. (1974). Synthetic English speech by rule. Computing Science Technical Report 14, Bell Labs, Murray Hill, New Jersey.

O'Shaughnessy, D., Lennig, M., Mermelstein, P. and Divay, M. (1981). Simulation of a French reading machine for the blind. *Proc Canadian Man-Computer Communication Conference*, 217–222, Waterloo, June.

Sherwood, B.A. (1978). Fast text-to-speech algorithms for Esperanto, Spanish, Italian, Russian and English. *Int J Man-Machine Studies*, **10**(6) 669–692, November.

Vanderslice, R. (1968). Synthetic elocution. *Working Papers in Phonetics*, **8**, University of California, Los Angeles, February.

Wilks, Y. (1975). An intelligent analyzer and understander of English. *Communications of the Association for Computing Machinery*, **18**(5) 264–274, May.

Young, S.J. and Fallside, F. (1980). Synthesis by rule of prosodic features in word concatenation systems. *Int J Man-Machine Studies*, **12**(3) 241–258, April.

9.5 Further Reading

Books on pronunciation give surprisingly little help in designing a text-to-speech procedure. The best aid is a good on-line dictionary and flexible software to search it and record rules, examples and exceptions. Here are some papers that describe existing systems.

Ainsworth, W.A. (1974). A system for converting text into speech. *IEEE Trans Audio and Electroacoustics*, **AU-21**, 288–290.

Colby, K.M., Christinaz, D. and Graham, S. (1978). A computer-driven, personal, portable, and intelligent speech prosthesis. *Computers and Biomedical Research*, **11**, 337–343.

Elovitz, H.S., Johnson, R.W., McHugh, A. and Shore, J.E. (1976). Letter-to-sound rules for automatic translation of English text to phonetics. *IEEE Trans Acoustics, Speech and Signal Processing*, **ASSP-24**(6) 446–459, December.

Kooi, R. and Lim, W.C. (1978). An on-line minicomputer-based system for reading printed text aloud. *IEEE Trans Systems, Man and Cybernetics*, **SMC-8**, 57–62, January.

Umeda, N. and Teranishi, R. (1975). The parsing program for automatic text-to-speech synthesis developed at the Electrotechnical Laboratory in 1968. *IEEE Trans Acoustics, Speech and Signal Processing*, **ASSP-23**(2) 183–188, April.

Umeda, N. (1976). Linguistic rules for text-to-speech synthesis. *Proc Institute of Electrical and Electronic Engineers*, **64**(4) 443–451, April.

10

DESIGNING THE MAN–COMPUTER DIALOGUE

Interactive computers are being used more and more by non-specialist people without much previous computer experience. As processing costs continue to decline, the overall expense of providing highly interactive systems becomes increasingly dominated by terminal and communications equipment. Taken together, these two factors highlight the need for easy-to-use, low-bandwidth interactive terminals that make maximum use of the existing telephone network for remote access.

Speech output can provide versatile feedback from a computer at very low cost in distribution and terminal equipment. It is attractive from several points of view. Terminals (telephones) are invariably in place already. People without experience of computers are accustomed to their use, and are not intimidated by them. The telephone network is cheap to use and extends all over the world. The touch-tone keypad (or a portable tone generator) provides a complementary data input device which will do for many purposes until the technology of speech recognition becomes better developed and more widespread. Indeed, many applications (especially information retrieval ones) need a much smaller bandwidth from user to computer than in the reverse direction, and voice output combined with restricted keypad entry provides a good match to their requirements.

There are, however, severe problems in implementing natural and useful interactive systems using speech output. The eye can absorb information at a far greater rate than can the ear. You can scan a page of text in a way which has no analogy in auditory terms. Even so, it is difficult to design a dialogue which allows you to search computer output visually at high speed. In practice, scanning a new report is often better done at your desk with a printed copy than at a computer terminal with a viewing program (although this is likely to change in the near future).

With speech, the problem of organizing output becomes even harder. Most of the information we learn using our ears is presented in a conversational way, either in face-to-face discussions or over the telephone. Verbal but non-conversational presentations, as in the university lecture theatre, are known to be a rather inefficient way of transmitting information. The degree of interaction is extremely high even in a telephone conversation, and communication relies heavily on speech gestures such as hesitations, grunts and pauses; on prosodic features such as intonation, pitch range, tempo and voice quality; and on conversational gambits such as interruption and long silence. I emphasized in the last two chapters the rudimentary state of knowledge about how to synthesize prosodic features, and the situation is even worse for the other, paralinguistic, phenomena.

There is also a very special problem with voice output, namely, the transient nature of the speech signal. If you miss an utterance, it's gone. With a visual display unit, at least the last few interactions usually remain available. Even then, it is not uncommon to look up beyond the top of the screen and wish that more of the history was still visible! This obviously places a premium on a voice response system's ability to repeat utterances. Moreover, the dialogue designer must do his utmost to ensure that the user is always aware of the current state of the interaction, for there is no opportunity to refresh the memory by glancing at earlier entries and responses.

There are two separate aspects to the man—computer interface in a voice response system. The first is the relationship between the system and the end user, that is, the "consumer" of the synthesized dialogue. The second is the relationship between the system and the applications programmer who creates the dialogue. These are treated separately in the next two sections. We will have more to say about the former aspect, for it is ultimately more important to more people. But the applications programmer's view is important, too; for without him no systems would exist! The technical difficulties in creating synthetic dialogues for the majority of voice systems probably explain why speech output technology is still greatly under-used. Finally we look at techniques for using small keypads such as those on touch-tone telephones, for they are an essential part of many voice response systems.

10.1 Programming Principles for Natural Interaction

Special attention must be paid to the details of the man—machine interface in speech-output systems. This section summarizes experience of human factors considerations gained in developing the remote telephone enquiry service described in Chapter 1 (Witten and Madams, 1977), which employs an ordinary touch-tone keypad for input in conjunction with synthetic voice response. Most of the principles which emerged were the result of natural evolution of the system, and were not clear at the outset. Basically, they stem from the fact that speech is both more intrusive and more ephemeral than writing, and so they are applicable in general to speech output information retrieval systems with keyboard or even voice input. Be warned, however, that they are based upon casual observation and speculation rather than empirical research. There is a desperate need for proper studies of user psychology in speech systems.

Echoing

Most alphanumeric input peripherals echo on a character-by-character basis. Although one can expect quite a high proportion of mistakes with unconventional keyboards, especially when entering alphabetic data on a basically numeric keypad, audio character echoing is distracting and annoying. If you type "123" and the computer echoes

"one ... two ... three"

after the individual key-presses, it is liable to divert your attention, for voice output is much more intrusive than a purely visual "echo".

Instead, an immediate response to a completed input line is preferable. This response can take the form of a reply to a query, or, if successive data items are being typed, confirmation of the data entered. In the latter case, it is helpful if the information can be generated in the same way that the user himself would be likely to verbalize it. Thus, for example, when entering numbers:

USER: "123#" (# is the end-of-line character)
COMPUTER: "One hundred and twenty-three."

For a query which requires lengthy processing, the input should be repeated in a neat, meaningful format to give the user a chance to abort the request.

Retracting Actions

Because commands are entered directly without explicit confirmation, it must always be easy for the user to revoke his actions. The utility of an "undo" command is now commonly recognized for any interactive system, and it becomes even more important in speech systems because it is easier for the user to lose his place in the dialogue and so make errors.

Interrupting

A command which interrupts output and returns to a known state should be recognized at every level of the system. It is essential that voice output be terminated immediately, rather than at the end of the utterance. We do not want the user to live in fear of the system embarking on a long, boring monologue that is impossible to interrupt! Again, the same is true of interactive dialogues which do not use speech, but becomes particularly important with voice response because it takes longer to transmit information.

Forestalling Prompts

Computer-generated prompts must be explicit and frequent enough to allow new users to understand what they are expected to do. Experienced users will "type ahead" quite naturally, and the system should suppress unnecessary prompts under these conditions by inspecting the input buffer before prompting. This allows the user to concatenate frequently-used commands into chunks whose size is entirely at his own discretion.

With the above-mentioned telephone enquiry service, for example, it was found that people often took advantage of the prompt-suppression feature to enter their user number, password, and required service number as a single keying sequence. As you become familiar with a service, you quickly and easily learn to forestall expected prompts by typing ahead. This provides a very natural way for the system to adapt itself automatically to the experience of the user. New users will naturally wait to be prompted, and proceed through the dialogue at a slower and more relaxed pace.

Suppressing unnecessary prompts is a good idea in any interactive system, whether or not it uses the medium of speech, although it is hardly ever done in conventional systems. It is particularly important with speech, however, because an unexpected or unwanted prompt is quite distracting, and it is not so easy to ignore it as it is with a visual display. Furthermore, speech messages usually take longer to present than displayed ones, so that the user is distracted for more time.

Information Units

Lengthy computer voice responses are inappropriate for conveying information, because attention wanders if one is not actively involved in the conversation. A sequential exchange of terse messages, each designed to dispense one small unit of information, forces the user to take a meaningful part in the dialogue. It has other advantages, too, allowing a higher degree of input-dependent branching, and permitting rapid recovery from errors.

The following example from the "Acidosis program", an audio response system designed to help physicians to diagnose acidosis, is a good example of what *not* to do.

"(Chime) A VALUE OF SIX-POINT-ZERO-ZERO HAS BEEN ENTERED FOR PH. THIS VALUE IS IMPOSSIBLE. TO CONTINUE THE PRO-

GRAM, ENTER A NEW VALUE FOR PH IN THE RANGE BETWEEN SIX-POINT-SIX AND EIGHT-POINT-ZERO (beep dah beep-beep)" (Smith and Goodwin, 1970).

The use of extraneous noises (for example, a "chime" heralds an error message, and a "beep dah beep-beep" requests data input in the form ⟨digit⟩⟨point⟩⟨digit⟩⟨digit⟩) was thought necessary in the Acidosis program to keep the user awake and help him with the format of the interaction. Rather than a long monologue like this, it seems much better to design a sequential interchange of terse messages, so that the caller can be guided into a state where he can rectify his error. For example,

CALLER: "6*00#"
COMPUTER: "Entry out of range"
CALLER: "6*00#" (persists)
COMPUTER: "The minimum acceptable pH value is 6.6"
CALLER: "9*03#"
COMPUTER: "The maximum acceptable pH value is 8.0"

This dialogue allows a rapid exit from the error situation in the likely event that the entry has simply been mis-typed. If the error persists, the caller is given just one piece of information at a time, and forced to continue to play an active role in the interaction.

Input Timeouts

In general, input timeouts are dangerous, because they introduce apparent acausality in the system seen by the user. A case has been reported where a user became "highly agitated and refused to go near the terminal again after her first timed-out prompt. She had been quietly thinking what to do and the terminal suddenly interjecting and making its own suggestions was just too much for her" (Gaines and Facey, 1975).

However, voice response systems lack the satisfying visual feedback of end-of-line on termination of an entry. Hence a timed-out reminder is appropriate if a delay occurs after some characters have been entered. This requires the operating system to support a character-by-character mode of input, rather than the usual line-by-line mode.

Repeat Requests

Any voice response system must support a universal "repeat last utterance" command, because old output does not remain visible. A fairly sophisticated facility is desirable, as repeat requests are very frequent in practice. They may be due to a simple inability to understand a response, to forgetting what was said, or to distraction of attention, which is especially common with office terminals.

In the telephone enquiry service two distinct commands were employed, one to repeat the last utterance in case of misrecognition, and the other to summarize the current state of the interaction in case of distraction. For the former, it is essential to avoid simply regenerating an utterance identical with the last. Some variation of intonation and rhythm is needed to prevent an annoying, stereotyped response. A second consecutive repeat request should trigger a paraphrased reply. An error recovery sequence could be used which presented the misunderstood information in a different way with more interaction, but experience indicates that this is of minor importance, especially if information units are kept small anyway. To summarize the current state of the interaction in response to the second type of repeat command necessitates the system maintaining a model of the user. Even a poor model, like a record of his last few transactions and their results, is well worth having.

Varied Speech

Synthetic speech is usually rather dreary to listen to. Successive utterances with identical intonations should be carefully avoided. Small changes in speaking rate, pitch range, and mean pitch level, all serve to add variety. Unfortunately, little is known at present about the role of intonation in interactive dialogue, although this is an active research area and new developments can be expected (for a detailed report of a recent research project relevant to this topic see Brown et al., 1980). However, even random variations in certain parameters of the pitch contour are useful to relieve the tedium of repetitive intonation patterns.

10.2 The Applications Programming Environment

The comments in the last section are aimed at the applications programmer who is designing the dialogue and constructing the interactive system. But what kind of environment should *he* be given to assist with this work?

The best help the applications programmer can have is a speech generation method which makes it easy for him to enter new utterances and modify them on-line in cut-and-try attempts to render the man-machine dialogue as natural as possible. This is perhaps the most important advantage of synthesizing speech by rule from a textual representation. If encoded versions of natural utterances are stored, it becomes quite difficult to make minor modifications to the dialogue in the light of experience with it, for a recording session must be set up to acquire new utterances. This is especially true if more than one voice is used, or if the voice belongs to a person who cannot be recalled quickly by the programmer to augment the utterance library. Even if it is his own voice there will still be delays, for recording speech is a real-time job which usually needs a stand-alone processor, and if data compression is used, a substantial amount of computation will be needed before the utterance is in a useable form.

The broad phonetic input required by segmental speech synthesis-by-rule systems is quite suitable for utterance representation. Utterances can be entered quickly from a standard computer terminal, and edited as text files. Programmers must acquire skill in phonetic transcription, but this is a small inconvenience. The art is easily learned in an interactive situation where the effect of modifications to the transcription can be heard immediately. If allophones must be represented explicitly in the input, then the programmer's task becomes considerably more complicated because of the combinatorial explosion in trial-and-error modifications.

Plain text input is also quite suitable. A significant rate of error is tolerable if immediate audio feedback of the result is available, so that the operator can adjust his text to suit the pronunciation idiosyncrasies of the program. But it is acceptable, and indeed preferable, if prosodic features are represented explicitly in the input rather than being assigned automatically by a computer program.

The application of voice response to interactive computer dialogue is quite different to the problem of reading aloud from text. We have seen that a major concern with reading machines is how to glean information about intonation, rhythm, emphasis, tone of voice, and so on, from an input of ordinary English text. The significant problems of semantic processing, utilization of pragmatic knowledge, and syntactic analysis do not, fortunately, arise in interactive information retrieval systems. In these, the end user is communicating with a program which has been created by a person who knows what he wants it to say. Thus the major difficulty is in *describing* the prosodic features rather than *deriving* them from text.

Speech synthesis by rule is a subsidiary process to the main interactive procedure. It would be unwise to allow the updating of resonance parameter tracks to be interrupted by other calls on the system, and so the synthesis process needs to be executed in real time. If a stand-alone processor is used for the interactive dialogue, it may be able to handle the synthesis rules as well. In this case the speech-by-rule program could be a library procedure, if the system is implemented in a compiled language. An interesting alternative with an interpretive-language implementation, such as Basic, is to alter the language interpreter to add a new command, "speak", which simply transfers a string representing an utterance to an asynchronous process which synthesizes it. However, there must be some way for an interpreted program to abort the current synthesis in the event of an interrupt signal from the user.

If the main computer system is time-shared, the synthesis-by-rule procedure is best executed by an independent processor. For example, a 16-bit microcomputer controlling a hardware formant synthesizer has been used to run the ISP system in real time without too much difficulty (Witten and Abbess, 1979). An important task is to define an interface between the two which allows the main process to control relevant aspects of the prosody of the speech in a way which is appropriate to the state of the interaction, without having to bother about such things as matching the intonation contour to the utterance and the details of syllable rhythm. Halliday's notation appears to be quite suitable for this purpose.

If there is only one synthesizer on the system, there will be no difficulty in addressing it. One way of dealing with multiple synthesizers is to treat them as assignable devices in the same way that non-spooling peripherals are in many operating systems. Notice that the data rate to the synthesizer is quite low if the utterance is represented as text with prosodic markers, and can easily be handled by a low-speed asynchronous serial line.

The Votrax ML-I synthesizer which is discussed in the next chapter has an interface which interposes it between a visual display unit and the serial port that connects it to the computer. The VDU terminal can be used quite normally, except that a special sequence of two control characters will cause Votrax to intercept the following message up to another control character, and interpret it as speech. The fact that the characters which specify the spoken message do not appear on the VDU screen means that the operation is invisible to the user. However, this transparency can be inhibited by a switch on the synthesizer to allow visual checking of the sound-segment character sequence.

Votrax buffers up to 64 sound segments, which is sufficient to generate isolated spoken messages. For longer passages, it can be synchronized with the constant-rate serial output using the modem lines of the serial interface, together with appropriate device-driving software.

This is a particularly convenient interfacing technique in cases when the synthesizer should always be associated with a certain terminal. As an example of how it can be used, one can arrange files each of whose lines contain a printed message, together with its Votrax equivalent bracketed by the appropriate control characters. When such a file is listed, or examined with an editor program, the lines appear simultaneously in spoken and typed English.

If a phonetic representation is used for utterances, with real-time synthesis using a separate process (or processor), it is easy for the programmer to fiddle about with the interactive dialogue to get it feeling right. For him, each utterance is just a textual string which can be stored as a string constant within his program just as a VDU prompt would be. He can edit it as part of his program, and "print" it to the speech synthesis device to hear it. There are no more technical problems to developing an interactive dialogue with speech output than there are for a conventional interactive program. Of course, there are more human problems, and the points discussed in the last section should always be borne in mind.

10.3 Using the Keypad

One of the greatest advantages of speech output from computers is the ubiquity of the telephone network and the possibility of using it without the need for special equipment at the terminal. The requirement for input as well as output obviously presents something of a problem because of the restricted nature of the telephone keypad.

Figure 10.1 shows the layout of the keypad. Signalling is achieved by dual-frequency tones. For example, if key 7 is pressed, sinusoidal components at 852 Hz and 1209 Hz are transmitted down the line. During the process of dialling these are received by the telephone exchange equipment, which assembles the digits that form a number and attempts to route the call appropriately. Once a connection is made, either party is free to press keys if desired and the signals will be transmitted to the other end, where they can be decoded by simple electronic circuits.

Dial telephones signal with closely-spaced dial pulses. One pulse is generated for a "1", two for a "2", and so on. (Obviously, ten pulses are

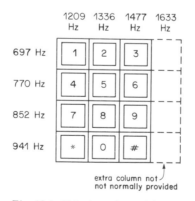

Fig. 10.1. Telephone keypad layout.

generated for a "0", rather than none!) Unfortunately, once the connection is made it is difficult to signal with dial pulses. They cannot be decoded reliably at the other end because the telephone network is not designed to transmit such low frequencies. However, hand-held tone generators can be purchased for use with dial telephones. Although these are undeniably extra equipment, and one purpose of using speech output is to avoid this, they are very cheap and portable compared with other computer terminal equipment.

The small number of keys on the telephone pad makes it rather difficult to use for communicating with computers. Provision is made for 16 keys, but only 12 are implemented; the others may be used for some military purposes. Of course, if a separate tone generator is used then advantage can be taken of the extra keys, but this will introduce incompatibility with those who use unmodified touch-tone phones. More sophisticated terminals are available which extend the keypad, such as the Displayphone of Northern Telecommunications. However, they are designed as a complete communications terminal, and contain their own visual display as well.

Keying Alphabetic Data

Figure 10.2 shows the near-universal scheme for overlaying alphabetic letters on to the telephone keypad. Since more than one symbol occupies each key, it is obviously necessary to have multiple keystrokes per character if the input sequence is to be decodable as a string of letters. One way of doing this is to depress the appropriate button the number of times corresponding to the position of the letter on it. For example, to enter the letter "L" the user would key the "5" button three times in rapid succession. Keying rhythm must be used to distinguish the four entries "J J J" "J K" "K J" and "L", unless one of the bottom three buttons is used as a separator. A different method is to use "*", "0" and "#" as shift keys to indicate

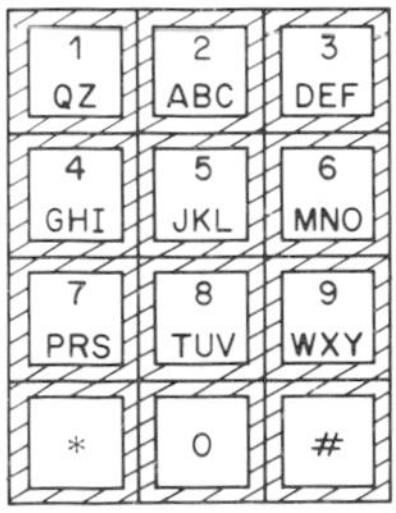

Fig. 10.2. Alphabetic layout.

whether the first, second, or third letter on a key is intended. Then "#5" would represent "L". Alternatively, the shift could follow the key instead of preceding it, so that "5#" represented "L".

If numeric as well as alphabetic information may be entered, a mode-shift operation is commonly used to switch between numeric and alphabetic modes.

The relative merits of these three methods, multiple depressions, shift key prefix, and shift key suffix, have been investigated experimentally (Kramer, 1970). The results were rather inconclusive. The first method seemed to be slightly inferior in terms of user accuracy. It seemed that preceding rather than following shifts gave higher accuracy, although this is perhaps rather counter-intuitive, and may have been fortuitous. The most useful result from the experiments was that users exhibited significant learning behaviour, and a training period of at least two hours was recommended. Operators were found able to key at rates of at least three to four characters per second, and faster with practice.

If a greater range of characters must be represented, then the coding problem becomes more complex. Figure 10.3 shows a keypad which can be used for entry of the full 64-character standard upper-case ASCII alphabet (Shew, 1975). The system is intended for remote vocabulary updating in a phonetically-based speech synthesis system. There are three modes of operation: numeric, alphabetic and symbolic. These are entered by "##", "**" and "*0" respectively. Two function modes, signalled by "#0" and "#*", allow some rudimentary line-editing and monitor facilities to be incorporated. Line-editing commands include character and line delete, and two kinds of read-back commands: one tries to pronounce the words in a line and the other spells out the characters. The monitor commands allow the user to repeat the effect of the last input line as though he had entered it again, to order the system to read back the last complete output line, and to query time and system status.

Incomplete Keying of Alphanumeric Data

It is obviously going to be rather difficult for the operator to key alphanumeric information unambiguously on a 12-key pad. In the description of the telephone enquiry service in Chapter 1, it was mentioned that single-key entry can be useful for alphanumeric data if the ambiguity can be resolved by the computer. If a multiple-character entry is known to refer to an item on a given list the characters can be keyed directly according to the coding scheme of Fig. 10.2.

Under most circumstances no ambiguity will arise. For example, Table 10.1 shows the keystrokes that would be entered for the first fifty 5-letter

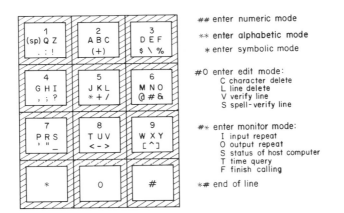

Fig. 10.3. Keyboard for entering the 64-character upper-case ASCII alphabet (after Shew, 1975).

words in an English dictionary. Only two clashes occur: between "adore" and "afore", and "agate" and "agave". As a more extensive example, in a dictionary of 24 500 words, just under 2000 ambiguities (8% of words) were discovered. Such ambiguities would have to be resolved interactively by the system explaining its dilemma, and asking the user for a choice. Notice incidentally that although the keyed sequences do not have the same lexicographic order as the words, no extra cost will be associated with the table-searching operation if the dictionary is stored in inverted form, with each legal number pointing to its English equivalent or equivalents.

A command language syntax is also a powerful way of disambiguating keystrokes entered. Figure 10.4 shows the keypad layout for a telephone voice calculator (Newhouse and Sibley, 1969). This calculator provides the standard arithmetic operators, ten numeric registers, a range of pre-defined mathematical functions, and even the ability for a user to enter his own functions over the telephone. The number representation is fixed-point,

Table 10.1. Keying equivalents of some words.

aback	22225#	abide	22433#	adage	23243#	adore	23673#	after	23837#
abaft	22238#	abode	22633#	adapt	23278#	adorn	23676#	again	24246#
abase	22273#	abort	22678#	adder	23337#	adult	23858#	agape	24273#
abash	22274#	about	22688#	addle	23353#	adust	23878#	agate	24283#
abate	22283#	above	22683#	adept	23378#	aeger	23437#	agave	24283#
abbey	22239#	abuse	22873#	adieu	23438#	aegis	23447#	agent	24368#
abbot	22268#	abyss	22977#	admit	23648#	aerie	23743#	agile	24453#
abeam	22326#	acorn	22676#	admix	23649#	affix	23349#	aglet	24538#
abele	22353#	acrid	22743#	adobe	23623#	afoot	23668#	agony	24669#
abhor	22467#	actor	22867#	adopt	23678#	afore	23673#	agree	24733#

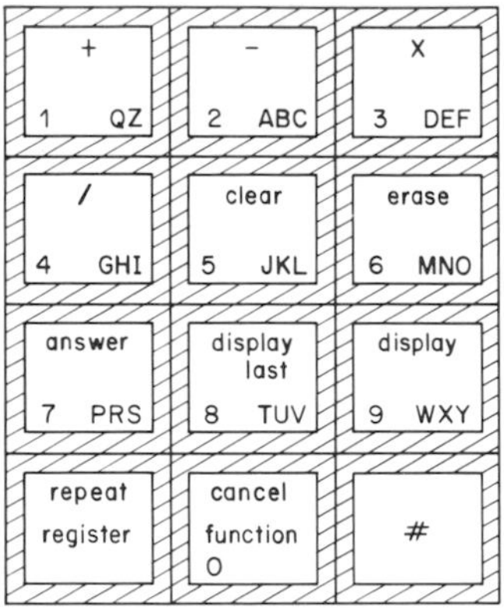

Fig. 10.4. Keypad layout for a telephone calculator (after Newhouse and Sibley, 1969).

with user control (through a system function) over the precision. Input of numbers is free format.

Despite the power of the calculator language, the dialogue is defined so that each keystroke is unique in context and never has to be disambiguated explicitly by the user. Table 10.2 summarizes the command language syntax in an informal and rather heterogeneous notation. A calculation is a sequence of operations followed by an EXIT function call. There are twelve different operations, one for each button on the keypad. Actually, two of them (*cancel* and *function*) share the same key so that "#" can be reserved for use as a separator; but the context ensures that they cannot be confused by the system.

Six of the operations give control over the dialogue. There are three different "repeat" commands; a command (called *erase*) which undoes the effect of the last operation; one which reads out the value of a register; and one which aborts the current utterance. Four more commands provide the basic arithmetic operations of add, subtract, multiply and divide. The operands of these may be keyed literal numbers, or register values, or function calls. A further command clears a register.

It is through functions that the extensibility of the language is achieved. A function has a name (like SIN, EXIT, MYFUNC) which is keyed with an appropriate single-key-per-character sequence (namely 746, 3948, 693862 respectively). One function, DEFINE, allows new ones to be entered. Another, LOOP, repeats sequences of operations. TEST incorporates arithmetic testing. The details of these are not important: what is interesting is the evident power of the calculator.

For example, the keying sequence

5 # 1 1 2 3 # 2 1 . 2 # 9 # 6 # 2 1 . 4 #

Table 10.2. Syntax for a telephone calculator.

construct	definition	explanation
⟨calculation⟩		a sequence of ⟨operation⟩s followed by a call to the system function $EXIT$
⟨operation⟩	⟨add⟩ OR ⟨subtract⟩ OR ⟨multiply⟩ OR ⟨divide⟩ OR ⟨function⟩ OR ⟨clear⟩ OR ⟨erase⟩ OR ⟨answer⟩ OR ⟨display-last⟩ OR ⟨display⟩ OR ⟨repeat⟩ OR ⟨cancel⟩	
⟨add⟩	+ ⟨value⟩ # OR + # ⟨function⟩	
⟨subtract⟩ ⟨multiply⟩ ⟨divide⟩		similar to ⟨add⟩
⟨value⟩ ⟨numeric-value⟩	⟨numeric-value⟩ OR *register* ⟨single-digit⟩	a sequence of keystrokes like 1 . 2 3 4 or 1 2 3 . 4 or 1 2 3 4
		some functions do not need the ⟨value⟩ part
⟨function⟩ ⟨name⟩	*function* ⟨name⟩ # ⟨value⟩ #	a sequence of keystrokes like SIN or $EXIT$ or $MYFUNC$
⟨clear⟩	*clear register* ⟨single-digit⟩ #	clears one of the 10 registers
⟨erase⟩	*erase* #	undoes the effect of the last operation
⟨answer⟩	*answer register* ⟨single-digit⟩ #	reads the contents of a register
⟨display-last⟩ ⟨display⟩ ⟨repeat⟩		these provide "repeat" facilities
⟨cancel⟩		aborts the current utterance

would be decoded as

clear + 123 − 1.2 *display erase* − 1.4.

One of the difficulties with such a tight syntax is that almost any sequence will be interpreted as a valid calculation: syntax errors are nearly impossible. Thus a small mistake by the user can have a catastrophic effect on the calculation. Here, however, speech output gives an advantage over conventional character-by-character echoing on visual displays. It is quite adequate to echo syntactic units as they are decoded, instead of echoing keys as they are entered. It was suggested earlier in this chapter that confirmation of entry should be generated in the same way that the user would be likely to verbalize it himself. Thus the synthetic voice could respond to the above keying sequence as shown in the second line, except that the *display* command would also state the result (and possibly summarize the calculation so far). Numbers could be verbalized as "one hundred and twenty-three" instead of as "one ... two ... three". (Note, however, that this will make it necessary to await the "#" terminator after numbers and function names before they can be echoed.)

10.4 References

Brown, G., Currie, K.L. and Kenworthy, J. (1980). "Questions of intonation", Croom Helm, London.

Gaines, B.R. and Facey, P.V. (1975). Some experience in interactive system development and application. *Proc Institute of Electrical and Electronic Engineers,* **63**(6) 894–911, June.

Kramer, J.J. (1970). Human factors problems in the use of pushbutton telephones for data entry. *Proc Symposium on Human Factors in Telephony,* 241–258, VDE-Verlay GmbH, Berlin.

Newhouse, A. and Sibley, R.A. (1969). On the use of very low cost terminals. *Proc International Conference on Remote Data Processing,* Paris, March.

Shew, E.S.Y. (1975). What's next for the pushbutton telephone as an IO device. *Canadian Datasystems,* 45–48, May.

Smith, S.L. and Goodwin, N.C. (1970). Computer-generated speech and man-computer interaction *Human Factors,* **12,** 215–223, April.

Witten, I.H. and Madams, P.H.C. (1977). The Telephone Enquiry Service: a man–machine system using synthetic speech. *Int J Man–Machine Studies,* **9**(4) 449–464, July.

Witten, J.H. and Abbess, J. (1979). A microcomputer-based real-time speech synthesis-by-rule system. *Int J Man–Machine Studies,* **11**(5) 585–620, September.

10.5 Further Reading

There are no books which relate techniques of man–computer dialogue to speech interaction. The best I can do is to guide you to some of the standard works on interactive techniques.

Gilb, T. and Weinberg, G.M. (1977). "Humanized input", Winthrop, Cambridge, Massachusetts.

This book is subtitled "techniques for reliable keyed input", and considers most aspects of the problem of data entry by professional key operators.

Martin, J. (1973). "Design of man–computer dialogues", Prentice-Hall, Englewood Cliffs, New Jersey.

Martin concerns himself with all aspects of man–computer dialogue, and the book even contains a short chapter on the use of voice response systems.

Smith, H.T. and Green, T.R.G. (editors) (1980). "Human interaction with computers", Academic Press, London and New York.

A recent collection of contributions on man–computer systems and programming research.

11

COMMERCIAL SPEECH OUTPUT DEVICES

This chapter takes a look at four speech output peripherals that are available today. It is risky in a book of this nature to descend so close to the technology as to discuss particular examples of commercial products, for such information becomes dated very quickly. Nevertheless, having covered the principles of various types of speech synthesizer, and the methods of driving them from widely differing utterance representations, it seems worthwhile to see how these principles are embodied in a few products actually on the market.

Developments in electronic speech devices are moving so fast that it is hard to keep up with them, and the newest technology today will undoubtedly be superseded next year. Hence I have not tried to choose examples from the very latest technology. Instead, this chapter discusses synthesizers which exemplify rather different principles and architectures, in order to give an idea of the range of options which face the system designer.

Three of the devices are landmarks in the commerical adoption of speech technology, and have stood the test of time. Votrax was introduced in the early 1970s, and has been re-implemented several times since in an attempt to cover different market sectors. The Computalker appeared in 1976. It was aimed primarily at the burgeoning computer hobbies market. One of its most far-reaching effects was to stimulate the interest of hobbyists, always eager for new lost-cost peripherals, in speech synthesis; and so provide a useful new source of experimentation and expertise which will undoubtedly help this heretofore rather esoteric discipline to mature. Computalker is certainly the longest-lived and probably still the most popular hobbyist's speech synthesizer. The Texas Instruments speech synthesis chip brought speech output technology to the consumer. It was the first single-chip speech synthesizer, and is still the biggest seller. It forms the heart of the "Speak 'n Spell" talking toy which appeared in toyshops in the summer of 1978. Although talking calculators had existed several years before, they were exotic gadgets rather than household toys.

11.1 Formant Synthesizer

The Computalker is a straightforward implementation of a serial formant synthesizer. A block diagram of it is shown in Fig. 11.1. In the centre is the main vocal tract path, with three formant filters whose resonant frequencies can be controlled individually. A separate nasal branch in parallel with the oral one is provided, with a nasal formant of fixed frequency. It is less important to allow for variation of the nasal formant frequency than it is for the oral ones, because the size and shape of the nasal tract is relatively fixed. However, it is essential to control the nasal amplitude, in particular to turn it off during non-nasal sounds. Computalker provides independent oral and nasal amplitude parameters.

Unvoiced excitation can be passed through the main vocal tract through the aspiration amplitude control AH. In practice, the voicing amplitudes AV and AN will probably always be zero when AH is non-zero, for physiological constraints prohibit simultaneous voicing and aspiration. A second unvoiced excitation path passes through a fricative formant filter whose resonant frequency can be varied, and has its amplitude independently controlled by AF.

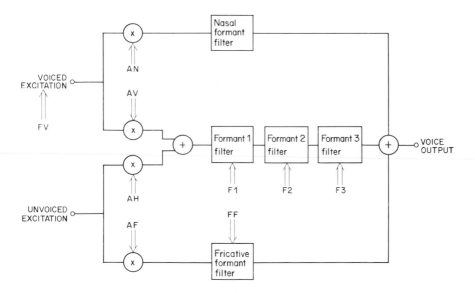

Fig. 11.1. Block diagram of the Computalker formant synthesizer.

Control Parameters

Table 11.1 summarizes the nine parameters which drive Computalker. Four of them control amplitudes, while the others control frequencies. In the latter case the parameter value is logarithmically related to the actual frequency of the excitation (FV) or resonance (F1, F2, F3, FF). The ranges over which each frequency can be controlled is shown in the Table. An independent calibration of one particular Computalker has shown that the logarithmic specifications are met remarkably well.

Each parameter is specified to Computalker as an 8-bit number. Parameters are addressed by a 4-bit code, and so a total of 12 bits is transferred in parallel to Computalker from the computer for each parameter update. Parameters 9 to 14 are unassigned ("reserved for future expansion" is the official phrase), and the last parameter, SW, governs the position of an audio on–off switch.

Computalker does not contain a clock that is accessible to the user, and so the timing of parameter updates is entirely up to the host computer. Typically, a 10 msec interval between frames is used, with interrupts generated by a separate timer. In fact the frame interval can be anywhere between 2 msec and 50 msec, and can be changed to alter the rate of speaking. However, it is rather naïve to view fast speech as slow speech speeded up by a linear time compression, for in human speech production, the rhythm changes and elisions occur in a rather more subtle way. Thus it is not particularly useful to be able to alter the frame rate.

Table 11.1. Computalker control parameters.

address	meaning	width	range
0 AV	amplitude of voicing	8 bits	
1 AN	nasal amplitude	8 bits	
2 AH	amplitude of aspiration	8 bits	
3 AF	amplitude of frication	8 bits	
4 FV	fundamental frequency of voicing	8 bits logarithmic	75– 470 Hz
5 F1	formant 1 resonant frequency	8 bits logarithmic	170– 1450 Hz
6 F2	formant 2 resonant frequency	8 bits logarithmic	520– 4400 Hz
7 F3	formant 3 resonant frequency	8 bits logarithmic	1700– 5500 Hz
8 FF	fricative resonant frequency	8 bits logarithmic	1700–14000 Hz
9	not used		
10	not used		
11	not used		
12	not used		
13	not used		
14	not used		
15 SW	audio on-off switch	1 bit	

At each interrupt, the host computer transfers values for all of the nine parameters to Computalker, a total of 108 data bits. In theory, perhaps, it is only necessary to transmit those parameters whose values have changed; but in practice all of them should be updated regardless. This is because the parameters are stored for the duration of the frame in analogue sample-and-hold devices. Essentially, the parameter value is represented as the charge on a capacitor. In time (and it takes only a short time) the values drift. Although the drift over 10 msec is insignificant, it becomes very noticeable over longer time periods. If parameters are not updated at all, the result is a "whoosh" sound up to maximum amplitude, in a period of a second or two. Hence it is essential that Computalker be serviced by the computer regularly, to update all its parameters. The audio on–off switch is provided so that the computer can turn off the sound directly if another program, which does not use the device, is to be run.

Filter Implementation

It is hard to get definite information on the implementation of Computalker. Because it is a commercial device, circuit diagrams are not published. It is certainly an analogue rather than a digital implementation. The designer suggests that a configuration like that of Fig. 11.2 is used for the formant filters (Rice, 1976). Control is obtained over the resonant frequency by varying the resistance at the bottom in sympathy with the parameter value. The middle two operational amplifiers can be modelled by a resistance

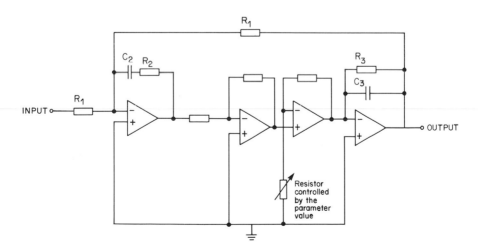

Fig. 11.2. Formant filter circuit for Computalker.

$-R/k$ in the forward path, where k is the digital control value. This gives the circuit in Fig. 11.3, which can be analysed to obtain the transfer function

$$-\frac{k}{R\,R_1C_2C_3} \cdot \frac{R_2C_2s + 1}{s^2 + \left(\dfrac{1}{R_3C_3} + \dfrac{kR_2}{R\,R_1C_3}\right)s + \dfrac{k}{R\,R_1C_2C_3}}.$$

This expression has a DC gain of -1, and the denominator is similar to those of the analogue formant resonators discussed in Chapter 5. However, unlike them the transfer function has a numerator which creates a zero at

$$s = -\frac{1}{R_2C_2}.$$

If R_2C_2 is sufficiently small, this zero will have negligible effect at audio frequencies, and the filter has the following parameters:

$$\text{centre frequency:}\quad \frac{1}{2\pi}\left(\frac{k}{R\,R_1C_2C_3}\right)^{1/2}\ \text{Hz}$$

$$\text{bandwidth:}\quad \frac{1}{2\pi}\left(\frac{1}{R_3C_3} + \frac{kR_2}{R\,R_1C_3}\right)\ \text{Hz.}$$

Note first that the centre frequency is proportional to the square root of the control value k. Hence a non-linear transformation must be implemented on the control signal, after D/A conversion, to achieve the required logarithmic relationship between parameter value and resonant frequency. The formant bandwidth is not constant, as it should be (see Chapter 5), but depends upon the control value k. This dependency can be minimized by selecting component values such that

$$\frac{kR_2}{R\,R_1C_3} \ll \frac{1}{R_3C_3}$$

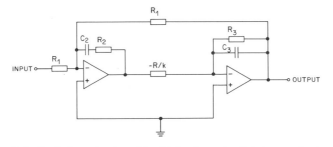

Fig. 11.3. Equivalent circuit to Fig. 11.2, where the digital control value is k.

for the largest value of k which can occur. Then the bandwidth is solely determined by the time constant R_3C_3.

The existence of the zero can be exploited for the fricative resonance. This should have zero DC gain, and so the component values for the fricative filter should make the time-constant R_2C_2 large enough to place the zero sufficiently near the frequency origin.

Market Orientation

As mentioned above, Computalker is designed for the computer hobbies market. Figure 11.4 shows a photograph of the device. It plugs into the S-100 bus which has been a *de facto* standard for hobbyists for several years, and has recently been adopted as a standard by the Institute of Electrical and Electronic Engineers. This makes it immediately accessible to many microcomputer systems.

An inexpensive synthesis-by-rule program, which runs on the popular 8080 microprocessor, is available to drive Computalker. The input is coded in a machine-readable version of the standard phonetic alphabet, similar to that which was introduced in Chapter 2 (Table 2.1). Stress digits may appear in the transcription, and the program caters for five levels of stress. The punctuation mark at the end of an utterance has some effect on pitch. The program is perhaps remarkable in that it occupies only 6 Kbyte of storage (including phoneme tables), and runs on an 8-bit microprocessor (but not in real time). It is, however, *un*remarkable in that it produces rather poor speech. According to a demonstration cassette, "most people find the speech

Fig. 11.4. The Computalker speech synthesizer.

to be readily intelligible, especially after a little practice listening to it", but this seems extremely optimistic. It also cunningly insinuates that if you don't understand it, you yourself may share the blame with the synthesizer: after all, *most* people do! Nevertheless, Computalker has made synthetic speech accessible to a large number of home computer users.

11.2 Sound-segment Synthesizer

Votrax was the first fully commercial speech synthesizer, and at the time of writing is still the only off-the-shelf speech output peripheral (as distinct from reading machine) which is aimed specifically at synthesis-by-rule rather than storage of parameter tracks extracted from natural utterances. Figure 11.5 shows a photograph of the Votrax ML-I.

Votrax accepts as input a string of codes representing sound segments, each with additional bits to control the duration and pitch of the segment. In the earlier versions (e.g. model VS-6) there are 63 sound segments, specified by a 6-bit code, and two further bits accompany each segment to provide a 4-level control over pitch. Four pitch levels are quite inadequate

Fig. 11.5. The Votrax ML-I speech synthesizer.

to generate acceptable intonation contours for anything but isolated words spoken in citation form. However, a later model (ML-I) uses an 8-level pitch specification, as well as a 4-level duration qualifier, associated with each sound segment. It provides a vocabulary of 80 sound segments, together with an additional code which allows local amplitude modifications and extra duration alterations to following segments. A further, low-cost model (VS-K) is now available which plugs in to the S-100 bus, and is aimed primarily at computer hobbyists. It provides no pitch control at all and is therefore quite unsuited to serious voice response applications. The device has recently been packaged as an LSI circuit (model SC-01), using analogue switched-capacitor filter technology.

One point where the ML-I scores favourably over other speech synthesis peripherals is the remarkably convenient engineering of its computer interface, which was outlined in the previous chapter.

The internal workings of Votrax are not divulged by the manufacturer. Figure 11.6 shows a block diagram at the level of detail that they supply. It seems to be essentially a formant synthesizer with analogue function generators and parameter smoothing circuits that provide transitions between sound segments.

Sound Segments

The 80 segments of the high-range ML-I model are summarized in Table 11.2. They are divided into phoneme classes according to the classification discussed in Chapter 2. The segments break down into the following categories. (Numbers in parentheses are the corresponding figures for VS-6.)

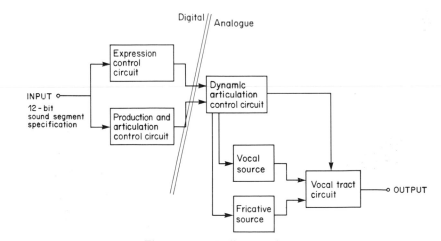

Fig. 11.6. Block diagram of Votrax.

Table 11.2. Votrax sound segments and their durations.

	Votrax		duration (msec)	test word
i	I		118	hid
	I1	(sound equivalent of I)	83	
	I2	(sound equivalent of I)	58	
	I3	(allophone of I)	58	
	.I3	(sound equivalent of I3)	83	
	AY	(allophone of I)	65	
e	EH		118	head
	EH1	(sound equivalent of EH)	70	
	EH2	(sound equivalent of EH)	60	
	EH3	(allophone of EH)	60	
	.EH2	(sound equivalent of EH3)	70	
	A1	(allophone of EH)	100	
	A2	(sound equivalent of A1)	95	
aa	AE		100	had
	AE1	(sound equivalent of AE)	100	
o	AW		235	hod
	AW2	(sound equivalent of AW)	90	
	AW1	(allophone of AW)	143	
u	OO		178	hood
	OO1	(sound equivalent of OO)	103	
	IU	(allophone of OO)	63	
a	UH		103	hud
	UH1	(sound equivalent of UH)	95	
	UH2	(sound equivalent of UH)	50	
	UH3	(allophone of UH)	70	
	.UH3	(sound equivalent of UH3)	103	
	.UH2	(allophone of UH)	60	
ar	AH1		143	hard
	AH2	(sound equivalent of AH1)	70	
aw	O		178	hawed
	O1	(sound equivalent of O)	118	
	O2	(sound equivalent of O)	83	
	.O	(allophone of O)	178	
	.O1	(sound equivalent of .O)	123	
	.O2	(sound equivalent of .O)	90	
uu	U		178	who'd
	U1	(sound equivalent of U)	90	
er	ER		143	heard
ee	E		178	heed
	E1	(sound equivalent of E)	118	
r	R		90	
	.R	(allophone of R)	50	
w	W		83	
	.W	(allophone of W)	83	

Table 11.2 (continued).

	Votrax		duration (msec)	test word
l	L		105	
	L1	(allophone of L)	105	
y	Y		103	
	Y1	(allophone of Y)	83	
m	M		105	
b	B		70	
p	P		100	
	.PH	(aspiration burst for use with P)	88	
n	N		83	
d	D		50	
	.D	(allophone of D)	53	
t	T		90	
	DT	(allophone of T)	50	
	.S	(aspiration burst for use with T)	70	
ng	NG		120	
g	G		75	
	.G	(allophone of G)	75	
k	K		75	
	.K	(allophone of K)	80	
	.X1	(aspiration burst for use with K)	68	
s	S		90	
z	Z		70	
sh	SH		118	
	CH	(allophone of SH)	55	
zh	ZH		90	
	J	(allophone of ZH)	50	
f	F		100	
v	V		70	
th	TH		70	
dh	THV		70	
h	H		70	
	H1	(allophone of H)	70	
	.H1	(allophone of H)	48	
silence	PA0		45	
	PA1		175	
	.PA1		5	
	.PA2	(used to change amplitude and duration)	—	

11 (11) vowel sounds which are representative of the phonological vowel classes for English

 9 (7) vowel allophones, with slightly different sound qualities from the above

20 (15) segments whose sound qualities are identical to the segments above, but with different durations

22 (22) consonant sounds which are representative of the phonological consonant classes for English

11 (6) consonant allophones

 4 (0) segments to be used in conjunction with unvoiced plosives to increase their aspiration

 2 (2) silent segments, with different pause durations

 1 (0) very short silent segment (about 5 msec).

Somewhat under half of the 80 elements can be put into one-to-one correspondence with the phonemes of English; the rest are either allophonic variations or additional sounds which can sensibly be combined with certain phonemes in certain contexts. The Votrax literature, and consequently Votrax users, persists in calling all elements "phonemes", and this can cause considerable confusion. I prefer to use the term "sound segment" instead, reserving "phoneme" for its proper linguistic use.

The rules which Votrax uses for transitions between sound segments are not made public by the manufacturer, and are embedded in encapsulated circuits in the hardware. They are clearly very crude. The key to successful encoding of utterances is to use the many non-phonemic segments in an appropriate way as transitions between the main segments which represent phonetic classes. This is a tricky process, and I have heard of one commercial establishment giving up in despair at the extreme difficulty of generating the utterances it wanted. It probably explains the proliferation of letter-to-sound rules for Votrax which have been developed in research laboratories (Colby *et al.*, 1978; Elovitz *et al.*, 1976; McIlroy, 1974; Sherwood, 1978). Nevertheless, with luck, skill, and especially persistence, excellent results can be obtained. The ML-I manual (Votrax, 1976) contains a list of about 625 words and short phrases, and they are usually clearly recognizable.

Duration and Pitch Qualifiers

Each sound segment has a different duration. Table 11.2 shows the measured duration of the segments, although no calibration data is given by Votrax. As mentioned earlier, a 2-bit number accompanies each segment to modify its duration, and this was set to 3 (least duration) for the measurements. The qualifier has a multiplicative effect, shown in Table 11.3.

As well as the 2-bit rate qualifier, each sound segment is accompanied

Table 11.3. Effect of the 2-bit per-segment rate qualifier.

rate qualifier	multiply duration in Table 11.2 by
3	1.00
2	1.11
1	1.22
0	1.35

by a 3-bit pitch specification. This provides a linear control over fundamental frequency, and Table 11.4 shows the measured values. The quantization interval varies from one to two semitones. Votrax interpolates pitch from phoneme to phoneme in a highly satisfactory manner, and this permits surprisingly sophisticated intonation contours to be generated considering the crude 8-level quantization.

The notation in which the Votrax manual defines utterances gives duration qualifiers and pitch specifications as digits preceding the sound segment, and separated from it by a slash (/). Thus, for example,

$$14/THV$$

defines the sound segment THV with duration qualifier 1 (multiplies the 70 msec duration of Table 11.2 by 1.22 (from Table 11.3) to give 85 msec) and pitch specification 4 (81 Hz). This representation of a segment is transformed into two ASCII characters before transmission to the synthesizer.

Converting a Phonetic Transcription to Sound Segments

It would be useful to have a computer procedure to produce a specification for an utterance in terms of Votrax sound segments from a standard phonetic

Table 11.4. Effect of the 3-bit per-segment pitch specifier.

pitch specifier	pitch (Hz)
0	57.5
1	64.1
2	69.4
3	75.8
4	80.6
5	87.7
6	94.3
7	100.0

transcription. This could remove much of the tedium from utterance preparation by incorporating the contextual rules given in the Votrax manual. Starting with a phonetic transcription, each phoneme should be converted to its default Votrax representative. The resulting "wide" Votrax transcription must be transformed into a "narrow" one by application of contextual rules. Separate rules are needed for

— vowel clusters (diphthongs)
— vowel transitions (i.e. consonant-vowel and vowel-consonant, where the vowel segment is altered)
— intervocalic consonants
— consonant transitions (i.e. consonant-vowel and vowel-consonant, where the consonant segment is altered)
— consonant clusters
— stressed-syllable effects
— utterance-final effects.

Stressed-syllable effects (which include extra aspiration for unvoiced stops beginning stressed syllables) can be applied only if stress markers are included in the phonetic transcription.

To specify a rule, it is necessary to give a *matching part* and a *context*, which define at what points in an utterance it is applicable, and a *replacement part* which is used to replace the matching part. The context can be specified in mathematical set notation using curly brackets. For example,

$$\{G\ SH\ W\ K\}\ OO \qquad IU\ OO$$

states that the matching part OO is replaced by IU OO, after a G, SH, W, or K. In fact, allophonic variations of each sound segment should also be accepted as valid context, so this rule will also replace OO after .G, CH, .W, .K, or .X1 (Table 11.2 gives allophones of each segment).

Table 11.5 gives some rules that have been used for this purpose. They were derived from careful study of the hints given in the ML-I manual (Votrax, 1976). Classes such as "voiced" and "stop-consonant" in the context specify sets of sound segments in the obvious way. The beginning of a stressed syllable is marked in the input by ".syll". Parentheses in the replacement part have a significance which is explained in the next section.

Handling Prosodic Features

We know from Chapter 8 the vital importance of prosodic features in synthesizing lifelike speech. To allow them to be assigned to Votrax utterances, an intermediate output from a prosodic analysis program like ISP can be used. For example,

1 *dh i s i z* / **d zh aa k s* /*h aa u s*;

which specifies "this is Jack's house" in a declarative intonation with emphasis on the "Jack's", can be intercepted in the following form:

.syll *dh* 50 (0 110) *i* 60 *s* 90 (0 99) *i* 60 *z* 60 (50 110) .syll *d* 50 (0 110) *zh* 50 *aa* 90   *k* 120 (10 90) *s* 90 .syll *h* 60 *aa* 140 *u* 60 *s* 140 ˆ 50 (40 70).

Syllable boundaries, pitches, and durations have been assigned by the procedures given earlier (Chapter 8). A number always follows each phoneme to specify its duration (in msec). Pairs of numbers in parentheses define a pitch specification at some point during the preceding phoneme: the first number of the pair defines the time offset of the specification from the beginning of the phoneme, while the second gives the pitch itself (in Hz). This form of utterance specification can then be passed to a Votrax conversion procedure.

The phonetic transcription is converted to Votrax sound segments using the method described above. The "wide" Votrax transcription is

.syll THV I S I Z .syll D ZH AE K S .syll H AE OO S PA0;

which is transformed to the following "narrow" one according to the rules of Table 11.5:

.syll THV I S I Z .syll D J (AE EH3) K S .syll H1 (AH1 .UH2) (O U) S PA0.

The duration and pitch specifications are preserved by the transformation in their original positions in the string, although they are not shown above. The next stage uses them to expand the transcription by adjusting the segments to have durations as close as possible to the specifications, and computing pitch numbers to be associated with each phoneme.

Correct duration-expansion can, in general, require a great amount of computation. Associated with each sound segment is a set of elements with the same sound quality but different durations, formed by attaching each of the four duration qualifiers of Table 11.3 to the segment and any others which are sound-equivalents to it. For example, the segment Z has the duration-set

{3/Z 2/Z 1/Z 0/Z}

with durations

{70 78 85 95}

msec respectively, where the initial numerals denote the duration qualifier. The segment I has the much larger duration-set

{3/I2 2/I2 1/I2 0/I2 3/I1 2/I1 1/I1 0/I1 3/I 2/I 1/I 0/I}

Table 11.5. Contextual rules for Votrax sound segments.

vowel clusters		
EH I	A1 AY	; *e i*—hey
UH OO	O U	; *uh u*—ho
AE I	(AH1 EH3) I	; *aa i*—hi
AE OO	(AH1 .UH2) (O U)	; *aa u*—how
AW I	(O UH) E	; *o i*—hoi
I UH	E I	; *i uh*—here
EH UH	(EH A1) EH	; *e uh*—hair
OO UH	OO UH	; *u uh*—poor
Y U	Y1 (IU U)	

vowel transitions	
{F M B P} O	(.O1 O)
{L R} EH	(EH3 EH)
{B K T D R} UH	(UH3 UH)
{T D} A1	(EH3 A1)
{T D} AW	(AH1 AW)
{W} I	(I3 I)
{G SH W K} OO	(IU OO)
AY {K G T D}	(AY Y)
E {M T}	(E Y)
I {M T}	(I Y)
E {L}	(I3 UH)
EH {R N S D T}	(EH EH3)
I {R T}	(I I3)
AE {S N}	(AE EH)
AE {K}	(AE EH3)
A1 {R}	(A1 EH1)
AH1 {R P K}	(AH1 UH)
AH1 {ZH}	(AH1 EH3)

intervocalics	
{voiced} T {voiced}	DT

consonant transitions	
L {EH}	L1
H {U OO IU}	H1

consonant clusters	
B {stop-consonant}	(B PA0)
P {stop-consonant}	(P PA0)
D {stop-consonant}	(D PA0)
T {stop-consonant}	(T PA0)
DT {stop-consonant}	(T {A0)
G {stop-consonant}	(G PA0)
K {stop-consonant}	(K PA0)
{D T} R	(.X1 R)
K R	.K (.X1 R)
{consonant} R	.R
{consonant} L	L1
K W	.K .W
D ZH	D J
T SH	T CH

Table 11.5 (continued).

---

initial effects
        {.syll} P {vowel}   (P .PH)
        {.syll} K {vowel}   (K .H1)
        {.syll} T {vowel}   (T .S)
        {.syll} L   L1
        {.syll} H {U OO O AW AH1}   H1
terminal effects
        E {PA0   (E Y)

---

with durations

{58 64 71 78 83 92 101 112 118 131 144 159},

because segments I1 and I2 are sound-equivalents to it. Duration assignment is a matter of selecting elements from the duration-set whose total duration is as close as possible to that desired for the segment. It happens that Votrax deals sensibly with concatenations of more than one identical plosive, suppressing the stop burst on all but the last. Although the general problem of approximating durations in this way is computationally demanding, a simple recursive exhaustive search works in a reasonable amount of time because the desired duration is usually not very much greater than the longest member of the duration-set, and so the search terminates quite quickly.

At this point, the role of the parentheses which appear on the right-hand side of Table 11.5 becomes apparent. Because durations are only associated with the input phonemes, which may each be expanded into several Votrax segments, it is necessary to keep track of the segments which have descended from a single phoneme. Target durations are simply spread equally across any parenthesized groups to which they apply.

Having expanded durations, mapping pitches on to the sound segments is a simple matter. The ISP system for formant synthesizers (Chapters 7 and 8) uses linear interpolation between pitch specifications, and the frequency which results for each sound segment needs to be converted to a Votrax specification using the information in Table 11.4.

After applying these procedures to the example utterance, it becomes

14/THV 14/I1 03/S 14/I1 04/Z 04/D 04/J 33/AE 33/EH3 02/K 02/K 02/S 02/H1 01/AH2 01/.UH2 31/O2 31/U1 01/S 10/S 30/PA0 30/PA0.

In several places, shorter sound-equivalents have been substituted (I1 for

I, AH2 for AH1, O2 for O, and U1 for U), while doubling-up also occurs (in the K, S, and PA0 segments).

The speech which results from the use of these procedures with the Votrax synthesizer sounds remarkably similar to that generated by the ISP system which uses parametrically-controlled synthesizers. Formal evaluation experiments have not been undertaken, but it seems clear from careful listening that it would be rather difficult, and probably pointless, to evaluate the Votrax conversion algorithm, for the outcome would be completely dominated by the success of the original pitch and rhythm assignment procedures.

11.3 Linear Predictive Synthesizer

The first single-chip speech synthesizer was introduced by Texas Instruments (TI) in the summer of 1978 (Wiggins and Brantingham, 1978). It was a remarkable development, combining recent advances in signal processing with the very latest in VLSI technology. Packaged in the *Speak 'n Spell* toy (Fig. 11.7), it was a striking demonstration of imagination and prowess in integrated electronics. It gave TI a long lead over its competitors and surprised many experts in the speech field. Overnight, it seemed, digital speech technology had descended from research laboratories with their expensive and specialized equipment into a $50.00 consumer item. Naturally

Fig. 11.7. Speak 'n Spell toy.

TI did not sell the chip separately but only as part of their mass-market product; nor would they make available information on how to drive it directly. Only recently when other similar devices appeared on the market did they unbundle the package and sell the chip.

The Speak 'n Spell Toy

The TI chip (TMC0280) uses the linear predictive method of synthesis, primarily because of the ease of the speech analysis procedure and the known high quality at low data rates. Speech researchers, incidentally, sometimes scoff at what they perceive to be the poor quality of the toy's speech; but considering the data rate used (which averages 1200 bits per second of speech) it is remarkably good. Anyway, although it is not uncommon to misunderstand a word, I have never heard a child complain! Two 128 Kbit read-only memories are used in the toy to hold data for about 330 words and phrases (lasting between 3 and 4 minutes) of speech. At the time (mid-1978) these memories were the largest that were available in the industry. The data flow and user dialogue are handled by a microprocessor, which is the fourth LSI circuit in the photograph of Fig. 11.8.

A schematic diagram of the toy is given in Fig. 11.9. It has a small display which shows upper-case letters. (Some teachers of spelling hold that the lack of lower case destroys any educational value that the toy may have.) It has a full 26-key alphanumeric keyboard with 14 additional control keys.

Fig. 11.8. Circuitry inside the *Speak 'n Spell* toy.

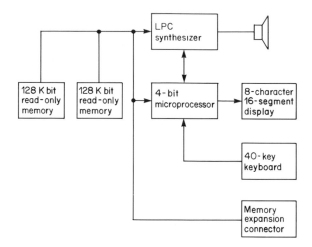

Fig. 11.9. Block diagram of the *Speak 'n Spell* toy.

(This is the toy's Achilles' heel, for the keys fall out after extended use. More recent toys from TI use an improved keyboard.) The keyboard is laid out alphabetically instead of in QWERTY order; possibly missing an opportunity to teach kids to type as well as spell. An internal connector permits vocabulary expansion with up to 14 more read-only memory chips. Controlling the toy is a 4-bit microprocessor (a modified TMS1000). However, the synthesizer chip does not receive data from the processor. During speech, it accesses the memory directly and only returns control to the processor when an end-of-phrase marker is found in the data stream. Meanwhile the processor is idle, and cannot even be interrupted from the keyboard. Moreover, in one operational mode ("say-it"), the toy embarks upon a long monologue and remains deaf to the keyboard; it cannot even be turned off. Any three-year-old will quickly discover that a sharp slap solves the problem! A useful feature is that the device switches itself off if unused for more than a few minutes. A fascinating account of the development of the toy from the point of view of product design and market assessment has been published (Frantz and Wiggins, 1981).

Control Parameters

The lattice filtering method of linear predictive synthesis (see Chapter 6) was selected because of its good stability properties and guaranteed performance with small word sizes. The lattice has 10 stages. All the control parameters are represented as 10-bit fixed-point numbers, and the lattice operates with an internal precision of 14 bits (including sign).

There are twelve parameters for the device: ten reflection coefficients, energy and pitch. These are updated every 20 msec. However, if 10-bit values were stored for each, a data rate of 120 bits every 20 msec, or 6 Kbit/s, would be needed. This would reduce the capacity of the two read-only memory chips to well under a minute of speech: perhaps 65 words and phrases. But one of the desirable properties of the reflection coefficients which drive the lattice filter is that they are amenable to quantization. A non-linear quantization scheme is used, with the parameter data addressing an on-chip quantization table to yield a 10-bit coefficient.

Table 11.6 shows the number of bits devoted to each parameter. There are 4 bits for energy, and 5 bits for pitch and the first two reflection coefficients. Thereafter the number of bits allocated to reflection coefficients decreases steadily, for higher coefficients are less important for intelligibility than lower ones. (Note that using a 10-stage filter is tantamount to allocating *no* bits to coefficients higher than the tenth.) With a 1-bit "repeat" flag, whose role is discussed shortly, the frame size becomes 49 bits. Updated every 20 msec, this gives a data rate of just under 2.5 Kbit/s.

The parameters are expanded into 10-bit numbers by a separate quantization table for each one. For example, the five pitch bits address a 32-word look-up table which returns a 10-bit value. The transformation is logarithmic in this case, the lowest pitch being around 50 Hz and the highest 190 Hz. As shown in Table 11.6, a total of 216 10-bit words suffices to hold all twelve quantization tables; and they are implemented on the synthesizer chip. To provide further smoothing of the control parameters, they

Table 11.6. Bit allocation for Speak 'n Spell chip.

parameter	bits	quantization table size (10-bit words)	
energy	4	16	4 energy = 0 means 4-bit frame
pitch	5	32	
repeat flag	1	—	10 repeat flag = 1 means 10-bit frame
k1	5	32	
k2	5	32	
k3	4	16	
k4	4	16	28 pitch = 0 (unvoiced) means 28-bit frame
k5	4	16	
k6	4	16	
k7	4	16	
k8	3	8	
k9	3	8	
k10	3	8	49 otherwise 49-bit frame
	49 bits	216 words	

are interpolated linearly from one frame to the next at eight points within the frame.

The raw data rate of 2.5 Kbit/s is reduced to an average of 1200 bit/s by further coding techniques. First, if the energy parameter is zero the frame is silent, and no more parameters are transmitted (4-bit frame). Secondly, if the "repeat" flag is 1, all reflection coefficients are held over from the previous frame, giving a constant filter but with the ability to vary amplitude and pitch (10-bit frame). Finally, if the frame is unvoiced (signalled by the pitch value being zero) only four reflection coefficients are transmitted, because the ear is relatively insensitive to spectral detail in unvoiced speech (28-bit frame). The end of the utterance is signalled by the energy bits all being 1.

Chip Organization

The configuration of the lattice filter is shown in Figure 11.10. The "two-multiplier" structure (Chapter 6) is used, so the 10-stage filter requires 19 multiplications and 19 additions per speech sample. (The last operation in the reverse path at the bottom is not needed.) Since a 10 kHz sample rate is used, just 100 μsec are available for each speech sample. A single 5 μsec adder and a pipelined multiplier are implemented on the chip, and multiplexed among the 19 operations. The latter begins a new multiplication every 5 μsec, and finishes it 40 μsec later. These times are within the capability of p-channel MOS technology, allowing the chip to be produced at low cost. The time slot for the 20'th, unnecessary, filter multiplication is used for an overall gain adjustment.

The final analogue signal is produced by an 8-bit on-chip D/A converter which drives a 200 milliwatt speaker through an impedance-matching transformer. These constitute the necessary analogue low-pass desampling filter.

Figure 11.11 summarizes the organization of the synthesis chip. Serial data enters directly from the read-only memories, although a control signal from the processor begins synthesis and another signal is returned to it upon

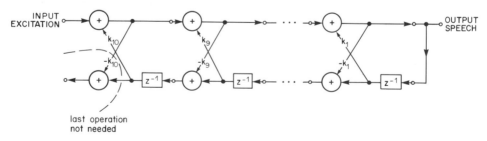

Fig. 11.10. Lattice filter used in the TI speech synthesis chip.

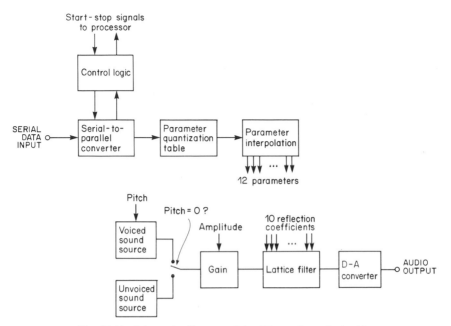

Fig. 11.11. Schematic diagram of the TI speech synthesis chip.

termination. The data is decoded into individual parameters, which are used to address the quantization tables to generate the full 10-bit parameter values. These are interpolated from one frame to the next. The lower part of the figure shows the speech generation subsystem. An excitation waveform for voiced speech is stored in read-only memory and read out repeatedly at a rate determined by the pitch. The source for unvoiced sounds is hard-limited noise provided by a digital pseudo-random bit generator. The sound source that is used depends on whether the pitch value is zero or not: notice that this precludes mixed excitation for voiced fricatives (and the sound is noticeably poor in words like "zee"). A gain multiplication is performed before the signal is passed through the lattice synthesis filter, described earlier.

11.4 Programmable Signal Processors

The TI chip has a fixed architecture, and is destined forever to implement the same vocal tract model: a 10'th order lattice filter. A more recent device, the Programmable Digital Signal Processor (Caldwell, 1980) from Telesensory Systems allows more flexibility in the type of model. It can serve as a digital formant synthesizer or a linear predictive synthesizer, and the order of model (number of formants, in the former case) can be changed.

Before describing the PDSP, it is worth looking at an earlier microprocessor which was designed for digital signal processing. Some industry observers have said that this processor, the Intel 2920, is to the analogue design engineer what the first microprocessor was to the random logic engineer way back in the mists of time (early 1970s).

The "Analogue Microprocessor"

The 2920 is a digital microprocessor. However, it contains an on-chip D/A converter, which can be used in successive approximation fashion for A/D conversion under program control, and its architecture is designed to aid digital signal processing calculations. Although the precision of conversion is 9 bits, internal arithmetic is done with 25 bits to accommodate the accumulation of round-off errors in arithmetic operations. An on-chip programmable read-only memory holds a 192-instruction program, which is executed in sequence with no program jumps allowed. This ensures that each pass through the program takes the same time, so that the analogue waveform is regularly sampled and processed.

The device is implemented in n-channel MOS technology, which makes it slightly faster than the pMOS *Speak 'n Spell* chip. At its fastest operating speed, each instruction takes 400 nsec. The 192-instruction program therefore executes in 78.6 μsec, corresponding to a sampling rate of almost 13 kHz. Thus the processor can handle signals with a bandwidth of 6.5 kHz, ample for high-quality speech. However, a special EOP (end of program) instruction is provided which causes an immediate jump back to the beginning. Hence if the program occupies less than 192 instructions, faster sampling rates can be used. For example, a single second-order formant resonance requires only 14 instructions and so can be executed at over 150 kHz.

Despite this speed, the 2920 is only marginally capable of synthesizing speech. Table 11.7 gives approximate numbers of instructions needed to do some subtasks for speech generation (Hoff and Li, 1980). The parameter entry and data distribution procedure collects 10 8-bit parameters from a serial input stream, at a frame rate of 100 frames/s. The parameter data rate is 8 Kbit/s, and the routine assumes that the 2920 performs each complete cycle in 125 μsec to generate sampled speech at 8 kHz. Therefore one bit of parameter data is accepted on every cycle. The glottal pulse program generates an asymmetrical triangular waveform (Chapter 5), while the noise generator uses a 17-bit pseudo-random feedback shift register. About 30% of the 192-instruction program memory is consumed by these

Table 11.7. 2920 instruction counts for typical
speech subsystems.

task	instructions
parameter entry and data distribution	35–40
glottal pulse generation	8
noise generation	11
lattice section	20
formant filter	14

essential tasks. A two-multiplier lattice section takes 20 instructions, and
so only six sections can fit into the remaining program space. It may be
possible to use two 2920s to implement a complete 10 or 12'th order lattice,
but the results of the first stage must be passed to the second by transmitting
analogue or digital data between each of the 2920s analogue ports; not a
terribly satisfactory method.

Since a formant filter occupies only 14 instructions, up to nine of them
would fit in the program space left after the above-mentioned essential
subsystems. Although other necessary house-keeping tasks may reduce this
number substantially, it does seem possible to implement a formant synthesizer on a single 2920.

The Programmable Digital Signal Processor

Whereas the 2920 is intended for general signal-processing jobs, Telesensory
Systems' PDSP (Programmable Digital Signal Processor) is aimed specifically at speech synthesis. It comprises two separate chips, a control unit
and an arithmetic unit. To build a synthesizer these must be augmented
with external memory and a D/A converter, arranged in a configuration like
that of Fig. 11.12.

The control unit accepts parameter data from a host computer, one byte
at a time. The data is temporarily held in buffer memory before being

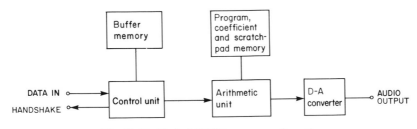

Fig. 11.12. Typical PDSP system configuration.

serialized and passed to the arithmetic unit. Notice that for the 2920 we assumed that parameters were presented to the chip already serialized and precisely timed: the PDSP control unit effectively releases the host from this high-speed real-time operation. But it does more. It generates both a voiced and an unvoiced excitation source and passes them to the arithmetic unit, to relieve the latter of the general-purpose programming required for both these tasks and allow its instruction set to be highly specialized for digital filtering.

The arithmetic unit has rather a peculiar structure. It accommodates only 16 program steps and can execute the full 16-instruction program at a rate of 10 kHz. The internal word-length is 18 bits, but coefficients and the digital output are only 10 bits. Each instruction can accomplish quite a lot of work. Figure 11.13 shows that there are four separate blocks of store in addition to the program memory. One location of each block is automatically associated with each program step. Thus on instruction 2, for example, two 18-bit scratchpad registers MA(2) and MB(2), and two 10-bit coefficient registers A1(2) and A2(2), are accessible. In addition five general registers, curiously numbered R1, R2, R5, R6, R7, are available to every program step.

Each instruction has five fields. A single instruction loads all the general

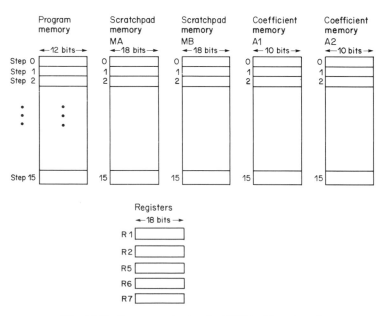

Fig. 11.13. Store organization for PDSP arithmetic unit.

registers and simultaneously performs two multiplications and up to three additions. The fields specify exactly which operands are involved in these operations.

The instructions of the PDSP arithmetic unit are really very powerful. For example, a second-order digital formant resonator requires only two program steps. A two-multiplier lattice stage needs only one step, and a complete 12-stage lattice filter can be implemented in the 16 steps available. An important feature of the architecture is that it is quite easy to incorporate more than one arithmetic unit into a system, with a single control unit. Intermediate data can be transferred digitally between arithmetic units since the D/A converter is off-chip. A four-multiplier normalized lattice (Chapter 6) with 12 stages can be implemented on two arithmetic units, as can a lattice filter which incorporates zeros as well as poles, and a complex series/ parallel formant synthesizer with a total of 12 resonators whose centre frequencies and bandwidths can be controlled independently (Klatt, 1980).

How this device will fare in actual commercial products is yet to be seen. It is certainly much more sophisticated than the TI Speak 'n Spell chip, and a complete system will necessitate a much higher chip count and consequently more expense. Telesensory Systems are committed to producing a text-to-speech system based upon it for use both in a reading machine for the blind and as a text-input speech-output computer peripheral.

11.5 References

Caldwell, J.L. (1980). Programmable synthesis using a new 'Speech Microprocessor'. *Proc International Conference on Acoustics, Speech and Signal Processing*, 868–871, April.

Colby, K.M., Christinaz, D. and Graham, S. (1978). A computer-driven, personal, portable, and intelligent speech prosthesis. *Computers and Biomedical Research*, **11**, 337–343.

Elovitz, H.S., Johnson, R.W., McHugh, A. and Shore, J.E. (1976). Letter-to-sound rules for automatic translation of English text to phonetics. *IEEE Trans Acoustics, Speech and Signal Processing*, **ASSP-24**(6) 446–459, December.

Frantz, G. and Wiggins, R. (1981). The development of 'Solid State Speech' technology at Texas Instruments. *IEEE Acoustics, Speech and Signal Processing Newsletter*, **53**, 34–38, March.

Hoff, M.E. and Li, W. (1980). Software makes a big talker out of the 2920 microcomputer. *Electronics*, 102–107, January 31.

Klatt, D.H. (1980). Software for a cascade/parallel formant synthesizer *J Acoustical Society of America* (3) 971–995, 67, March.

McIlroy, M.D. (1974). Synthetic English speech by rule. Computing Science Technical Report 14, Bell Labs, Murray Hill, New Jersey.

Rice, D.L. (1976). Friends, humans and countryrobots: lend me your ears. *Byte*, **12**, 16–24.

Sherwood, B.A. (1978). Fast text-to-speech algorithms for Esperanto, Spanish, Italian, Russian and English. *Int J Man–Machine Studies*, **10**(6) 669–692, November.
Votrax (1976). ML-I multilingual voice system. Vocal Interface Division, Federal Screw Works, Troy, Michigan.
Wiggins, F. and Brantingham, L. (1978). Three-chip system synthesizes human speech. *Electronics*, 109–116, August 31.

INDEX